Managing Change in IT Outsourcing

TECHNOLOGY, WORK AND GLOBALIZATION

The Technology, Work and Globalization series was developed to provide policy makers, workers, managers, academics and students with a deeper understanding of the complex interlinks and influences between technological developments, including information and communication technologies, work organizations and patterns of globalization. The mission of the series is to disseminate rich knowledge based on deep research about relevant issues surrounding the globalization of work that is spawned by technology.

Also in the series:

MANAGING CHANGE IN IT OUTSOURCING
Albert Plugge

ADVANCED OUTSOURCING PRACTICE
Mary C. Lacity and, Leslie P. Willcocks

ENTERPRISE MOBILITY
Carsten Sørensen

GLOBAL SOURCING OF BUSINESS AND IT SERVICES
Leslie P. Willcocks and Mary C. Lacity

ICT AND INNOVATION IN THE PUBLIC SECTOR
Francesco Contini and Giovan Francesco Lanzara

EXPLORING VIRTUALITY WITHIN AND BEYOND ORGANIZATIOINS
Niki Panteli and Mike Chaisson

KNOWLEDGE PROCESSES IN GLOBALLY DISTRIBUTED CONTEXTS
Julia Kotlarsky, Ilan Oshri and Paul C. van Fenema

GLOBAL CHALLENGES FOR IDENTITY POLICIES
Edgar Whitley and Ian Hosein

E-GOVERNANCE FOR DEVELOPMENT
A Focus on India
Shirin Madon

OFFSHORE OUTSOURCING OF IT WORK
Mary C. Lacity and Joseph W. Rottman

OUTSOURCING GLOBAL SERVICES
Ilan Oshri, Julia Kotlarsy and Leslie P. Willcocks

BRICOLAGE, CARE AND INFORMATION
Chrisanthi Avgerou, Giovan Francesco Lanzara and Leslie Wilcocks

e-GOVERNANCE FOR DEVELOPMENT
Shirin Madon

CHINA'S EMERGING OUTSOURCING CAPABILITIES
Mary C. Lacity, Leslie P. Willcocks and Yingqin Zheng

GOVERNING THROUGH TECHNOLOGY
Information Nets and Social Practice
Jannis Kallinikos

Managing Change in IT Outsourcing

Towards a Dynamic Fit Model

Albert Plugge

palgrave
macmillan

First published 2012 by
PALGRAVE MACMILLAN

Palgrave Macmillan in the UK is an imprint of Macmillan Publishers Limited, registered in England, company number 785998, of Houndmills, Basingstoke, Hampshire RG21 6XS.

Palgrave Macmillan in the US is a division of St Martin's Press LLC, 175 Fifth Avenue, New York, NY 10010.

Palgrave Macmillan is the global academic imprint of the above companies and has companies and representatives throughout the world.

Palgrave® and Macmillan® are registered trademarks in the United States, the United Kingdom, Europe and other countries.

ISBN 978–1–137–03044–3

This book is printed on paper suitable for recycling and made from fully managed and sustained forest sources. Logging, pulping and manufacturing processes are expected to conform to the environmental regulations of the country of origin.

A catalogue record for this book is available from the British Library.

A catalog record for this book is available from the Library of Congress.

10 9 8 7 6 5 4 3 2 1
21 20 19 18 17 16 15 14 13 12

Printed and bound in Great Britain by
CPI Antony Rowe, Chippenham and Eastbourne

Contents

List of Tables

List of Figures

Series Editors' Preface

We launched this series in 2006 to provide policy makers, workers, managers, academics and students with a deeper understanding of the complex interlinks and influences among technological developments, including in information and communication technologies (ICT), work, organizations and globalization. We have always felt that technology is all too often positioned as the welcome driver of globalization. The popular press neatly packages technology's influence on globalization with snappy soundbites, such as 'Any work that can be digitized will be globally sourced'. Cover stories report Indians doing US tax returns, Moroccans developing software for the French, Filipinos answering UK customer service calls, and the Chinese doing everything for everybody. Most glossy cover stories assume that all globalization is progressive, seamless, intractable, and leads to unmitigated good. But what we are experiencing in the twenty-first century in terms of the interrelationships between technology, work and globalization is both profound and highly complex.

The mission of this series is to disseminate rich knowledge based on deep research about relevant issues surrounding the globalization of work that is spawned by technology. To us, substantial research on globalization considers multiple perspectives and levels of analyses. We seek to publish research based on in-depth study of developments in technology, work and globalization and their impacts on and relationships with individuals, organizations, industries and countries. We welcome perspectives from business, economics, sociology, public policy, cultural studies, law and other disciplines that contemplate both larger trends and micro-developments from Asian, African, Australia and Latin American, as well as North American and European viewpoints.

As of this writing, we have 14 books published or under contract. These books are introduced below.

1. *Global Sourcing of Business and IT Services* by Leslie P. Willcocks and Mary C. Lacity is the first book in the series. The book is based on over 1,000 interviews with clients, providers and advisers and 15 years of study. The specific focus is on developments in outsourcing, offshoring and mixed sourcing practices from client and provider perspectives in a globalizing world. We found many organizations struggling. We also found some organizations adeptly creating global sourcing networks that are agile, effective and

cost-efficient. But they did so only after a tremendous amount of trial and error and close attention to details. All our participant organizations acted in a context of fast moving technology, rapid development of supply-side offerings, and ever changing economic conditions.

2. *Knowledge Processes in Globally Distributed Contexts* by Julia Kotlarsky, Ilan Oshri and Paul van Fenema examines the management of knowledge processes of global knowledge workers. Based on substantial case studies and interviews, the authors – along with their network of co-authors – provide frameworks, practices and tools that consider how to develop, coordinate and manage knowledge processes in order to create synergetic value in globally distributed contexts. Chapters address knowledge sharing, social ties, transactive memory, imperative learning, work division and many other social and organizational practices to ensure successful collaboration in globally distributed teams.

3. *Offshore Outsourcing of IT Work* by Mary C. Lacity and Joseph W. Rottman explores the practices for successfully outsourcing IT work from Western clients to offshore providers. Based on over 200 interviews with 26 Western clients and their offshore providers in India, China and Canada, the book details client-side roles of chief information officers, programme management officers and project managers and identifies project characteristics that differentiated successful from unsuccessful projects. The authors examine ten engagement models for moving IT work offshore and describe proven practices to ensure that offshore outsourcing is successful for both client and provider organizations.

4. *Exploring Virtuality Within and Beyond Organizations* by Niki Panteli and Mike Chiasson argues that there has been a limited conceptualization of virtuality and its implications on the management of organizations. Based on illustrative cases, empirical studies and theorizing on virtuality, this book goes beyond the simple comparison between the virtual and the traditional to explore the different types, dimensions and perspectives of virtuality. Almost all organizations are virtual, but they differ theoretically and substantively in their virtuality. By exploring and understanding these differences, researchers and practitioners gain a deeper understanding of the past, present and future possibilities of virtuality. The collection is designed to be indicative of current thinking and approaches, and provides a rich basis for further research and reflection in this important area of management and information systems research and practice.

5. *ICT and Innovation in the Public Sector* by Francesco Contini and Giovan Francesco Lanzara examines the theoretical and practical issues of implementing innovative ICT solutions in the public sector. The book is based on

a major research project sponsored and funded by the Italian government (Ministry of University and Research) and coordinated by Italy's National Research Council and the University of Bologna during the years 2002–06. The authors, along with a number of co-authors, explore the complex interplay between technology and institutions, drawing on multiple theoretical traditions such as institutional analysis, actor–network theory, social systems theory, organization theory and transaction costs economics. Detailed case studies offer realistic and rich lessons. These cases studies include e-justice in Italy and Finland, e-bureaucracy in Austria, and Money Claim On-Line in England and Wales.

6. *Outsourcing Global Services: Knowledge, Innovation, and Social Capital* edited by Ilan Oshri, Julia Kotlarsky and Leslie P. Willcocks assembles the best work from the active participants in the *Information Systems Workshop on Global Sourcing* which began in 2007 in Val d'Isere, France. Because the quality of the contributions was exceptional, we invited the programme chairs to edit a book based on the best papers at the conference. The collection provides in-depth insights into the practices that lead to success in outsourcing global services. Written by internationally acclaimed academics, it covers best practices on IT outsourcing, business process outsourcing and netsourcing.

7. *Global Challenges for Identity Policies* by Edgar Whitley and Ian Hosein provides a perfect fit for the series in that the authors examine identity policies for modern societies in terms of the political, technical and managerial issues needed to prevent identity fraud and theft. The scale of the problem exceeds political boundaries and the authors cover national identity policies in Europe and the rest of the world. Much of the book provides in-depth discussion and analysis of the United Kingdom's National Identity Scheme. The authors provide recommendations for identity and technical policies.

8. *E-Governance for Development* by Shirin Madon examines the rapid proliferation of e-Governance projects aimed at introducing ICT to improve systems of governance and thereby to promote development. In this book, the author unpacks the theoretical concepts of development and governance in order to propose an alternative conceptual framework, which encourages a deeper understanding of macro- and micro-level political, social and administrative processes within which e-Governance projects are implemented. The book draws on more than 15 years of research in India during which time many changes have occurred in terms of the country's development ideology, governance reform strategy and ICT deployment.

9. *Bricolage, Care and Information Systems,* edited by Chrisanthi Avgerou, Giovan Francesco Lanzara and Leslie P. Willcocks, celebrates Claudio Ciborra's

Legacy in Information Systems Research. Claudio Ciborra was one of the most innovative thinkers in the field of information systems. He was one of the first scholars who introduced institutional economics in the study of IS; he elaborated new concepts, such as 'the platform organization', 'formative contexts'; and he contributed to the development of a new perspective altogether through Heideggerian phenomenology. This book contains the most seminal work of Claudio Ciborra and work of other authors who were inspired by his work and built upon it.

10. *China's Emerging Outsourcing Capabilities* edited by Mary C. Lacity, Leslie P. Willcocks and Yingqin Zheng marks the tenth book in the series. The Chinese government has assigned a high priority to science and technology as its future growth sectors. China has a national plan to expand the information technology outsourcing (ITO) and business process outsourcing (BPO) sectors. Beyond the hopes of its leaders, is China ready to compete in the global ITO and BPO markets? Western companies are increasingly interested in extending their global network of ITO and BPO services beyond India and want to learn more about China's ITO and BPO capabilities. In this book, we accumulate the findings of the best research on China's ITO and BPO sector by the top scholars in the field of information systems.

11. *The Outsourcing Enterprise: From Cost Management to Collaborative Innovation* is by Leslie Willcocks, Sara Cullen and Andrew Craig. The central question answered in this book is 'How does an organization leverage the ever growing external services market to gain operational, business, and strategic advantage?' The book covers the foundations of mature outsourcing enterprises that have moved outsourcing to the strategic agenda by building the relationship advantage, selecting and levering suppers, keeping control through core retained capabilities, and collaborating to innovate. The book provides proven practices used by mature outsourcing enterprises to govern, design, and measure outsourcing. The final chapter presents practices on how mature outsourcing enterprises prepare for the next generation of outsourcing.

12. *Governing through Technology* by Jannis Kallinikos is thoughtful scholarship that examines the relationships among information, technology, and social practices. The author discusses the regulative regime of technology, and issues of human agency control and complexity in a connected world. He provides a valuable counter-perspective to show that social practices are, in part, unmistakably products of technologies, that technologies are, through historical processes, embedded in the social fabric, and that, if technological determinism is naive, the notion of the regulative regime of technology remains alive and well into the internet age.

13. *Enterprise Mobility: Tiny Technology with Global Impact on Information Work* by Carsten Sørensen explores how mobile technologies are radically changing the way work is done in organizations. The author defines enterprise mobility as the deployment of mobile information technology for organizational purposes. The author contrasts how large technology projects in organizations, such as enterprise resource planning (ERP) implementations, will increasingly be managed differently because of mobile technology. The introduction of mobile technology supporting organizational information work will often be driven by individuals, small teams, or as part of departmental facilitation of general communication services.

14. *Collaboration in Outsourcing: A Journey to Quality*, edited by Sjaak Brinkkemper and Slinger Jansen, is based on an integrated programme of outsourcing research at Utrecht University in the Netherlands. The book is written for practitioners based on interviews and case studies in many global outsourcing firms including Cisco, IBM, Deloitte, Infosys, Logica, and Partni – to name just a few. The 16 chapters are short, tight, and written to communicate best practices quickly. The chapters cover the topics of governance, knowledge management, relationship management, and new trends in software development outsourcing.

In addition to the books already published and under contract, we have several other manuscripts under review but always need more. We encourage other researchers to submit proposals to the series, as we envision a protracted need for scholars to deeply and richly analyse and conceptualize the complex relationships among technology, work and globalization. Please follow the submissions guidelines on the Palgrave website (www.palgrave-usa.com/Info/Submissions.aspx). Stephen Rutt (email: s.rutt@palgrave.com) is the publishing director for the series (to be updated at proof).

Leslie P. Willcocks
Mary C. Lacity
September 2011

Acknowledgements

Many people contributed to the realization of this book, and I am grateful for all the support I have received from them. First, I would like to thank Professor Rene Wagenaar, who passed away unexpectedly. René, I would like to thank you for your confidence and giving me the opportunity to start my PhD. With regard to my scientific development I would like to thank Professors Yao-Hua Tan and Harry Bouwman and Dr Gerard Wijers. Many thanks for your commitment and your valuable comments which encouraged my academic growth. Moreover, I would like to thank my colleagues in the ICT section of our faculty for their support, cooperation and contribution to my research. Without any doubt I would like to emphasize my thanks to Piet Mul, whose considerable effort to review and strengthen my manuscript is much appreciated.

I would like to take the opportunity to thank the executive management and employees of the providers studied in this volume. Their ability and willingness to cooperate gave me the opportunity to conduct my research, through which many other interested parties are able to obtain new insights.

Furthermore, I want to express my thanks to the organizers and participants of the Global Sourcing Workshop. Their knowledge and experience in the field of (out)sourcing helped to deepen my scientific understanding. In particular, I would like to thank Leslie Willcocks, Ilan Oshri, Julia Kotlarsky and Joe Rottman for their initiative to organize the Workshop. A word of special thanks goes out to the scientific experts who were willing to send me a 'personal quote' based on their experience in the field of outsourcing. These quotes eloquently describe situations that can be recognized by all who are involved in outsourcing arrangements.

Most of all I would like to thank my wife Marijke, who enabled me to start and complete my research and book and to whom I owe so much. During the previous years I have 'outsourced' a lot of work to you, which you managed perfectly. A true example that a successful relationship can only be built on love and trust!

Grateful acknowledgement is given to the following for permission to reprint:

Figure 1.1 from T. Kern and L.P. Wilcocks, *The Relationship Advantage: Information Technologies, Sourcing, and Management* (Oxford: Oxford University

Press, 2001). Copyright © 2001 by Oxford University Press. By permission of Oxford University Press

Figure 2.1 from T. Kern and L.P. Willcocks, 'Exploring Relationships in Information Technology Outsourcing: The Interaction Approach ', *European Journal of Information Systems*, 11, 3–19. Copyright © 2002 by Tribune Media Services .By permission of Tribune Media Services.

Figure 2.2 from D. Feeny, M.C. Lacity and L.P. Willcocks, 'Taking the Measure of Outsourcing Providers', *MIT Sloan Management Review*, Spring, 46, 3, 41–8. Copyright © 2005 by John Wiley & Sons Ltd .By permission of John Wiley & Sons Ltd.

Figure 2.3 from by A. Neely, C. Adams, M. Kennerley, *The Performance Prism: The Scorecard for Measuring and Managing Business Success* (London: Prentice Hall, Pearson Education Limited, 2000). Copyright © 2001 by Pearson Education Ltd. By permission of Pearson Education Ltd.

Introduction

Suppliers also need to work on their strategies and capabilities if they are to sustain the more collaborative relationships that clients increasingly demand, and deliver meaningfully on an innovation as well as a cost and service agenda.

(Leslie Willcocks)

Providers' challenges

The provision of IT outsourcing services has shown a rapid increase over the last two decades. Because a growing number of firms now outsource their IT function, the IT landscape is becoming increasingly varied, with a wide range of outsourcing arrangements. Important aspects that affect outsourcing arrangements include relationship models, contract management, offshoring, and success/failure scenarios. Since these aspects have a significant effect on service provider organizations, regular communication among clients and providers becomes more important. Clients have to deal with market dynamism, uncertainty and change in their environment, influencing client organization strategy, focus, needs, and market positioning. Therefore, clients are likely to discuss market developments and business needs with their service providers on a regular basis. This illustrates the relevance of the dyadic inter-firm relationship between service providers and client organizations. However, few studies in the field of outsourcing relations include the views of providers which is in sharp contrast to the overwhelming amount of research that focuses on the client side. The focus in this book is on IT outsourcing from the provider perspective. Providers face serious challenges in their relationship with clients in IT outsourcing arrangements. In particular, service providers are struggling to offer sustainable *IT performance* for their clients. A lack of provider performance will result in disturbances on the client side.

The quality of service delivery is decreasing while there will be an increase in the costs of abrogating the lack of provider performance. Furthermore, the lack of provider performance could also have a negative business impact on the client as the time-to-market of products and or services increases. On the other hand, market developments on the client side also change over time.

One explanation for the identified lack of sustainable performance has to be found in *capabilities* that are lacking on the provider side, as well as in how these capabilities are *organized*. Clients need to gain access to relevant provider capabilities, while at the same time providers are incapable of performing at a sustainably high level. This results consequently in a tension in the relationship between outsourcing partners. Depending on the client organization, different dimensions have to be taken into account in organizing provider capabilities. Because a client's situation is subject to change, the supporting organizational structure of an IT provider may also change over time. In this book we argue that IT outsourcing providers who manage to establish a fit between capabilities and their own organizational structure are less subject to changes enforced to them as a result of client developments.

Through an analysis of three case studies, this book shows how the concept of fit between sourcing capabilities and organizational structure can be established. Moreover, the case studies revealed relevant factors that can provide insights for provider's executive management into how they can manage changes in outsourcing arrangements.

The main objectives of this book

This book offers IT outsourcing providers a perspective into how to establish a *dynamic fit* between *sourcing capabilities* and their own *organizational structure*. As a result, service providers are less susceptible to changes in their clients' environment. However, the establishment of a dynamic fit is not sufficient. There is also a need for the continuous monitoring of the provider's performance. IT providers who monitor their clients' developments are expected to be able to adapt to changing client circumstances and realize a sustainable performance.

The key objectives of the book are to:

1 Monitor and assess changing client circumstances in IT outsourcing arrangements.
2 Assess the impact of key client developments on service providers' sourcing capabilities.
3 Assess the impact of key client developments on service providers' organizational structures.

4 Identify what aspects influence the performance of service providers towards their clients.
5 Develop a dynamic fit approach that provides insight in the interplay between client developments, sourcing capabilities and organizational structural dimensions, as well as creating a deeper understanding of their effect on the provider's performance.

Definitions

The term outsourcing has been used in the literature in various ways. Some authors have emphasized the contribution by external vendors related to physical and/or human resources associated with components of the IT infrastructure in the user organization. Others specifically focused on the field of IT outsourcing addressing the commissioning of a third party to manage a client organization's IT assets, people and/or activities. We apply the definition of IT outsourcing as defined by Kern (1997) who argue that:

> *IT outsourcing is a decision taken by an organization to contract out or sell the organization's IT assets, people, and/or activities to a third party provider, who in exchange provides and manages assets and services for monetary return over an agreed time period.*

To prevent the use of the inaccurate terms 'outsourcing' and 'offshoring' we use the following definitions as stated by Oshri et al. (2009).

> *Outsourcing is defined as contracting with a service provider for the management and completion of a certain amount of work, for a specified length of time, cost, and level of service.*
>
> *Offshoring refers to the relocation of organizational activities (e.g. IT, finance and accounting, back office, human resources) to a wholly owned subsidiary or an independent service provider in another country.*

Since these definitions are applicable to the field of Information Technology, highlighting the role and position of the service provider, our research will make use of these definitions.

Demarcation

Although the client–provider outsourcing relationship is our starting point, the focal point of this book is the service provider organization. Our aim is to address both the sourcing capabilities and the organizational structure from an organizational perspective. The interaction of both aspects with respect to sourcing performance is also investigated at an organizational level. In addition to the effect of organizational capabilities and organizational structure on sourcing performance, it is important to discuss the interplay between sourcing capabilities and structure in order to interpret these interactions. Therefore, we will look at the nature of, and interaction between, organizational sourcing capabilities and organizational structure in some detail.

With regard to our organizational approach, we make a distinction between various levels of organizational structures as applied by a provider. At a business level we can recognize a generic organizational structure to support the core competences of the firm such as sales, procurement and HR. Furthermore, at a functional level IT providers apply another organizational structure to facilitate the delivery of IT outsourcing services to their clients such as workplace and office automation services and application development services. This structure can be considered to be a specialized form of organizational structure applied within the general organizational structure of an IT provider. In our research, this specialized form of organizational structure is used as a unit of observation. Moreover, the capabilities that are applied by a service provider to support this specific organizational structure also differ from their core competences and what Feeny et al. (2005) refers to as sourcing capabilities. Therefore, we specifically address sourcing capabilities that are applied to support outsourcing arrangements to clients and the way in which these sourcing capabilities are organized.

In this book we focus on IT outsourcing service providers. The scope of IT includes services such as communication networks, office automation, infrastructure management, application maintenance and application development. This scope, which is perceived in the market as mature services, makes it possible to compare the different IT service providers with each other according to the organization of their sourcing capabilities. With respect to an outsourcing arrangement from a provider perspective, we can identify two main phases – namely the transition phase and the delivery phase. To obtain a comprehensive view of the performance of an IT outsourcing service provider it is worthwhile addressing both phases within an IT provider organization. In an attempt to define the boundaries of this book, other forms or types of outsourcing will not be taken into consideration. The explanation for this demarcation is that, for instance Business Process Outsourcing compared to IT outsourcing, is such a different concept with other accents that the results will be too diffuse and too limited to extract any conclusions.

Contribution

Our research contributes to IT outsourcing providers by increasing their awareness of the relevance of establishing a dynamic fit that will improve their sourcing performance significantly. Market analysis (for example, KPMG EquaTerra, International Association of Outsourcing Professionals) based on longitudinal comparisons between providers demonstrated that providers have difficulties to cater to clients' business need and adapt their IT services. Consequently, providers are still struggling to offer a sustainable performance which may result in disputes with their clients. Providers can gain insights about which determinants will affect their sourcing performance towards clients. In particular, more in-depth knowledge about the ways in which sourcing capabilities and organizational dimensions affect each other is valuable to understand performance issues. The way in which providers' capabilities and their organizational structural dimensions are intertwined provide insights into how providers are able to adapt these main constructs. By strengthening their sourcing capabilities they are able to cater to clients' business needs. Moreover, developing an organizational structure that reflects the client's environment contributes to an aligned governance mechanism. In doing so, providers are able to increase their maturity and provide a sustainable performance. This study also helps providers to create more insights into how client developments can be monitored and assessed. These insights can be applied to start the adaptation process related to capabilities and organizational structures. Furthermore, from a managerial perspective, the providers' executive management is provided with insights into which determinants can be influenced by management in order to establish a sustainable performance.

The structure of this book

First, in Chapter 1 we sketch the sourcing background to highlight the relevance of IT outsourcing. The aim of Chapter 2, which describes the theoretical background of our research, is to identify appropriate theories related to establishing a dynamic fit. Chapter 3 addresses a preliminary research into client–provider relationships investigating relevant client developments that occurred during IT outsourcing arrangements. Chapters 4, 5, and 6 discuss our case studies that refer to a domestic provider, an offshore provider, and a global provider respectively. Based on the empirical descriptive case studies, in Chapter 7 we will conduct a cross-case analysis to identify the implications for our research model. Then, in Chapter 8 the results of our quantitative research are described that is conducted to test the relationships between the constructs as mentioned in Chapter 2. In Chapter 9 we discuss the conclusions and practical implications.

1
Overview of the Sourcing Background

Outsourcing arrangements are dynamic in nature and so are the structures, capabilities and value developed and extracted from them over time.

(Ilan Oshri)

Introduction

The provisioning of IT outsourcing services has shown a particularly rapid increase over the past two decades. A historic perspective on outsourcing shows that from the 1980s large companies started to contract out parts of IT-related tasks to third parties. During this period third parties could offer just a few elementary services, including technical consultancy and training. Applying recent taxonomy, this period can be defined as a preliminary phase of outsourcing, as third parties focused more of their efforts on outtasking. The first real phase of outsourcing, which approximately comprises the decade of the 1990s, was the result of a technology push. During this period companies aimed to contract out parts (or even their entire IT function) to third parties. Third parties, also called suppliers, focused on providing technologically driven solutions. Since companies in these days were aimed primarily at buying a technical solution, adding value related to their business was not in the scope of their considerations. Agreements between companies and suppliers were therefore considered to be more transaction-oriented. As a consequence, companies paid more attention to the specific task of managing the supply side. Kodak's decision in 1989 to outsource their data center to IBM and DEC can be considered to be a landmark in the field of IT outsourcing (Loh and Venkatraman, 1992). Ever since the 'Kodak effect' IT outsourcing has been seen from an industry perspective as the supplier market at the early 1990s developed significantly. Hence, a new industry arose. The shift from hiring personnel to delivering technology solutions has had a great effect on suppliers such as providing integral solutions and building long-term relationships. This outsourcing phase was popularized by the market as Outsourcing 1.0. During the second phase, which encompasses the decade 2000 to 2010, the maturity of suppliers increased significantly as they focused on providing IT services instead of technology solutions. It was during this period that suppliers were considered as providers by the market. Agreements between companies and providers changed and became more service-oriented. At the same time companies experienced that they needed to align their demand and supply sides to ensure the delivery of IT services. This development had a significant influence on their organization. Summarizing this second phase the market has popularized this era as Outsourcing 2.0.

Reflecting on the growth in IT outsourcing since the 1990s it can be observed that three major forces have changed the vision and strategy of both firms and providers, namely: (1) globalization; (2) deregulation; and (3) consolidation (Holway, 1998). For decades many firms regarded their IT function to be a core competence that should form a part of their in-house capabilities. As a result of *globalization* firms are being forced to focus on their core business activities in order to remain competitive. Business activities that are useful and non-critical can be considered to be a commodity and can therefore be outsourced. From the perspective of the provider, concepts such as nearshoring and offshoring were introduced that are encouraged by the major force of globalization. Moreover, outsourcing firms such as Accenture, CSC, and TCS have extended their global reach by establishing strategic arrangements with other providers in order to cater to client's growing needs to provide a wide range of IT services. *Deregulation* is another driver that changed the field of outsourcing. Domestic or international legislation affected firms in various industries by changing or even cancelling market legislation. For example, the telecommunications industry in Europe underwent dramatic changes when the European Union decided to liberalize the telecommunication market in 1987. Telecom operators faced fierce competition while they had to make a shift from delivering technical solutions towards services. Consequently, these firms were forced to focus on their core businesses and they decided to outsource their non-critical business activities. Since the 1990s we have seen that many telecom operators have decided to outsource parts of their IT function. In addition, *consolidations* are considered to be an important force that have had a significant influence on firms and providers. As most firms have to grow to survive in the market, they decided to merge with their competitors or acquire companies that could enable them to secure a competitive advantage. In the field of

IT we have also seen various consolidations. Examples include HP, which merged with EDS in 2008, and Wipro, which acquired Infocrossing in 2007. Recently, Capgemini has acquired Artesys, a small French Service Integrator dedicated to enabling cloud projects. When applying a consolidation strategy firms are able to enter new markets and gain access to new clients while offering a wider range of services. Another consolidation rationale for firms is to increase their market share in order to achieve a stronger position in the market. These three forces have acted in combination to generate the growth of and demand for IT outsourcing.

Since research companies apply various criteria to measure the growth of outsourcing it is difficult to obtain consistent information. Back in 1989, global Information Technology Outsourcing (ITO) was estimated to be a market between $9 and $12 billion. By the end of 2009, global ITO revenues exceeded US$250 billion (Oshri et al., 2009). The growth of ITO was not only limited to domestic IT spend. In particular, the IT spend is growing in low-cost countries, such as Poland, India, and the Philippines. The underlying compound annual growth rate (CAGR) of the outsourcing market has been approximately 7 per cent in the 2008–2009 period (Gartner, 2009). The economic recession from 2009 has had an impact on the growth of the outsourcing market, causing a delay. As illustrated by the analyst companies IDC and Gartner this is only a temporary phenomenon. Over the next few years the growth of the outsourcing market is expected to continue. The offshore provisioning of IT outsourcing services has also shown a rapid increase over the past decade while it is expected to continue to grow. A study carried out by McKinsey and National Association of Software and Service Companies (NASSCOM) estimates that the Information Technology and Enterprise Solutions (ITES) market in India is likely to reach $142 billion in 2009. We observe, however, that the Enterprise Solutions market is considered to be much wider than simply Information Technology as it also contains other components (for example, printers and payment equipment). Therefore, it is difficult to compare all of these market figures. Carmel and Tjia (2005), who carried out an intensive study of the Indian market, suggest that India will continue to play a dominant role in the global ITO market. As firms decide to offshore their IT activities, they benefit from reduced cost, improved lead times, process streamlining, and strategic repositioning (Beulen and Ribbers, 2003; Beulen et al., 2006). In this context firms face new issues such as cultural differences, language barriers, time zones (Carmel and Espinosa, 2011) and geopolitical risks (Jones, 2009). Because of these barriers regular communication among firms and service providers becomes increasingly important. The key driver for offshoring and nearshoring is primarily cost savings.

In terms of sourcing locations, currently most of the offshoring services are provided from India, which is one of the most popular offshoring countries, commonly referred to as the BRIC nations (Brazil, Russia, India and China). In Europe, countries such as Hungary, Ireland, Poland and Russia also provide suitable locations for nearshoring.

IT outsourcing in the early 1990s started with the contracting out of those parts of the IT function that were more supportive in nature. As the value that IT offers cannot easily be attributed within a firm IT costs were regarded as simply overheads. IT was essential, but was nevertheless considered from a cost perspective. However, as a result of increased competition firms shifted their business strategy as they reduced risks and concentrated on their core competencies. As a result, firms developed a focus strategy by adding value to their businesses to create a competitive advantage in the market. Today many firms consider outsourcing to be a strategic option for a number of reasons: access to external capabilities, benefit from providers' economy of scale, increased flexibility and an increased time-to-market (De Looff, 1997; DiRomualdo and Gurbaxani, 1998). Kern and Willcocks (2001) developed a strategic decision-making matrix on outsourcing (Figure 1.1), which can also be applied to the field of IT. The authors described the relation between the competitive position of a firm and the contribution of activities to business operations. While a firm considers parts of their IT function to be a commodity, however useful it may be, outsourcing is recommended. After all, retaining these IT activities in-house results in less added value for the firm. On the other hand, business activities that enable a firm to differ from their competitors and are considered as critical need to stay in-house. When a firm consider their IT function to be a commodity but nevertheless critical to their business operations the authors nominate this option as a 'qualifier'. Practice shows that firms divide their IT function in multiple domains in which parts are qualified to contract out to third parties. The fourth option concerns an IT function that is considered as a differentiator and only useful to the business. Discussing the latter option firms have to assess if the IT function, or parts of the function, can be transformed to add value to their businesses. In doing so, firms need to keep this function in-house. Contrary, when an IT function cannot be migrated to a critical contribution firms have to discontinue this activity and outsource the function.

Today, IT outsourcing is considered by both researchers and practitioners to be a multidisciplinary environment. The outsourcing of IT within a firm involves various disciplines, including organizational structures, governance, finance, HR, legal and, of course, Information Technology. Furthermore, many of these disciplines are intertwined. For example, the transfer of a

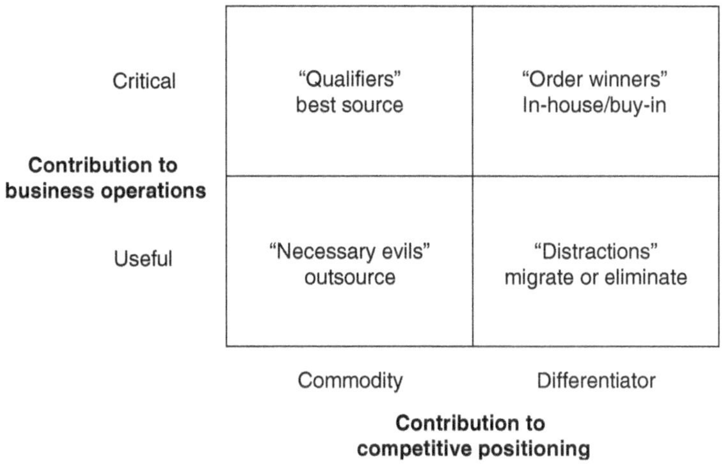

Figure 1.1 Decision-making matrix on outsourcing
Source: Kern and Willcocks (2001).

firm's IT staff to a service provider is related to the area of Human Resource (HR) as agreements need to be made about employment conditions and fringe benefits such as pension plans. In addition, the outsourcing of a firm's IT function affects the boundaries of a firm and thus their organizational structure. Therefore, firms have to pay attention to manage the coherence of an outsourcing arrangement instead of strictly managing individual disciplines. Due to the importance of these disciplines, contracting out an IT function will result in a major process of organizational change. Examples of related risks comprise business interruptions, an increased time-to-market and a growth in the level of resource inflexibility. As is illustrated by market research, the average outsourcing contract length is stabilizing at between three and five years. Hence, switching providers during the contract period will result in high switching costs that could often form an unbridgeable barrier. Considering these various disciplines firms are facing both internal and external developments that lead to a number of more general challenges affecting their organization. To illustrate some general challenges we have included some examples.

- *The rise of Business Process Outsourcing.* The trend towards the outsourcing of business processes to external providers leads to a more output-oriented service. At the same time firms have to decide to bundle their business processes and IT function towards one single provider (total outsourcing) or divide their services between separate providers (selective outsourcing).

- *The complexity of outsourcing deals.* Because of the rise of selective outsourcing, firms apply new governance models to manage multiple providers. As a result of implementing a selective sourcing strategy, firms' complexity with regard to IT governance will increase as topics such as tasks and responsibilities needs to be determined.
- *Aligning a firm's demand and supply side.* Firms that outsource IT activities need to develop and retain certain capabilities to manage the execution of the IT outsourcing strategy successfully. For example, firms that have outsourced their application maintenance to a service provider should be able to absorb this application maintenance, which requires knowledge and experience. This relates to structural issues around managing the demand and supply of application maintenance as part of a firm's capabilities. Practice shows that firms are struggling how to manage their demand and supply side effectively.
- *Compliancy demands.* Companies remain responsible to comply with legislation even when specific activities or processes have been outsourced to third parties. With regard to IT infrastructure large companies have to comply with legislation to, for instance, data storage, recording personal identity files or recording financial transactions.
- *The combination of internal shared service centres and external service providers.* Combining two types of delivery organizations, an internal shared service centre and an external IT outsourcing provider, a firm becomes responsible for managing both delivery organizations. The coordinating department, the sourcing management organization, needs to be organized separately. The rationale behind this choice is that the sourcing management organization is responsible for aligning both business needs and delivery solutions, regardless of whether the service delivery is supported internally or externally.

As a result of the developments that arise from the multidisciplinary nature of outsourcing, firms developed strategies to shape arrangements with their service providers. The next section will highlight the main flavours of current outsourcing arrangements.

Studying the IT outsourcing domain

So in order to create a better understanding on outsourcing arrangements we describe the main outsourcing strategies that are applied in the market. Research has taken three major types of strategies into consideration: total outsourcing, selective or multiple-provider outsourcing and strategic alliances.

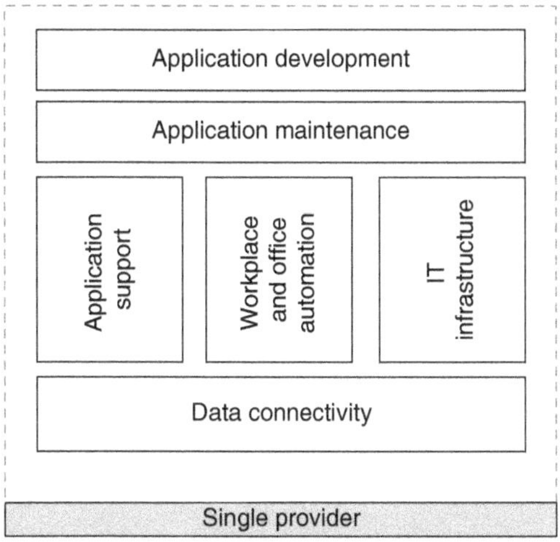

Figure 1.2 Total outsourcing

Total outsourcing

This strategy, which was popular in the 1990s, can be defined as the strategy to outsource more than 70 per cent of an organization's IT functions, most commonly to a single large provider. The motivation for companies to opt for a total outsourcing arrangement (see Figure 1.2) is for predominantly strategic reasons such as concentration on core business activities in order to create market advantage. This type of decision involves the transfer of a significant number of IT staff from a firm to a third party. The firm receives a large payment for the transferred assets while the provider receives a long-term guarantee to deliver IT services. However, Kern and Willcocks (2001) found out that this can be achieved by outsourcing contracts that are focusing primarily on cost reduction, but often at the expense of IT operational services and business strategic inflexibilities. Although there has been a reduction in total outsourcing arrangements, companies still choose for this type of decision. In 2005 Volkswagen, for instance, announced its intention to outsource their complete IT department, worth $3 billion on a seven-year contract, to T-Systems in order to enhance sales growth and profitability.

Selective outsourcing

Although the large multi-million/billion, long-term contracts sound impressive, research has unveiled that selective outsourcing is the more common practice. When applying a selective outsourcing strategy, firms divide their IT function into various logical-oriented domains that can easily be transferred

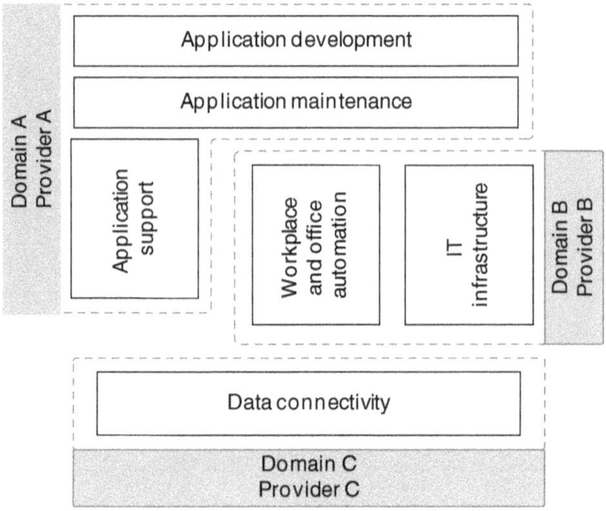

Figure 1.3 Selective outsourcing

to the market. For each domain a firm can select an appropriate provider that fits in with the required type of service (see Figure 1.3). The rationale behind this approach is that providers are having difficulties in excelling in all IT domains such as application development, workplace automation and data communication networks. There are several differences between total outsourcing and selective outsourcing. Bringing in multiple providers will reduce the dependency on a single provider to support all IT domains and, therefore, mitigates the risks. Moreover, firms can switch from providers per domain without changing their complete landscape. Practice shows that firms who divide their landscape into different domains are able to focus more easily on innovation initiatives in order to improve a certain domain. This approach encourages competition between the providers at the same time. The downside of this strategy is that the sourcing management organization of a firm has to spend more time on coordinating the multiple providers. In 2005 the Dutch grocer Royal Ahold adopted this strategy and outsourced their IT function, worth $500 million based on a five-year arrangement, to multiple providers. Ahold developed a framework with its providers outlining how the providers have to work together, while one of the providers (for example, EDS) has an additional coordinating role as service integrator.

Strategic alliance

Originally, the rationale for initiating a strategic alliance covers aspects such as developing new products/services, entering new markets and mitigating risks. When establishing a strategic alliance, firms and providers bring in staff and assets to accomplish a new company delivering IT services. The key advantage of a strategic alliance when compared to a total outsourcing strategy is to reduce the risks of a single provider or multiple providers because the client is able to influence and control the strategy of the provider. At the same time risks and rewards can be shared between both firm and provider. Another reason is that a firm also gains access to specialist skills of the provider. Establishing a strategic alliance enables firms to create a competitive advantage in the market. Literature reveals examples of strategic alliances such as Xerox-EDS, Mutual Life Insurance and CSC and the Canadian Imperial Bank of Commerce (CIBC) and Hewlett Packard (HP). Practice shows that in these cases arrangements typically endure for a period of 7 up to 10 years. Literature reveals that various terms are used to describe this arrangement: from 'partnership' to 'strategic partnership' and 'strategic alliance'.

IT outsourcing provider industry

To understand the position and the approach of service providers within the distinguished strategic arrangements it is necessary to study their background. From the perspective of service providers, IT outsourcing has undergone many changes, starting with a service bureau model in the 1960s via ASP's to Software as a Service in the 21st century. The way in which providers offer IT outsourcing services depends on both the context and their background. With regard to the context, new entrants have created a fierce competition in which providers have to distinguish themselves from their competitors by offering value-added services.

Many providers who are active in the outsourcing industry at present initially did not set out with outsourcing as a target market and, as such, their heritage is an important factor in terms of understanding both their interest in and aptitude for outsourcing. The IT value chain encompasses various layers from data connectivity to consulting services (see Figure 1.4). Each provider offered IT services that relate to specific layers in the IT value chain. The growth of the IT outsourcing market encouraged providers to expand their service portfolio as they developed and introduced new IT services. Depending on their original position, providers positioned themselves either higher or lower in the IT value chain. This resulted in fierce competition between providers as they experienced competition in relation to their own core competences. On the other hand, to some extent providers were opportunistic and copied their competitors in developing new IT services (Lacity and Hirschheim, 1993). This is a clear example of the 'bandwagon'

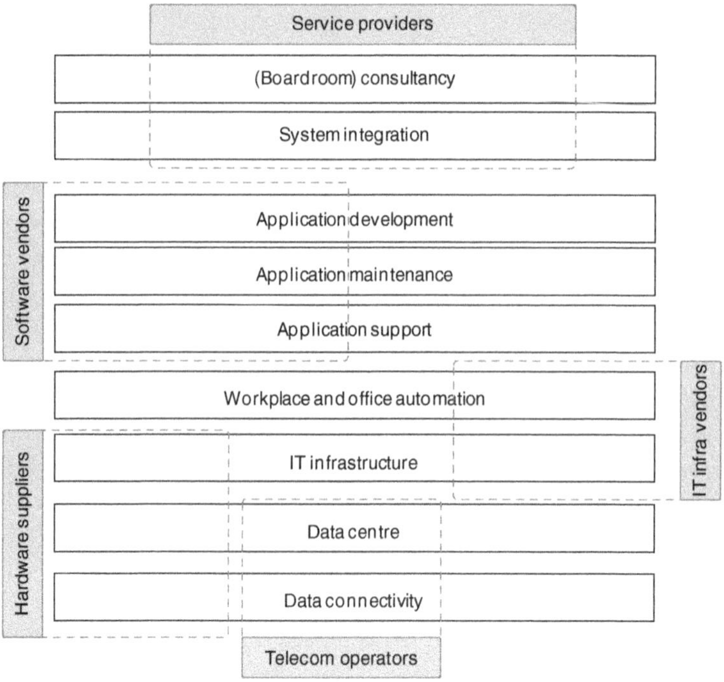

Figure 1.4 IT providers' domains

effect and provider strategies of keeping their options open. The market for outsourcing providers, which has been the subject of previous study, can be categorized into five different types: service providers, software vendors, IT infrastructure vendors, hardware suppliers, and Telecom operators. These categories are illustrated in Figure 1.4.

Providers that belong to the first category, service providers, deliver traditional software development services and often play an important role as a system integrator (examples include companies such as Accenture, CSC, HP/EDS). They are often characterized by a large number of highly trained professionals delivering value-added services. Service providers with a consulting background tend to focus more on business relationships and advise on strategic information systems. These companies have a competitive advantage as they have extensive experience with business issues. However, research (Michell and Fitzgerald, 1997) shows that service companies are moving towards more operational services and the actual development of software. This development means a downward integration in order to deliver a full range of IT services with a wide scope ranging strategic to operational.

Software vendors such as SAP and Oracle, which belong to the second category, have developed by providing custom systems design, development and implementation. As they often have a more domestic or regional reach, they feel both the pressure of service providers from above and also of traditional hardware suppliers from below. This 'stuck-in-the-middle' position forces them to expand both upwards and downwards to prevent their role from decreasing over time. Most of the software vendors have created long-term relationships and management responsibility for package software with their clients. By offering application management services they are able to expand their natural business. The development of software vendors to integrate traditional services with more consulting services and operational services strengthens their position in the IT outsourcings marketplace.

IT infrastructure vendors form the fourth category of providers. A number of IT infrastructure providers are the former IT departments of large companies offering their services to external clients (for example, Barclays Computer Operations, Philips Communication). Their main focus is to provide system management services such as hardware (server farms), software and local and wide area networks. Traditionally, they offer desktop services, applications and maintenance as well as the implementation of new applications. Many companies that originally fit in this target area have evolved by delivering software development and integration services. Through a renewed focus on high-margin services, this combination forms a starting point for a strong position in the value chain of providing IT outsourcing services. One example of an IT department shifting to the external market is Philips Communication, a subsidiary of Royal Philips Electronics. Philips's focus on core business activities led in 1996 to a situation in which the operational IT services were separated from the company. Through a merger with BSO/Origin in 1996 and later with Atos in 2000, Atos Origin was established by delivering IT services which focused on the European market. Recently, Atos Origin acquired Siemens IT Solutions in 2011, changing their name to Atos.

Of all sectors, hardware suppliers (for example, IBM and HP) went through the biggest challenges to survive in the marketplace. As a result of the commoditization of the hardware market and the resulting decline in their margins, hardware suppliers had to leave their hardware-centred position and move upwards in the value chain, providing vertically integrated IT services. This radical change from delivering hardware to delivering outsourcing services has helped to reshape the industry. Traditional hardware suppliers had good relationships with client IT departments and thus operational activities. However, by moving upwards in the value chain, they had to establish new relationships with business management and improve their understanding of business processes. The most striking example of a new position in the value chain is IBM. Having been established initially as a traditional hardware supplier they changed their business strategy on the basis of the vision that both business and IT within companies will converge. By establishing a new corporation, Integrated Systems Solutions Corporation (ISSC), they were able to focus on delivering vertically integrated IT outsourcing services from consulting to hardware maintenance. IBM has demonstrated the success of their change in business strategy; at present they are the global market leader in IT outsourcing services.

Telecom operators such as Deutsche Telekom and British Telecom can be regarded as the fifth category of providers. Focusing originally on delivering hardware and infrastructure services, they felt the pressure as a result of market developments when these products and services became a commodity. As a result of decreasing margins it was necessary to adopt a new approach. This was based on delivering communication solutions instead of infrastructure, for example call centre services, which include IT functionality as well as staff. Some operators, such as BT and T-Systems, moved towards IT integration services, while others focused on delivering ASP services. One example of a telecom operator that changed their strategy is the merger between KPN and Getronics in 2007 through which KPN gained entrance to the service industry, thereby expanding their service portfolio.

By moving upwards or downwards through the IT value chain, providers will face important consequences. The first consequence is a change in the provider capabilities. The proposition of new services, for instance application development, requires new skills, which must be either developed or acquired. When a provider pays insufficient attention to the required capabilities, the client satisfaction is at stake. Moreover, there is yet another effect that will influence the capacity of the provider, the increasing dependency on an overall IT service integrator. Because of the rise of selective outsourcing, large companies decide to position an overall IT service integrator between their internal departments and the different subcontractors to coordinate and integrate the IT services. The result of this model is an increase of complexity with regard to the cooperation between customer, overall service integrator and subcontractors. The relationship of a provider with both client and overall service integrator can be dual, an operational relation towards the overall service integrator and a financial relation towards the client. This means that the provider has to shift from a traditional one-to-one relationship into a one-to-many relationship model. Because of changes in their service portfolio and increased levels of cooperation with their competitors, providers need to adapt to ensure the continuous delivery of high-quality services over time. Research reveals that this results in a tension in the relationship between providers and clients.

Conclusion

In this chapter we described the IT outsourcing provider industry and relevant sourcing models from a historical perspective. With the introduction of new sourcing strategies, such as nearshoring and offshoring, providers are able to provide IT services based on geographically dispersed locations. This provides both opportunities and challenges as this development will affect providers, dealing with their sourcing capabilities and the way in which they organize their resources. As a result, they have to adapt to changes that occur on the client side or within their own organization.

2
Managing Change

Changing the interorganizational or international division of labour has brought the potential for productivity increases to a new frontier. But the more you divide, the more you need to coordinate. The success in outsourcing and offshoring depends on the way you divide the labour and how effectively you coordinate its outcomes.

(Armin Heinzl)

Direction for developing a dynamic fit

The contribution of sourcing capabilities and organizational structure to sourcing performance is a domain where the notion of fit is particularly relevant. The concept of fit, match or congruence has a long tradition in strategic literature (Porter, 1980, 1991; Zajac et al., 2000). Initially, the view on fit was static, being focused on the relation between environmental factors and organizational structure, and common across organizations in similar environments. In more recent views fit is seen as a dynamic process, focused on multivariate relations between organizational factors and organizational contingencies in order to explain organizational strategy. Organizational performance is the consequence of fit between two or more factors such as strategy, environment, technology, structure, and culture (Burns and Stalker, 1961). The fundamental view of fit propounded by strategic management researchers and organization theorists is a 'dynamic search that seeks to align the organization with its environment and to arrange resources internally in support of that alignment' (Miles and Snow, 1978). In organization theory and strategic management literature the focus is on the relation between environment opportunities and threats, industry and competitive analyses (Porter, 1980, 1991), organizational strength (Barney, 1991) and strategy. In this book we focus specifically on a dynamic fit between sourcing capabilities and organizational structure.

Venkatraman (1989) proposed a framework that comprises six different perspectives from which fit can be defined and studied: moderation, mediation, matching, covariation, profile deviation, and gestalts. This framework represents fit-based relationships classifying the perspectives along three dimensions: the degree of specificity of the functional form of fit, the number of variables in the equation, and the presence of a criterion variable. First, with regard to our research, the degree of specificity of the theoretical relationship indicates a precise functional form of fit. The underlying variables of the fit relationship under study, which are the constructs sourcing capabilities and organizational structure, can be described in a precise form, as two specific variables are involved in our research. Previous studies of Gupta and Govindarajan (1984) and Miller and Friesen (1984) also explored the fit between two variables. As our study indicates two variables, the number in the equation is limited and, based on Venkatraman's classificatory framework, it can be described as few. This relates to the second dimension. In our study, the construct performance can be seen as a criterion variable. This means that the third dimension is a part of a criterion-specific relationship.

When mapping the six distinct perspectives of Venkatraman's framework we can determine that the notion of fit as moderation is closely aligned to our research. According to the moderation perspective, the impact that the predictor variable has on a criterion variable is dependent on a third variable, the moderator. In our study, the predictor relates to sourcing capabilities while the criterion variable relates to performance. The moderator relates to organizational structure. We argue that according to our theory the impact of the predictor (sourcing capabilities) varies across the different levels of the moderator (organizational structure). In other words, the organizational structure can be viewed categorically, taking the various dimensions into account (for example, the locus of decision-making, hierarchy). Moreover, the moderator will affect the strength of the relation between the predictor (sourcing capabilities) and the criterion variable (performance). In our study we clearly specify the type of fit and the number of variables. We theoretically underpin our study and discuss the results with respect to the theory and the selected perspective of fit. This is consistent with the previous research of Bergeron et al. (2001).

We focus on the fit between the sourcing capabilities that IT outsourcing providers have to make available, that fit their internal organizational processes and structure. Additional insight is needed into the changes client organizations have to deal with that might influence providers' capabilities. We use, based on the approach in Zajac et al. (2000), the concept of dynamic fit if changes in sourcing capabilities occur in a beneficial way with adaptations in the organizational processes and structure of decision-making.

Environment and capabilities

There are frequent changes in the environment of organizations, forming new opportunities and threats for firms that operate in this environment. To cope with these changes a firm may choose to adapt its behaviour. Usually, firms have a certain degree of resilience built into their organization in order to cater for smaller, predictable changes such as small shifts in products, markets and resources. However, as soon as changes in the environment lead to changes within the strategy, the adaptation of the organization will take considerably more time (Volberda, 2003). So it is of key importance for a firm to know what changes take place in their environment, and which resources and capabilities need to be adjusted. What is relevant for businesses in general is also relevant for outsourcing service providers and their clients. Changes in the environment of the client will affect their behaviour, and therefore these changes are also relevant for the provider and the sourcing capabilities that they have to deliver.

Environment

Although IT outsourcing relationships have received some attention in the literature (McFarlan and Nolan, 1995; Kern and Willcocks, 2000, 2001, 2002), all of the studied relationships showed a limited scope as the context of the relationship was neglected. In addition to the context, behaviour and structural dimensions, the Inter Organizational Relationship (IOR) theory examines the conditions of a dyadic inter-firm relationship (Kern and Willcocks, 2001). The IOR is particularly valuable in analysing interorganizational coordination and cooperation (Bensaou and Venkatraman, 1996; Cunningham and Tynan, 1993). However, when studying relationships we can recognise multiple dimensions that are not all covered by the IOR theory. Following a review of the literature on IT outsourcing relationships, Hakansson (1982) developed an 'Interaction Approach' that has been derived from the IOR theory. The 'Interaction Approach' draws upon inter-organizational theory, and has received empirical validation in literature on both marketing (Hakansson, 1982) and IT (Cunningham and Tynan, 1993; Leek et al., 2000). In addition to the Hakansson 'Interaction Approach', Kern and Willcocks (2002) argue that most of the literature focused either on behaviour or management aspects,

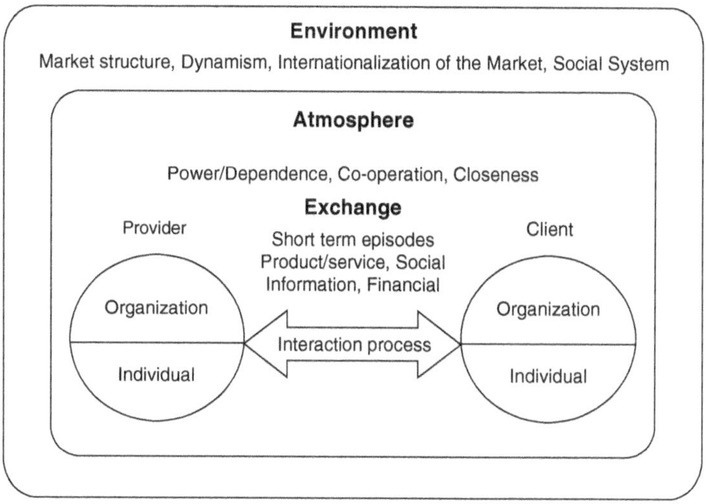

Figure 2.1 Interaction Approach adopted from Hakansson (1982)

but none focused on the interaction, the structure and the context. Building on the work of Kern and Willcocks, the 'Interaction Approach' in relationships is used during empirical research as a fundamental tool for exploring client developments. Figure 2.1 illustrates the basic interaction model based on dyadic client–provider arrangements.

The 'Interaction Approach' can be divided into three categories of variables that influence the interaction between both parties: their mutual environment, the atmosphere and the exchange process. Using Hakansson's 'Interaction Approach', the model shown in Figure 2.1 provides a more comprehensive and holistic view of the client environment. Furthermore, from the perspective of relationships, the IOR theory can be useful to identify how important clients experience the impact of key developments on provider capabilities.

Capabilities

The field of strategic management focuses on the reasons that firms have for making different strategic choices and, subsequently, the effect that these choices have on their performance. Research regarding capabilities and firm performance is commonly based on resource-based (RBV) reasoning (Wernerfelt, 1984; Barney, 1986). The RBV focuses on concepts such as technological capabilities, organizational structures, managerial competence, and firm performance (Barney, 1991). The RBV shifts the emphasis from the firm's competitive environment, as discussed by Porter (1980), towards its resources – that is, the firm's capabilities with regard to the execution of its strategy. The main argument of the RBV is that firms possess resources that contribute to the achievement of both a competitive advantage and long-term performance (Penrose, 1959; Wernerfelt, 1984; Barney, 1991; Grant, 1991). When a firm develops unique advantages in the market which are difficult to compete with, the foundation for a competitive advantage is grounded. Barney (1991) argued that sustained competitive advantage is derived from resources and capabilities a firm controls that are valuable, rare, imperfectly imitable and not substitutable. Building on previous research, Barney (1995) argues that sustained competitive advantage is based on three motivations: (1) some resources and capabilities can only be developed over long periods of time (that is, path dependency); (2) it may not always be clear how to develop these capabilities in the short to medium term (that is, causal ambiguity); and (3) some resources and capabilities cannot be bought and sold (that is, social complexity). The available literature shows (Henderson and Cockburn, 1994; Barney and Arikan, 2001) that firms that build their strategies on path-dependent, causally ambiguous, socially complex and intangible assets outperform firms that build their strategies only on tangible assets.

When studying the literature we come across the use of a wide variety of concepts. Therefore it is useful to clarify and define the relevant terms. Prahalad and Hamel (1990) popularized the concept of organizational core competence and stated that core competences are comparatively more durable than simple capabilities. The distinction between core competences and capabilities is that core competences comprise capabilities, whereas capabilities are not necessarily core competences. Core competences refer to organizational processes engaged in by people that result in products and services and endure over time as employees enter and exit the firm (Eisenhardt and Martin, 2000). The set of core competences of a firm is relatively stable as it cannot be changed on a short-term basis. Unlike core competences, capabilities do not remain constant. They will emerge, grow, mature and decline (Dierickx and Cool, 1989).

In our study, we define resources as assets that are owned and controlled by a firm as input for production. Examples of assets concerns people, properties and capital that can be acquired from the market (Sanchez, 1996; Wade and Hulland, 2004). Assets are defined as anything tangible or intangible a firm can use in its processes for developing or producing products and or services. A capability refers to the ability of a firm to perform a coordinated set of tasks to achieve a certain end result. Capabilities can be characterized as repeatable patterns of actions in the use of assets to develop products and or services to a market (Sanchez, 1996). Capabilities also include the aspect of processes, skills and know-how that are required to produce products or services. Moreover, capabilities can be considered as either 'operational' or 'dynamic'. Winter (2000: 983) defines an operational capability as 'a high-level routine, or collection of routines, that, together with its implementing input flows, confers upon an organization's management a set of decision options for producing significant outputs of a particular type'. In other words, an operational capability is based on processes and procedures to coordinate a number of tasks that are required to perform an activity. By contrast, dynamic capabilities involve adaptation and change as they build, integrate or reconfigure operational capabilities in order to respond to a changing business environment. Dynamic capabilities are often characterized as unique and idiosyncratic processes that emerge from path-dependent histories of individual firms (Teece et al., 1997; Zollo and Winter, 2002). Routines that relate to a capability may refer to the performance of individual tasks or the coordination of the individual tasks (Helfat and Peteraf, 2003). This relates to both individuals and teams.

Capabilities can be subdivided into the following relevant properties: tacitness, context specificity and temporality. Tacitness refers to the extent to which knowledge can be captured, codified and imitated (Polanyi, 1966). When an organization tries to imitate routines form their competitors, there is no guarantee that capabilities are also imitated because capabilities are developed by integrating different organizational routines within the context of the firm. Research (Ethiraj et al., 2005) empirically demonstrates that firm capabilities are often context-specific. Elements of this context-specificity include, for instance, the way in which providers capabilities are adapted to the client's organization and environment. As a result of their context dependency, it is difficult to transfer or replace capabilities from one context to another.

Sourcing capabilities

To this point we have not discussed sourcing capabilities in more detail. We define sourcing capability as the 'IT capabilities that refers to an assembly of skills, techniques, and know-how developed over time which enable an organization to acquire, deploy and leverage IT investments in pursuit of business strategies' (Lacity and Willcocks, 2001). As mentioned above, literature on IT provider sourcing capabilities has yielded only very limited research. Kern and Willcocks (2001) argue that IT providers need to have three types of organizational competences to support their relational advantage: customer awareness, business skills and service delivery. Feeny et al. (2005), which builds on earlier research (Kern and Willcocks, 2001, 2002),

Figure 2.2 IT provider competences and capabilities
Source: Feeny et al. (2005).

describes 12 provider sourcing capabilities that are related to three organizational competences: relationship, transformation, and delivery. These three organizational competence areas and accompanying sourcing capabilities are illustrated in Figure 2.2. The first organizational competence focuses on the relationship between provider and client, including topics like planning and contracting, organizational design, governance and leadership.

In many outsourcing arrangements, the provider has to balance a demanding client and the own organization that expects a profitable margin. The realization of a win–win situation is probably the most challenging factor in the relationship. The second organizational competence is related to the area of transformation. Relevant topics in this area are technology exploitation, process improvement, programme management and customer development. The third organizational competence, delivery, determines the extent to which a provider is able to react to a client's day-to-day needs with regard to operational services, and it includes topics such as business management, domain expertise, behaviour management and sourcing. On the one hand, a different set of sourcing capabilities is required during each phase of an outsourcing arrangement. This means that provider sourcing capabilities have to be organized and aligned with the clients' needs. In regular mutual meetings between client and provider, capability alignment can take place. On the other hand, the value and content of sourcing capabilities will change over time. As mentioned, Feeny et al. (2005) have subdivided the three organizational technology-oriented or organizational-oriented factors. This will lead to the following hypothesis:

> ***H 1c:** Exogenous client developments will lead to adjustment in service provider sourcing capabilities.*

Sourcing capabilities and organizational structure

As indicated earlier, the provider's sourcing capabilities need to be dynamic in nature in order to meet the client's demand. This requires that providers have to emphasize on the regular development of sourcing capabilities. To what extent sourcing capabilities needs to be developed depends on the type of market in which the provider is acting: moderately dynamic markets or very dynamic markets. First, moderately dynamic markets can be characterized as frequently changing but roughly predictable with linear paths. In most of the cases these markets are relatively stable, comprising clear boundaries and well-known players (for example, competitors, customers). Secondly, in very dynamic or so-called 'high-velocity' markets, changes are unpredictable and become non-linear. Very dynamic markets can be characterized by blurred market boundaries, unclear business models and shifting market players. In these circumstances, firms cannot rely on existing knowledge; rather, they have to rely on rapidly creating situation-dependent new knowledge. It will be clear that if capabilities are continuously scrutinized and flexibility and competence is required from employees, the organizational structure is also affected. An organization that requires its employees to be professionals has to adjust their organizational structure to accommodate these professionals.

With regard to the field of IT outsourcing, Transaction Cost Economics (TCE) has been applied to the discussion of sourcing decisions (Lacity et al., 1995; Watjatrakul, 2005), IT operations (Aubert et al., 2004) and costs (Barthélemy and Quélin, 2006). Williamson (1979) proposes that costs comprise not only production costs, the costs of capital, labour and material, but also transaction costs. This means that firms, and therefore decision-makers, have to consider integral costs (production costs plus transaction costs) when considering the production of services. Taking the aspect of economics and firm boundaries into account, the TCE is a form of organizational theory. The level of transaction costs depends on the specific characteristics of the services to be delivered, the economic aspects of the situation and the way the organization is structured. Previous research (Williamson, 1975, 1979) revealed that providers are able to produce goods or services at lower costs due to economies of scale that can be achieved via economies of scale. Because of this rationale IT outsourcing providers focus on the reduction of their average costs by allocating fixed costs over more units of output and by receiving discounts resulting from their bargaining power. Important determining factors that refer to outsourcing transactions concern the uncertainty surrounding the transaction and the specificity of the assets.

At any time, there is a level of uncertainty surrounding transactions. For instance, when a client is not willing or able to specify an IT service, this will lead, to some extent, to uncertainty on the provider side. Lacity and Willcocks (1995) describe the relationship between the uncertainty of the transaction and the coordination costs. The more uncertainty surrounds a transaction, the higher the coordination costs for a provider will become. Previous research (Speklé, 2001) defines uncertainty as the degree of specifiability of intended performance and predictability of the environment within which the contract is to be executed. On the other hand, it is impossible to anticipate on all future eventualities and to describe them in a contract. However, an important critique on the TCE is that the aspect of internal resources are neglected, specifically the influence of core competences of an organization. Therefore, we previously discussed the RBV in relation to the importance of capabilities. The second determinant factor that is important refers to asset specificity. The degree of customization (specific or non-specific) of the transaction type can be measured by the difference between costs of the asset and the value of its second-best use (Williamson, 1981). As asset specificity increases and contract protection clauses become more complex, they become increasingly costly to implement (Aubert et al., 2004). Investments in specific assets will lead to higher transaction costs; therefore a provider who is investing in specific assets is looking for guarantees from their client. For instance, by agreeing to a long-term outsourcing arrangement. In doing so, the client offers a reimbursement for the investments of the provider.

One of the TCE assumptions is the existence of a relationship between asset specificity and the complexity of governance structures. As Dyer (1997) stated: 'The standard (transaction cost) reasoning is that as asset specificity increases, more complex governance structures are required to eliminate or attenuate costly bargaining over profits from specialized assets.' When a firm does not possess the required competences for the internal production of services, they can acquire them with the acceptance of high transaction costs. Therefore, a firm has to enter a long-term relationship with an external provider and establish an appropriate coordination mechanism (governance structure). This coordination mechanism can be considered as a functional organizational structure that a firm applies to produce and transfer a product or service towards their clients. Williamson (1975) investigated the relationship between transaction costs and the degree of specificity.

Discussing both dimensions from the perspective of TCE, a firm may apply various coordination mechanisms to coordinate transactions. First, it is assumed that for non-specific assets, the market achieves economies of scale on production costs. Transaction costs are minimal as a firm does not have to monitor an external party. This means that a firm requires a coordination mechanism for offering standard solutions at a low cost. In other words, specific firm activities (for example, the IT function) can be outsourced to third parties. This coordination mechanism is often depicted as a Market form of coordination. When the degree of asset specificity varies, the mechanism to coordinate the transactions becomes more complex. As a result, the transaction costs increase proportionately. This relates to the term Hybrid form of coordination as described by Williamson (1975). Since asset specificity is mixed, the market can offer economies of scale for the standard part of transactions. So outsourcing firms' activities, for example the IT function, is still an option. When firms offer a complex set of different services to clients, the coordination mechanism to support clients is designed more specifically, which results in higher transaction costs. This is the Hierarchical form of coordination. Firm's hierarchies can realize economies of scale as assets are specialized to a single employee. This form of coordination refers to insourcing.

From the perspective of an IT service provider, Williamson's framework for categorizing coordination mechanisms can be applied to the determination of the impact on outsourcing arrangements. At a functional level service providers establish a specific organizational structure to facilitate the delivery of IT services to their clients. When highly standardized IT services are provided to clients, the providers' transaction costs are perceived as low as the degree of asset specificity is low. However, as there is an increased complexity in the coordination of the transactions, the transaction costs also experience a substantial increase. For example, a provider who supports different types of IT services to a client has to pay more attention towards monitoring, controlling and managing the IT services internally. This is related to organizational dimensions such as decision-making, communication and level of hierarchy. As clients have different types of contracted IT services (for example, single service or multiple services) and different markets in which they act (for example, static or dynamic), providers also have to differentiate their coordination mechanisms. Moreover, changing client circumstances may result in changes in the provider's organizational structure.

As the scope of our research includes various types of IT services (for example, networks, office automation, infrastructure management) some aspects of a provider's transaction are standardized while others are customized. This corresponds with the Hybrid form of coordination as described by Williamson (1975). Therefore, to be less susceptible to changes in their clients' environment, IT outsourcing providers have to establish a dynamic fit between sourcing capabilities and their own organizational structure.

Organizational structure dimensions

As discussed, the type of coordination mechanism is directly related to the applied organizational structure of a firm. Formal organizational structure and the roles that people play, including the competences and responsibilities involved, have been investigated extensively in organizational literature (Dalton et al., 1980; Koufteros and Vonderembse, 1998; Daft, 1995). An organization is a unit of formal positions, usually occupied by individuals, with explicit objectives, tasks, processes and assets (Bouwman et al., 2006) and is related to firm performance (Carmeli and Tishler, 2004). Providers that rely on the division of labour, as is the case for IT outsourcing providers, can only stay in business when they are able to organize their internal transaction of services more efficiently than other firms.

The existing literature suggests that the nature of organizational structure in industrial versus post-industrial firms can be regarded as mechanistic (inorganic) versus organic (Lawrence and Lorsch, 1967; Zammuto and O'Conner, 1992; Daft, 1995). Daft (1995) argues that the mechanistic paradigm is effective when environments have a high degree of certainty, technologies tend to be routine, organizations are designed to handle handling large volumes (for example, products or services) and employees are treated as just another resource. Internal forms tend to be vertical, functional and bureaucratic. The organic paradigm, on the other hand, is characterized by an unstable, even chaotic nature of the external environment. Typical features of these types of organizations include teamwork, face-to-face interactions, learning and innovation.

In this section, we address different dimensions of organizational structures that play a role in organizing tasks, processes and resources (capabilities). Previous research (Mintzberg, 1979) described five coordinating mechanisms to explain the fundamental ways in which organizations coordinate their work. Daft (1995) studied various organizational dimensions such as the level of formalization, specialization, standardization, the hierarchy of authority, and professionalism. Germain (1996) focuses on specialization and decentralization while other researchers (see, for example, Koufteros

Table 2.2 List of subdimensions for organizational structure

Dimension	Definition	Literature
Locus of decision-making	The degree to which decisions are made high versus low in the organizational hierarchy	Daft (1995), Damanpour (1991), Doll and Vonderembse (1991), Gerwin (1996), Germain et al. (1994), Nemetz and Fry 1988), Ruekert et al. (1985), Thompson (1965), Walton (1985), Zammuto and O'Conner (1992)
Level of hierarchy	The degree to which an organization has many versus few levels of management	Burns and Stalker (1961), Damanpour (1991), Doll and Vonderembse (1991), Hull and Hage (1982), Walton (1985)
Level of horizontal integration	The degree to which departments and workers are functionally specialized versus integrated in their works, skills and training	Davenport and Nohria (1994), Doll and Vonderembse (1991), Gerwin and Kolodny 1992), MacDuffie (1995), Vonderembse et al. (1997), Walton (1985)

and Vonderembse, 1998) emphasize centralization and formalization. Nahm et al. (2003) concentrate on the degree of centralization of the decision-making process, the formalization of rules and procedures and structural differentiation in their research into environmental uncertainty and organizational form. Among this variety of subdimensions for organizational structure, the three commonly discussed are deemed relevant to this study and are listed in Table 2.2. These subdimensions concern the locus of decision-making, the number of layers in the hierarchy, and the level of horizontal integration. Because a client's situation is subject to change, the supporting organizational structure and accompanying dimensions of the IT provider may also vary. Next, we discuss the three different organizational dimensions in more detail.

Locus of decision-making

The 'locus of decision-making' is the degree to which decisions are made higher or lower in the organizational hierarchy (Daft, 1995; Doll and Vonderembse, 1991; Germain, 1996). Firms that are operating in an uncertain environment should delegate decisions to the level at which employees are able to quickly adapt to changing circumstances and add value for their customers. When the level of organizational uncertainty is high, strategic decision-making authority can be centralized (Paswan et al., 1998), but operational decision-making authority should be decentralized. The lower the locus, the more decentralized the decision-making. An organic organizational structure would decentralize decision-making to the greatest extent possible (Zammuto and O'Conner, 1992; Daft, 1995). Our research is limited to just one domain: operational decentralization related to service decisions.

Number of layers in hierarchy

The 'number of layers in hierarchy' is the degree to which an organization has many versus few levels of management (Burns and Stalker, 1961; Walton, 1985). In a more traditional command and control model, an expanding hierarchy is necessary as a result of the need to control behaviour. In a commitment model, the management form tends to be flat, relies upon shared goals for control and lateral coordination, influences based on expertise and information rather than position and minimizes status difference. A characteristic of a flat organization is that this is a tacit asset that makes it easier to compete with other parties due to faster decision-making. However, the more layers in a firm and the wider the span of control, the more complex is the structure. On the one hand Burns and Stalker (1961) and Walton (1985) argue that organic organizations have only few layers in their hierarchy. On the other hand, mechanic organizations tend to exploit many layers in their organizational hierarchy.

Level of horizontal integration

The 'level of horizontal integration' is the degree to which departments and workers are functionally specialized versus integrated in their work, skills and training (Doll and Vonderembse, 1991; Davenport and Nohria, 1994). Firms that are based on production (for example, products) usually separate functional departments so that work can be carried out in a sequential manner. However, firms that are focusing on the provisioning of services will integrate functionalities of different departments and their employees. The justification for this choice is based on an adequate response to the changing environment and the needs of the client organization and therefore it adds value. Workers in service-oriented firms are being brought together in autonomous work teams, cross-functional teams and taskforces. Employees are usually cross-trained so that they have a better understanding of the overall processes and are able to respond quickly to changing business needs. As a result, mechanistic organizations have a low level of horizontal integration and organic organizations have a high level of horizontal integration.

competences into 12 capabilities. These sourcing capabilities are listed in Table 2.1. We argue that in order to cater to a client's need providers require dynamic sourcing capabilities. Based on the sourcing capabilities as discussed, we will investigate in our empirical research which provider sourcing capabilities are applied during the different sourcing phases (e.g. transition and delivery).

Now that we have introduced the core concepts based on the IOR and the RBV literature, we can formulate the following hypotheses, which will be tested in our quantitative study in Chapter 8.

Hypotheses

We argue that IT outsourcing providers have to reassess their sourcing capabilities on a regular basis and strengthen them when necessary to adapt to the changing circumstances that a client has to deal with. Therefore we pose our first hypothesis as follows:

> ***H 1a:*** *Outsourcing service provider's sensitivity to change and uncertainty a client has to deal with, will lead to adjustment in service provider sourcing capabilities.*

As a result of environmental uncertainty providers have to manage their internal processes in order to adapt their sourcing capabilities. This is related to both the ability and the willingness of service providers. In doing so, adaptability procedures can be applied to guide the internal adaptability process which in turn require regular attention and investments. The outsourcing provider's internal adaptability, that is, the responsiveness and adaptability of their employees, is a condition for the adjustment of sourcing capabilities. Management can promote employees to be aware of their role in being adaptive. Based on this assumption we pose the following hypothesis:

> ***H 1b:*** *Outsourcing service provider's internal focus on adaptability will lead to adjustment in service provider sourcing capabilities.*

Exogenous developments in the client environment may lead to a refocusing of activities. Since environmental developments increase over time, clients have to adapt to their environment regularly in order to innovate their businesses. Consequently, developments on the client side also affect clients' relation with the service provider, so that providers have to adapt their sourcing capabilities. For example, if innovation is high on the agenda of a client the service provider has to strengthen its sourcing capabilities that refer to technology-oriented or organizational-oriented factors. This will lead to the following hypothesis:

> ***H 1c:*** *Exogenous client developments will lead to adjustment in service provider sourcing capabilities.*

Sourcing capabilities and organizational structure

As indicated earlier, the provider's sourcing capabilities need to be dynamic in nature in order to meet the client's demand. This requires that providers have to emphasize on the regular development of sourcing capabilities. To what extent sourcing capabilities needs to be developed depends on the type of market in which the provider is acting: moderately dynamic markets or very dynamic markets. First, moderately dynamic markets can be characterized as frequently changing but roughly predictable with linear paths. In most of the cases these markets are relatively stable, comprising clear boundaries and well-known players (for example, competitors, customers). Secondly, in very dynamic or so-called 'high-velocity' markets, changes are unpredictable and become non-linear. Very dynamic markets can be characterized by blurred market boundaries, unclear business models and shifting market players. In these circumstances, firms cannot rely on existing knowledge; rather, they have to rely on rapidly creating situation-dependent new knowledge. It will be clear that if capabilities are continuously scrutinized and flexibility and competence is required from employees, the organizational structure is also affected. An organization that requires its employees to be professionals has to adjust their organizational structure to accommodate these professionals.

With regard to the field of IT outsourcing, Transaction Cost Economics (TCE) has been applied to the discussion of sourcing decisions (Lacity et al., 1995; Watjatrakul, 2005), IT operations (Aubert et al., 2004) and costs (Barthélemy and Quélin, 2006). Williamson (1979) proposes that costs comprise not only production costs, the costs of capital, labour and material, but also transaction costs. This means that firms, and therefore decision-makers, have to consider integral costs (production costs plus transaction costs) when considering the production of services. Taking the aspect of economics and firm boundaries into account, the TCE is a form of organizational theory. The level of transaction costs depends on the specific characteristics of the services to be delivered, the economic aspects of the situation and the way the organization is structured. Previous research (Williamson, 1975, 1979) revealed that providers are able to produce goods or services at lower costs due to economies of scale that can be achieved via economies of scale. Because of this rationale IT outsourcing providers focus on the reduction of their average costs by allocating fixed costs over more units of output and by receiving discounts resulting from their bargaining power. Important determining factors that refer to outsourcing transactions concern the uncertainty surrounding the transaction and the specificity of the assets.

At any time, there is a level of uncertainty surrounding transactions. For instance, when a client is not willing or able to specify an IT service, this will lead, to some extent, to uncertainty on the provider side. Lacity and Willcocks (1995) describe the relationship between the uncertainty of the transaction and the coordination costs. The more uncertainty surrounds a transaction, the higher the coordination costs for a provider will become. Previous research (Speklé, 2001) defines uncertainty as the degree of specifiability of intended performance and predictability of the environment within which the contract is to be executed. On the other hand, it is impossible to anticipate on all future eventualities and to describe them in a contract. However, an important critique on the TCE is that the aspect of internal resources are neglected, specifically the influence of core competences of an organization. Therefore, we previously discussed the RBV in relation to the importance of capabilities. The second determinant factor that is important refers to asset specificity. The degree of customization (specific or non-specific) of the transaction type can be measured by the difference between costs of the asset and the value of its second-best use (Williamson, 1981). As asset specificity increases and contract protection clauses become more complex, they become increasingly costly to implement (Aubert et al., 2004). Investments in specific assets will lead to higher transaction costs; therefore a provider who is investing in specific assets is looking for guarantees from their client. For instance, by agreeing to a long-term outsourcing arrangement. In doing so, the client offers a reimbursement for the investments of the provider.

One of the TCE assumptions is the existence of a relationship between asset specificity and the complexity of governance structures. As Dyer (1997) stated: 'The standard (transaction cost) reasoning is that as asset specificity increases, more complex governance structures are required to eliminate or attenuate costly bargaining over profits from specialized assets.' When a firm does not possess the required competences for the internal production of services, they can acquire them with the acceptance of high transaction costs. Therefore, a firm has to enter a long-term relationship with an external provider and establish an appropriate coordination mechanism (governance structure). This coordination mechanism can be considered as a functional organizational structure that a firm applies to produce and transfer a product or service towards their clients. Williamson (1975) investigated the relationship between transaction costs and the degree of specificity.

Discussing both dimensions from the perspective of TCE, a firm may apply various coordination mechanisms to coordinate transactions. First, it is assumed that for non-specific assets, the market achieves economies of scale on production costs. Transaction costs are minimal as a firm does not have to monitor an external party. This means that a firm requires a coordination mechanism for offering standard solutions at a low cost. In other words, specific firm activities (for example, the IT function) can be outsourced to third parties. This coordination mechanism is often depicted as a Market form of coordination. When the degree of asset specificity varies, the mechanism to coordinate the transactions becomes more complex. As a result, the transaction costs increase proportionately. This relates to the term Hybrid form of coordination as described by Williamson (1975). Since asset specificity is mixed, the market can offer economies of scale for the standard part of transactions. So outsourcing firms' activities, for example the IT function, is still an option. When firms offer a complex set of different services to clients, the coordination mechanism to support clients is designed more specifically, which results in higher transaction costs. This is the Hierarchical form of coordination. Firm's hierarchies can realize economies of scale as assets are specialized to a single employee. This form of coordination refers to insourcing.

From the perspective of an IT service provider, Williamson's framework for categorizing coordination mechanisms can be applied to the determination of the impact on outsourcing arrangements. At a functional level service providers establish a specific organizational structure to facilitate the delivery of IT services to their clients. When highly standardized IT services are provided to clients, the providers' transaction costs are perceived as low as the degree of asset specificity is low. However, as there is an increased complexity in the coordination of the transactions, the transaction costs also experience a substantial increase. For example, a provider who supports different types of IT services to a client has to pay more attention towards monitoring, controlling and managing the IT services internally. This is related to organizational dimensions such as decision-making, communication and level of hierarchy. As clients have different types of contracted IT services (for example, single service or multiple services) and different markets in which they act (for example, static or dynamic), providers also have to differentiate their coordination mechanisms. Moreover, changing client circumstances may result in changes in the provider's organizational structure.

As the scope of our research includes various types of IT services (for example, networks, office automation, infrastructure management) some aspects of a provider's transaction are standardized while others are customized. This corresponds with the Hybrid form of coordination as described by Williamson (1975). Therefore, to be less susceptible to changes in their clients' environment, IT outsourcing providers have to establish a dynamic fit between sourcing capabilities and their own organizational structure.

Organizational structure dimensions

As discussed, the type of coordination mechanism is directly related to the applied organizational structure of a firm. Formal organizational structure and the roles that people play, including the competences and responsibilities involved, have been investigated extensively in organizational literature (Dalton et al., 1980; Koufteros and Vonderembse, 1998; Daft, 1995). An organization is a unit of formal positions, usually occupied by individuals, with explicit objectives, tasks, processes and assets (Bouwman et al., 2006) and is related to firm performance (Carmeli and Tishler, 2004). Providers that rely on the division of labour, as is the case for IT outsourcing providers, can only stay in business when they are able to organize their internal transaction of services more efficiently than other firms.

The existing literature suggests that the nature of organizational structure in industrial versus post-industrial firms can be regarded as mechanistic (inorganic) versus organic (Lawrence and Lorsch, 1967; Zammuto and O'Conner, 1992; Daft, 1995). Daft (1995) argues that the mechanistic paradigm is effective when environments have a high degree of certainty, technologies tend to be routine, organizations are designed to handle handling large volumes (for example, products or services) and employees are treated as just another resource. Internal forms tend to be vertical, functional and bureaucratic. The organic paradigm, on the other hand, is characterized by an unstable, even chaotic nature of the external environment. Typical features of these types of organizations include teamwork, face-to-face interactions, learning and innovation.

In this section, we address different dimensions of organizational structures that play a role in organizing tasks, processes and resources (capabilities). Previous research (Mintzberg, 1979) described five coordinating mechanisms to explain the fundamental ways in which organizations coordinate their work. Daft (1995) studied various organizational dimensions such as the level of formalization, specialization, standardization, the hierarchy of authority, and professionalism. Germain (1996) focuses on specialization and decentralization while other researchers (see, for example, Koufteros

Table 2.2 List of subdimensions for organizational structure

Dimension	Definition	Literature
Locus of decision-making	The degree to which decisions are made high versus low in the organizational hierarchy	Daft (1995), Damanpour (1991), Doll and Vonderembse (1991), Gerwin (1996), Germain et al. (1994), Nemetz and Fry 1988), Ruekert et al. (1985), Thompson (1965), Walton (1985), Zammuto and O'Conner (1992)
Level of hierarchy	The degree to which an organization has many versus few levels of management	Burns and Stalker (1961), Damanpour (1991), Doll and Vonderembse (1991), Hull and Hage (1982), Walton (1985)
Level of horizontal integration	The degree to which departments and workers are functionally specialized versus integrated in their works, skills and training	Davenport and Nohria (1994), Doll and Vonderembse (1991), Gerwin and Kolodny 1992), MacDuffie (1995), Vonderembse et al. (1997), Walton (1985)

and Vonderembse, 1998) emphasize centralization and formalization. Nahm et al. (2003) concentrate on the degree of centralization of the decision-making process, the formalization of rules and procedures and structural differentiation in their research into environmental uncertainty and organizational form. Among this variety of subdimensions for organizational structure, the three commonly discussed are deemed relevant to this study and are listed in Table 2.2. These subdimensions concern the locus of decision-making, the number of layers in the hierarchy, and the level of horizontal integration. Because a client's situation is subject to change, the supporting organizational structure and accompanying dimensions of the IT provider may also vary. Next, we discuss the three different organizational dimensions in more detail.

Locus of decision-making

The 'locus of decision-making' is the degree to which decisions are made higher or lower in the organizational hierarchy (Daft, 1995; Doll and Vonderembse, 1991; Germain, 1996). Firms that are operating in an uncertain environment should delegate decisions to the level at which employees are able to quickly adapt to changing circumstances and add value for their customers. When the level of organizational uncertainty is high, strategic decision-making authority can be centralized (Paswan et al., 1998), but operational decision-making authority should be decentralized. The lower the locus, the more decentralized the decision-making. An organic organizational structure would decentralize decision-making to the greatest extent possible (Zammuto and O'Conner, 1992; Daft, 1995). Our research is limited to just one domain: operational decentralization related to service decisions.

Number of layers in hierarchy

The 'number of layers in hierarchy' is the degree to which an organization has many versus few levels of management (Burns and Stalker, 1961; Walton, 1985). In a more traditional command and control model, an expanding hierarchy is necessary as a result of the need to control behaviour. In a commitment model, the management form tends to be flat, relies upon shared goals for control and lateral coordination, influences based on expertise and information rather than position and minimizes status difference. A characteristic of a flat organization is that this is a tacit asset that makes it easier to compete with other parties due to faster decision-making. However, the more layers in a firm and the wider the span of control, the more complex is the structure. On the one hand Burns and Stalker (1961) and Walton (1985) argue that organic organizations have only few layers in their hierarchy. On the other hand, mechanic organizations tend to exploit many layers in their organizational hierarchy.

Level of horizontal integration

The 'level of horizontal integration' is the degree to which departments and workers are functionally specialized versus integrated in their work, skills and training (Doll and Vonderembse, 1991; Davenport and Nohria, 1994). Firms that are based on production (for example, products) usually separate functional departments so that work can be carried out in a sequential manner. However, firms that are focusing on the provisioning of services will integrate functionalities of different departments and their employees. The justification for this choice is based on an adequate response to the changing environment and the needs of the client organization and therefore it adds value. Workers in service-oriented firms are being brought together in autonomous work teams, cross-functional teams and taskforces. Employees are usually cross-trained so that they have a better understanding of the overall processes and are able to respond quickly to changing business needs. As a result, mechanistic organizations have a low level of horizontal integration and organic organizations have a high level of horizontal integration.

Hypotheses

We argue that improvements in sourcing capabilities have an influence on the level at which decisions are to be made. Dependent on the extent to which capabilities are adjusted providers have to define whether the locus of decision-making in the organization is determined to be either high or low.

> ***H 2a:*** *Adjustment in service provider sourcing capabilities will have an effect on organizational decision-making.*

In the same way we argue that an adjustment in service provider sourcing capabilities will influence the number of layers in the organization.

> ***H 2b:*** *Adjustment in service provider sourcing capabilities will lead to a reduction of organizational hierarchy.*

When there is a reduction in the number of layers in the hierarchy, fewer people are involved in the provisioning of IT services. Consequently, the level of horizontal integration of departments and employees will be functionally integrated. Therefore we hypothesize that:

> ***H 2c:*** *Adjustment in service provider sourcing capabilities will lead to horizontal integration.*

In analogy with hypothesis H1c that the provider's focus on client developments will affect its sourcing capabilities, we expect that in line with contingency theory (Galbraith, 1977), the organizational structure of the provider will also be adjusted. The organizational structure of providers is partly influenced by their external environment, that is, developments on the client side also affect the client's relationship with the service provider. The service provider might have to adjust the way decision-making is organized, the number of decision-making levels applied, and the degree of horizontal integration. Therefore, we hypothesize that:

> ***H 2d:*** *Exogenous client developments will lead to adjustment in service provider organizational structure.*

The organizational structure of providers is influenced in part by their external environment (Nahm et al., 2003). The extent to which the external environment influences the way decision-making is organized, the number of decision-making levels applied, and the degree of horizontal integration.

Organizational structure and performance

Several authors (Galbraith, 1977; Drazin and Van de Ven, 1985) have adopted a contingency perspective to examine the relationships between organizational strategy and structure and IT strategy and structure. Only a small number of the studies have undertaken an empirical examination of the impact of the fit between these variables and organizational performance. The organizational subdimensions, when well organized, are expected to provide positive contributions to the provider's performance. In this sense, the organizational structure of IT providers can be seen as intermediating the relationship between the developments with which the client has to deal, and the provider's sourcing capabilities that are designed to support these developments. Capabilities and organizational structure can be perceived as factors that have an influence on firm performance (King and Zeithaml, 2001). Capabilities and organizational structure form a combination of both tangible and intangible assets and, as argued by Barney (1991), will contribute to improvements in firm performance.

There is extensive literature on performance in the IS field (Feeny and Ives, 1990; Clemons and Row, 1991; Feeny et al., 2005). Much of this research suggests that the ability to leverage distinctive internal capabilities is related to environmental dynamism that affect a firm's performance and ultimately the sustainability of providing services (Schendel and Hofer, 1979; Lieberman and Montgomery, 1998; Levina and Ross, 2003). Since research on firm performance from the perspective of the RBV is manifold, it is necessary to focus on a specific part of performance. To be consistent with our research approach in this study we focus on organizational performance.

Addressing the aspect of performance, Kaplan and Norton (1992) proposed the business scorecard (BSC) to measure this concept. They argued that traditional financially oriented accounting measures offer a narrow and incomplete view of business performance. As a result they suggest that traditional measures are supplemented with non-financial perspectives that reflect customer satisfaction, internal business processes, and learning and growth perspectives. Martinsons et al. (1999) have developed a BSC for information systems that measured and evaluated IS activities from the following perspectives: business value, user orientation, internal process and future readiness. Despite its widespread use, the BSC does have some shortcomings. Neely and Adams (2000) noted the absence of a competitive dimension while later research (King and Zeithaml, 2001) emphasizes the importance of a relationship between competences and firm performance. Moreover, the BSC also lacks the perspective of the customer as a dimension to reflect

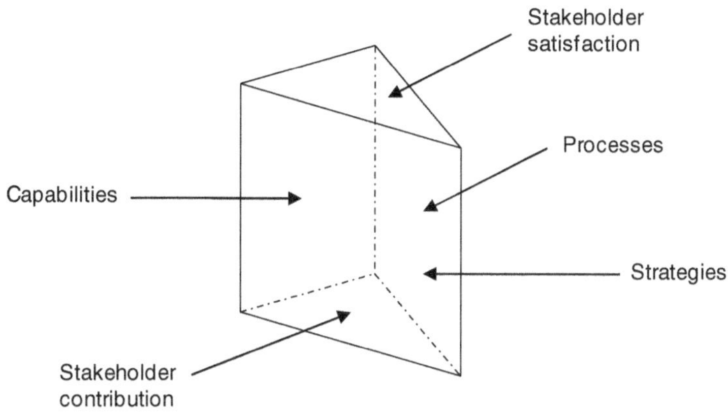

Figure 2.3 Comprehensiveness of the Performance Prism
Source: Neely et al. (2002).

the performance. Examples of these dimensions are generic strategic objectives according to cost, quality, delivery and flexibility. Considering these shortcomings the usability of the balanced scorecard from the perspective of our research is limited.

We need a framework that is multidimensional. Neely et al. (2002) have designed and developed the Performance Prism, which is a three-dimensional model based on five facets (for example, stakeholders, stakeholder contribution, capabilities, processes and strategies). Together they provide a set of measurement tools. To reflect the growing importance of satisfying stakeholder requirements, the Performance Prism adopts a stakeholder-centric view. Among the identified stakeholders are, for instance, clients, providers and employees. In essence, the Performance Prism, which is illustrated in Figure 2.3, looks at the interdependencies among stakeholders. The goal to which performance measurement continues is primarily to stakeholders and not to strategy, as is the case with the BSC.

Mapping the Performance Prism framework to IT service providers enables us to measure the research constructs at an organizational level. The Performance Prism dimensions encompass all research constructs. The Performance Prism can be regarded as multidimensional in that it provides a balanced analysis of the environment in which services are provided while highlighting various stakeholders and measuring internal strategies, processes and capabilities. As discussed earlier, in more recent views fit is seen as dynamic focusing on multivariate relations between organizational factors. Therefore, the Performance Prism framework aligns the multidimensional constructs of our research. The Prism facet *stakeholders* refers to our research construct client developments and the internal provider organization. This facet includes an external perspective as well as an internal perspective. Both clients and internal employees can be viewed as important stakeholders that might have an influence on the provider's organization. As we focus on changes in the client's environment we can use the Performance Prism to measure these changes and assess their impact on the provider's organization. The Prism facet *capabilities* relates directly to the research construct sourcing capabilities. As the Prism facets *stakeholders* and *capabilities* are interlinked, the influence of changing client circumstances on sourcing capabilities can be measured. The Prism facet of *processes* can be related to the construct organizational structure. Processes are required to guide the organizational dimensions are described in section 2.3. As the Prism facet *strategies* is interlinked with the facets *capabilities* and *processes* this means that this facet refers directly to the measurement of the fit between sourcing capabilities and organizational structure.

Using the Performance Prism framework in IT provider organizations allows for the identification and measurement of key sourcing capabilities and organizational structures that influence firm performance. As we emphasize the term sustainable performance, we apply the following definition:

> *A sustainable sourcing performance arise from a provider's ability to monitor and assess changing client circumstances, adapt their sourcing capabilities and organizational structure which result in a consistent high-quality service performance over time.*

Hypotheses

Sourcing capabilities embedded in an organizational structure that is aligned with the client environment are expected to contribute to the providers' sourcing performance. We argue that establishing this dynamic fit enables providers to establish a sustainable sourcing performance. By doing so, the organizational structure facilitates the provisioning of IT services, and contributes to the sustainable performance of an outsourcing service provider. However, the problem is that it is often difficult to measure the effect of capabilities and organizational structure on firm performance (Robins and Wiersema, 1995). As it is difficult to gather real data that refer to the providers' performance in empirical research we suggest monitoring the performance. The importance that is attributed to performance monitoring can be considered an alternative for direct measurements. The degree to which importance is attributed to performance monitoring is used as a proxy for high-level sustainable performance.

H 3a: *Decision-making is positively related to the monitoring of the performance of an outsourcing arrangement.*

H 3b: *Level of hierarchy is positively related to the monitoring of the performance of an outsourcing arrangement.*

H 3c: *Horizontal integration is positively related to the monitoring of the performance of an outsourcing arrangement.*

Next to the intermediated effects via capabilities and organizational structure of the attention for client developments, we also expect that employees will assume that client developments have a direct effect on the performance of providers. As a result of developments that occur on the client side, clients experience the effect of the provider's willingness and ability to respond to these developments and relate the outcome to the providers' sourcing performance. Again we use the monitoring as a proxy for this concept. Therefore, we hypothesize that:

H 3d: *Client developments an outsourcing service provider has to deal with will be positively related to the monitoring of the performance of an outsourcing arrangement.*

In Figure 2.4 we summarize the core constructs as discussed in a research model that forms the starting point for our empirical research. By testing the relationships between the core constructs as hypothesized, we can assess the role of sensitivity towards developments clients have to deal with and the impact on the provider's sourcing capabilities and organizational structure, and their interdependency, and in the end on outsourcing performance.

Conclusion

Based on a literature analysis, we can conclude that a dynamic fit model can be developed with existing theories and concepts. The dynamic fit model encompasses both sourcing capabilities and organizational structure. The dynamic fit model consists of predefined sourcing capabilities that are related to specific organizational dimensions while taking client developments into account. The outcome of the developed fit model is reflected in the construct sourcing performance. As mentioned earlier, the provider side of IT outsourcing arrangements is still under-researched. The results from our study will provide insights into how client development influence the provider's

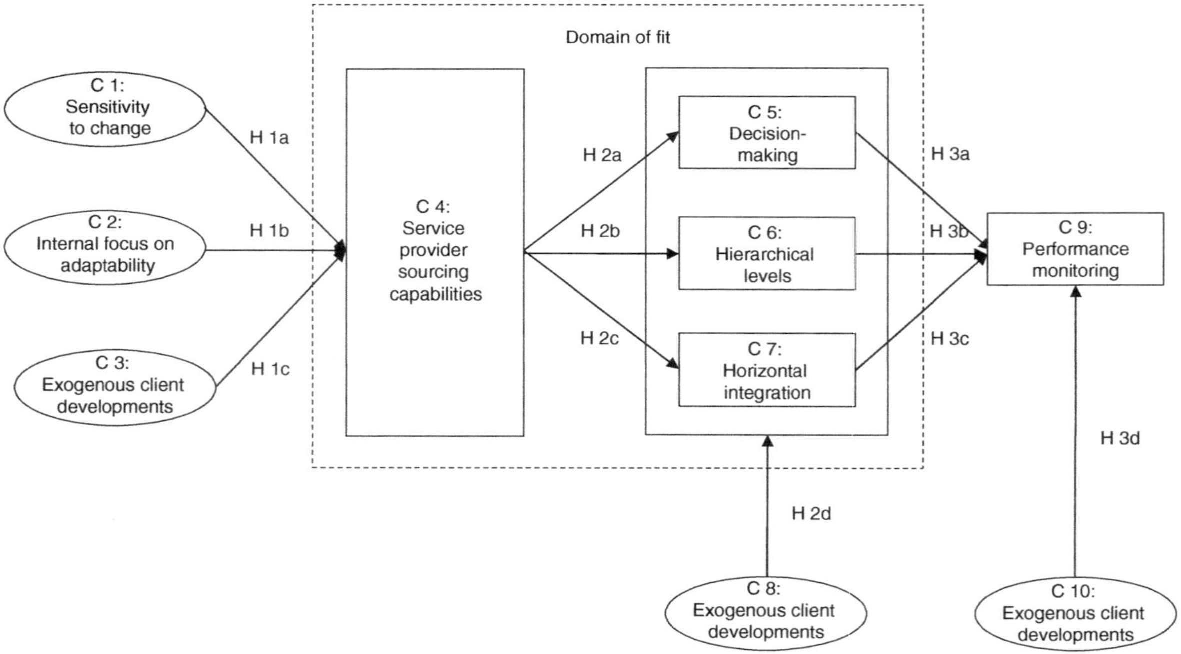

Figure 2.4 Research model

capabilities. Since the topic of adaptability of service providers involved in IT outsourcing arrangements has been the subject of little research, our work aims to contribute to the partial filling of this gap. In doing so, our research may reveal how providers' resources and capabilities evolve over time, adapting to ever-changing client needs. Our research can assist practitioners by developing an IT approach that can be applied to explain if providers are able to achieve a sustainable performance. In addition, we pay attention to the development of a multidimensional measure of sourcing performance.

3
Preliminary Research

When a high level of client-specific knowledge is required for task performance, the client is unlikely to achieve economic benefits from outsourcing when the supplier lacks prior experiences in the task domain.

(Jens Dibbern)

It is of key importance for an outsourcing provider to know what specific changes take place in their environment. Changes in the environment of the client will affect the behaviour of the provider, and therefore these changes are also relevant for the provider and the sourcing capabilities that they have to deliver. For this reason we conducted a preliminary exploratory research into client–provider relationships investigating relevant client developments that occurred in the course of IT outsourcing arrangements. This preliminary research forms the starting point to answer the first key objective: 'Monitor and asses changing client circumstances in IT outsourcing arrangements.' It is the intention of this study to use these insights derived from the study as a basis for further enquiry into IT provider organizations.

About this preliminary research

This preliminary research is derived from the study of five client organizations located in five different sectors of the Dutch business community (see Table 3.1). The data collection is generated through the conducting of in-depth interviews with an average of four participants in each client organization, including IT executives, sourcing managers, information managers, delivery managers and experts positioned across the firm. We applied a semi-structured interview as a research instrument and in addition to the interview data other relevant information such as documents and plans

Table 3.1 Case studies

Case studies	Industry	Sourcing strategy	Start of the deal	Length of the deal	Total size of the deal (million)	Number FTE transferred	Interviews with:		
							CIO	Vendor man.	IT man.
Company A	Banking	Selective	2002	5 years	Euro 1.800	2000	1	1	2
Company B	Retail	Selective	2002	5 years	Euro 467	800	1	2	1
Company C	Chemicals	Selective	1999	5 years	Euro 100	80		2	2
Company D	Telecommunications	Selective	2001	5 years	Euro 1.400	950	1	2	2
Company E	Manufacturing	Selective	2001	5 years	Dollar 1.000	500	1	1	2

were analysed. All of the respondents were interviewed in the Summer of 2006. The interviews varied from 60 minutes to 120 minutes in length and they were conducted via a semi-structured design with many open-ended questions. All of the interviews were then transcribed, and the text was confirmed by the respondents. Additional information was gathered from service catalogues, internal reports and outsourcing contracts.

The collected information was categorized into different subjects. Our first attempt at the theorization of these data involved the coding of the interviews using the method of categorized subjects. To maximize external validity, the study used replication logic to conduct and analyze the different case studies. All cases used predetermined questions for analysis. We clustered the findings in three consecutive parts: environmental developments, atmosphere developments and exchange process developments. As all of the different types of developments may have an impact on IT provider capabilities we started with the identification of the environment, followed by the atmosphere and, finally, the exchange process. We then addressed the impact on IT provider capabilities.

Although there are differences between these five client organizations, they were selected because of similarities of their IT outsourcing arrangements. All of the selected client organizations are market leaders in their specific market sector and operate in an intense and dynamic environments. Each client organization has at least four years' experience in managing the relationship with their providers. Their geographical scope varies from European to global. From an IT perspective, the outsourced IT activities include: office automation, business applications, software development and IT infrastructure. As a result of the broad approach several similarities and differences were identified and analyzed. During our interviews with the respondents we observed that all of the client organizations apply a selective sourcing strategy. While it is not yet possible to draw definitive conclusions from the investigated client organizations, the variations in the categories across the different industry sectors yield some interesting observations.

The relationship between clients and providers can be studied from several theoretical perspectives, including strategy, management and technology. In addition, aspects such as context and behaviour are important in any attempt to fathom this relationship. Therefore, this preliminary research is based on Hakansson's 'Interaction Approach' because this promotes a more comprehensive and holistic view of the client environment. Three categories were studied: environmental developments, atmosphere developments and developments that arise during the exchange of IT services. The results are indicative for the challenges and developments that both clients and providers have to go through.

Preliminary research findings

Category: Environmental developments

Client development 1: Globalization

We find that the effect of globalization has a significant influence on client organizations. As a result of fierce competition, the emergence of new entrants in the playing field and an expanding business strategy, globally operating client organizations focus increasingly on their core business activities. The investigated chemical company, for instance, observed a market shift towards Asia while at the same time new players were entering the market. In order to serve their customers and to sustain their businesses they were forced to open sales offices and even a production plant nearer to those customers. Service providers will be challenged to follow the client organization to new countries. It can be assumed that this will certainly have an impact on provider capabilities.

Client development 2: Market dynamics

The second identified key development is the influence of market dynamics. Acting in a competitive climate means that it is important for client organizations to respond to the changing business needs of their customers. The dynamics of the market – characterized by new entrants, fierce competition and regulation – will have a continuous impact on all aspects of companies' activities. The client organizations have to reduce their time-to-market in order to meet customer demands. In turn, the IT provider must be able to respond quickly. This requires a business mindset that anticipates new business needs. As a result, the provider needs to be more flexible as an organization and to increase the agility of its company.

Client development 3: Legislation

The third key development is in the area of legislation. From a market perspective, legislation applies to, for instance, the determined markets, the dimension of the market share and regulated client services. From a financial perspective, legislation such as the Sarbanes–Oxley Act has a substantial effect on companies. In addition to general legislation, firms that are market leaders also have to comply to specific legislation. The impression of the researched client organizations is that providers are struggling with the increasing amount of legislation, due to the level of details in the processes. Clients assume that insufficient provider capabilities are most often the cause for this struggle.

Category: Atmosphere developments

Client development 4: Sourcing strategy

Another key development is the client's sourcing strategy. In situations where the client has decided to implement a selective sourcing strategy, a competition model towards the provider is introduced. This competition model is based on the principle of a continuous challenging of the providers in order to get the best price/performance ratio when contracts are renewed or new contracts are tendered. This competition model results in a proactive role for the provider. Consequently, the provider cannot afford to lose their focus on the client organization, which is one of the objectives of the customer. This is a key development that will also have an impact on the provider's capabilities.

Client development 5: Innovation

One key development that will have a serious impact on the provider capabilities is the increasing interest of client organizations in innovation. In general, we found a growing need to share new innovative products and services. In particular, companies that are involved in the second-generation outsourcing arrangements are looking to add more value to the relationship and to discuss innovation. They have found that cost reduction alone cannot meet new business requirements. The term innovations refers to the improvement of business processes, procedures and technology. Companies in the banking and manufacturing market have even included innovation in some of their contracts. We found various strategies to address the need to innovate. Some client organizations apply a more structured approach, using contracts that specifically encourage providers to suggest innovative solutions, while other organizations apply a more ad hoc approach.

Category: Exchange developments

Client development 6: Architecture

Interestingly, clients ascribe value to the role of designing the IT architecture which can be identified as a key development. As a result of the division of the IT environment into separate entities and also as a result of applying a selective sourcing strategy, the role played by the IT architecture becomes increasingly important. Hence, entities, processes and interfaces have to be described in a detailed way to record the agreed responsibilities so that risks are mitigated and continuity is guaranteed. All client organizations are of the opinion that they need to work closely together with the architects on the provider side as in designing the IT landscape both client and provider have to be involved. During the interviews it appeared that IT architecture alignment is becoming increasingly important when more parties – client, overall provider integrator and subcontractors – are involved in defining the IT landscape. Therefore, architecture as a key development will affect not only the client organizations, but also the provider. This means that the provider needs to have the right architecture capabilities in-house in order to tune the IT services to the client architecture.

Client development 7: Required flexibility

Another key development that was found concerns the clients' requirements for the provider to be flexible. As indicated earlier, acting in a dynamic market requires a growing need for flexibility which will require a proactive attitude on the part of the providers. A rapid response to changing business needs demands a flexible mindset from the provider. Addressing the issue of flexibility, we have to distinguish between the expectations of a client and the performance of a provider. We find that clients expect a highly flexible provider organization at all levels, with proactive employees catering for all their needs. In practice, however, providers are struggling with flexibility for different reasons. Although flexibility may not have been seen as a value add in the acquisition phase of the outsourcing arrangement, the providers will still need to take this into account when delivering services for their client. An inadequate provider mindset with regard to flexibility will have a negative effect on the mutual relationship.

Focus

As a result of our empirical research of five client organizations we have identified seven developments that, from a client perspective, cause a significant impact on provider capabilities. To create an approach that is consistent with our other research constructs, we have decided to focus on client-related developments that are based on organizational aspects, and not to include either market-related or technological aspects. As a result, we have included *sourcing strategy*, *innovation* and *required flexibility* as client developments that will influence providers' sourcing capabilities. We will apply these three client developments in the selected case studies that will be discussed in Chapters 4 to 6.

Research perspective

Since there is only limited empirical research on fit, we conducted an empirical research study that is based on qualitative exploratory research. As the performance of IT outsourcing providers can change over time, it is necessary to carry out longitudinal research. Following a longitudinal approach over time, we have decided to determine the scope of measuring for a period of five years, which corresponds with the average outsourcing contract term in the market. By conducting a thorough investigation of the period of an outsourcing arrangement, longitudinal research will provide reliable insights into how the performance during the arrangement is affected by the fit between capabilities and organizational structure. Through conducting a longitudinal study we can determine if an IT provider is able to achieve a sustainable sourcing performance towards their customers. This leads to a more holistic view than if we take 'snaphots' at certain moments allowing us to have a real appreciation of the situation.

This study is based primarily on a multiple case study. We selected three service providers, namely a domestic provider, an offshore provider, and a global provider. Since outsourcing arrangements can be divided into three main phases, sales, transformation and delivery, providers' participants were selected because they were active in these phases. These outsourcing phases concern the identified sourcing competence related to relationship, transformation and delivery. In this way, the case study participants form a representative group related to the identified core constructs. The participants have several functions, including IT executives, business development managers, sales and account managers, transformation managers, service delivery managers, technical consultants and experts positioned across the firm. The interviewees were first selected from a strategic level as these are the personnel involved in decision-making. They are capable of discussing the relationship between capabilities, organizational structure and firm performance, so it was worthwhile discussing these topics with them. Secondly, due to their position they were able to look at their organization as a whole and to identify the relations between the researched topics and the processes that support them.

Conclusion

During an outsourcing arrangement providers experience various developments that occur in their clients' environment. In this chapter we explored relevant client developments that may affect providers' organization. In total seven key developments from the perspective of client organizations were found. These client developments comprise: globalization, market dynamics, legislation, sourcing strategy, innovation, architecture and required flexibility. To create focus we selected three client developments from an organizational perspective: sourcing strategy, innovation, required flexibility. These three client developments were used in our case studies. This chapter also elaborates the research perspective that is used.

4
Case Study: Domestic Provider

One should never outsource a problem that you don't understand. Fix the problem or understand clearly what the problem is and its source, before one outsources.

(Rudy Hirschheim)

This chapter introduces our first case study, which is a domestic IT outsourcing provider located in the Netherlands. We begin by discussing the context of the case study, and giving more background information about the provider under study. Following this we introduce a client case. This client case has been studied over a period of time and a number of critical episodes have been derived. These are described in the subsequent paragraphs. Based on the outcome of the client episodes we analyze our findings. These findings are clustered around the defined constructs. In our analysis we assess how these findings affect the provider's fit, influencing sourcing capabilities, organizational structure and performance. Finally, we conclude our findings and analysis with regard to this case study.

Context of the case study

The Dutch service provider is a specialist in the area of Information Technology. It employs the equivalent of 900 full-time equivalents (FTEs), 700 of whom are directly related to the firm and 200 of whom are interim professionals. The IT outsourcing services, which were introduced in 2001, fit well with customers ranging from the top 300 to the top 3,000 companies in the Netherlands. The provider does not currently support any customers in the top 300 due to the lack of fit with their businesses, size and geography. The provider has decided to focus on the delivery of IT services principally in the Dutch market with some services also offered in the Belgian market. The rationale behind this decision is that delivering IT services from an European perspective requires an adaptation with regard to geography, culture and operations. Rather than extending their IT services overseas, the company has decided to strengthen their home base in the Netherlands.

The business strategy of the provider is aimed at three focal points: creating customer intimacy, supporting limited market segments and achieving a cultural fit with its clients. With regard to customer intimacy, the firm's vision is to focus on the client's demand in providing IT services. In addition, the firm focuses on innovation aspects developing value-added services that ally with their customer intimacy goals. An example of such a value-added service is 'virtualization' which increases the flexibility of using a client's applications while decreasing the cost level. The Dutch service provider made a conscious decision to focus on four market segments: government, health care, trade and finance. Through their focus on these market segments, they have gained extensive knowledge and experience. They have taken the deliberate decision to develop and maintain a select IT service portfolio aligned with the supported market segments. Furthermore, it is their opinion that successful outsourcing arrangements are based on a cultural fit between client and firm. Therefore, behaviour and cooperation are key to the establishment of a sound arrangement.

With regard to the firm's outsourcing strategy, their IT service portfolio includes IT infrastructure, workplace automation, and application services. They are of the opinion that managing and operating an own data centre for their IT infrastructure and applications does not fit their IT strategy. As a result, they outsourced their data centre to a third party. Since they decided to focus on a select IT service portfolio, they have also transferred their specific SAP consulting department to a third party. The firm's technology strategy is focused on the development of a high-performance workplace and a Service Oriented Architecture (SOA). By applying this technology approach they are able to achieve an adaptive technology capability to meet client demand. The firm derived their IT strategy from their business strategy in order to ensure a sound alignment.

Client object under study

The client in our case study is a local government organization in the Netherlands. At the start of the millennium they started a major project, called 'Another government'. Their main objective was to improve local services to citizens and decrease their bureaucratic overheads by repealing redundant rules. The local government organization can be characterized as an official and stable organization. They decided to focus on core activities that resulted in the delivery of shared governmental services, such as building licences and health care facilities. In order to be able to adapt rapidly to new situations, the local government organization demanded a flexible IT environment. Consequently, they decided to outsource part of their IT activities.

Before the client started their outsourcing arrangement with our service provider, they had a negative experiment with a former outsourcing arrangement. In this first arrangement, the client outsourced its IT environment to a global provider. As a result they experienced a cultural gap between their own relative small organization (1,400 FTEs) and the provider organization (over 300,000 FTEs). Three factors contributed to the arrangement being experienced as failing. First, as the IT activities were outsourced for the first time, a lack of maturity was experienced in their own organization. Second, the global provider decided to withdraw from the governmental sector. Third, the client experienced the behaviour of the global provider as product driven, slow, and inflexible. Subsequently, the mutual relationship deteriorated and discussions were initiated to backsource the IT activities. After extensive discussions, both internal and external with a consulting firm, they decided to switch to a relatively smaller IT outsourcing firm in 2003, the provider under study. The scope of the outsourcing arrangement is based on a five-year contract and concerns IT infrastructure and data centre activities. The local governmental organization decided to support end-user services and helpdesk services themselves.

The client selected our provider taking into account three criteria: a cultural fit, a relationship based on equality, and an innovation drive. During the selection phase, the client specifically assessed the provider's competences to assure that they were able to adapt to changing circumstances. The identified competences included relationship management, technological know-how and a focus on cultural issues.

Episodes

We have studied the provider–client outsourcing arrangement to determine the extent to which the uncertainty of the client has an influence on the provider organization. From the perspective of the domestic provider we conducted an empirical study of the arrangement over time. We identified various minor and major client circumstances, hereafter called episodes. As a result, we clustered our findings around four important episodes. Each episode describes a situation that highlights a client development and the provider's response to this development. Through the study of these episodes we were able to determine the effect on the provider's fit and sourcing performance.

Episode 1: Transition phase

At the start of the outsourcing arrangement, the transition phase resulted in a real struggle. From the perspective of the client, the maturity level in managing their internal business needs (that is, demand) and external provider (that is, supply) was weak. Fierce discussions took place about governance aspects between client and provider, such as roles, responsibilities and decision-making. Also the interpretation of the contract caused difficulties. For example, as the architecture of IT domains and related boundaries were undefined, various discussions were conducted with regard to responsibilities, resulting in improvement plans to create clarity. However, no methodologies or frameworks were applied to execute these improvement projects, which caused some delay. The client experienced that a crucial role such as defining IT architecture is a core activity that must be retained in-house. The lack of the client's architecture capability resulted in the underperformance of IT applications, which were applied to support governmental services to citizens. As a result, there was a decline in the quality of governmental services.

The provider deployed various sourcing capabilities (*for example, governance, planning and contracting, consulting*) to support the client in increasing the overall maturity of their IT organization. At the start of the transition phase the provider placed too much focus on their technological capabilities. Less attention was paid to bringing in more relationship-oriented capabilities. Because the provider neglected the relationship capability this aspect resulted in a fall in the overall quality. Consequently, the client decided to bring a temporary end to the transition phase which caused a dispute with the provider. Subsequently, the provider developed an improvement plan that included the replacement of representatives by employees with better relationship capabilities. In addition, service management and consulting activities were applied in an attempt to increase performance and facilitate a qualitatively stable delivery process. This improvement plan contributed to a higher level of cooperation with the client and resulted in a restart of the transition phase.

> *Quality is important! Each client demands a tailor-made solution in their situation. However, we believe that our front-end towards the client must be based on customer intimacy while our back-office environment must focus on*

> *operational excellence to create efficiency. This approach definitely influences our capabilities. Clients do argue that they perceive this model as effective and are satisfied with regard to our flexibility and the willingness to adapt. (Source: an account manager)*

To complete the transition phase successfully the provider adapted their governance capability and planning and contracting capability. This contributed to the creation of a better mutual understanding and prevented the necessity for additional discussions. This resulted in the development of a more business-oriented relationship between provider and client.

Episode 2: Organizational change

In the second year of the arrangement, the client announced that they considered changing their sourcing management organization, which, in particular, affected their roles and responsibilities with regard to the alignment of demand and supply activities. For historical reasons, a decentralized sourcing management organization had been developed. All of the governmental departments were responsible for the management of their own IT environment and IT providers. Hence, a central department 'Information and Services' was established that became responsible for IT services. This prevented the government from facing an unmanageable IT infrastructure. At the same time a new IT manager was recruited who was experienced in the areas of both IT and outsourcing. He replaced personnel that were inexperienced in the area of outsourcing. It was the new IT manager's objective to invest in the maturity of the sourcing management organization (Information and Services) whereas the former management had ignored the importance of this area. As a result of this organizational change towards a more central position for sourcing management organization the provider struggled with the question of how to support the client both effectively and efficiently. In the end, our provider responded to this change by reorganizing their organizational dimensions.

> *In response to client's change towards a more central position of their sourcing management organization, we adapted our organizational structure and rearranged dimensions like decision-making and communication. Besides that, we strengthened our sourcing capabilities like process reengineering to achieve more flexibility. (Source: sales director)*

A client-oriented team, with dedicated responsibility for the delivery of IT services, was established in an attempt to improve the effectiveness of client support. Within the client-oriented team organizational dimensions were adapted. The introduction of the client team decreased the level of decision-making, limited the number of layers in the hierarchy and contributed to the development of more rapid communication. The provider developed a central focus, with their internal business unit Managed Services becoming ultimately responsible as a direct focal point for the client's central sourcing management organization. As a result of this change, the provider's adaptation to the client situation, there was an improvement in the performance of IT services.

Episode 3: Demand for close client–provider alignment

From a technological perspective the provider was able to support the client's IT services almost entirely remotely. However, the client's experience was that answering questions or solving issues via a remote helpdesk created a certain distance in the relationship. Moreover, some of the provider representatives who were closely involved in the service delivery were acting in strict accordance with the contract. Because of this behaviour various discussions arose about the relationship between the client and the provider. The client demanded the onsite presence of some of the provider's employees to improve the operational performance. Subsequently, the provider's representatives needed more focus on the client's demand. The provider selected eight representatives and stationed them on the client's premises on specific working days. The onsite provider's team consists of various roles and responsibilities in order to respond to all sorts of questions and assignments. It is their goal to support the client's employees by solving problems, responding to questions, and preparing and executing meetings. Moreover, the provider replaced some representatives (such as the service manager or the service coordinator) to ensure a more client-oriented focus. As the onsite team has been active for at least two years, the client experiences the provider's employees as being part of their own organization. From the client satisfaction reports, it appears that there has been a significant improvement in the provider's performance.

> *We definitely experience a relationship between our sourcing capabilities and the way we organize them. Towards the local government organization, eight of our own representatives are stationed at client's branch offices. This fits well within our existing governance structure. We made an agreement that the provider's onsite personnel stays for at least 2 years, resulting in tight relationships with client employees. (Source: a service coordinator)*

Episode 4: The provider's innovation approach

Monitoring changes in client circumstances, the provider identified that there were frequent changes in the IT infrastructure and applications landscape. As the result of changing political demands, new IT projects were initiated on a regular basis to provide new applications for civilians. These projects resulted in higher structural costs for IT and external interim professionals. The provider proactively proposed a reorientation of the IT infrastructure by applying an innovative solution. The provider increased the manageability of the server farms by introducing their adaptive virtual storage solution. However, the client had not allocated a separate innovation budget to cater for these new developments. The proposed provider's solution was funded through the annual reduction in IT infrastructure budgets. The client appreciated the proactive behaviour of the provider and agreed with this solution. The exploitation costs of the IT infrastructure services decreased and became predictable which made a positive contribution to the annual budget estimates. As the interviews showed, following the implementation of the virtualization solution the level of client satisfaction increased still further and became sustainable over time.

> *As client circumstances changed, we initiated the development of new IT services. For instance, we recognized a trend in the governmental arena to offer more e-services to civilians. So we suggested our client to develop a brand new web application for the department Civilian Affairs to support their services via the internet to civilians in the city. (Source: an account manager)*

The episodes and the responses of the service provider in our study are summarized in Table 4.1.

Table 4.1 Episode overview

Year	Event	Event description	Service provider response
2003	1	Transition struggle: discussion with regard to interfaces and responsibilities	Deployment of various capabilities
2004	2	Organizational change: from centralized to decentraized organizational structure	Reorganization of the relationship and delivery processes
2005	3	Demand for tight client-provider alignment	Introduction of an on-site delivery team
2006	4	Initiation of various IT infrastructure projects	Innovative solution based on virtualization

Analyses

Referring to our research model we will focus on the following constructs: client developments, sourcing competences, organizational structure, fit and sourcing performance.

Client developments

In discussing client developments as a starting point we take the three identified main client developments from our preliminary research. Starting with the client's sourcing strategy, we found that this development has an effect on the provider's sourcing competences. During the selection phase of the outsourcing project the client conducted a scan of the provider's competences and culture. The objective of this assessment was to ensure that our provider was able to provide a fit between the client's business culture and the required competences. This illustrates the importance of provider sourcing competences for the client. Interestingly, during the selection phase the original global provider also competed. However, as a result of their divergent culture, behaviour and sourcing capabilities the global provider was eliminated during the selection phase.

Studying the topic of innovation we found a difference between the interests of the end-users and those of the central sourcing management organization. From an end-user perspective we recognize a need for innovative solutions such as the integration of telecommunication services in the workplace environment. Nevertheless, the sourcing management organization, which is responsible for the profit and loss of all IT services, placed a low value on the area of innovation. This can be illustrated by the fact that no innovation budget was allocated for the initiation of new projects. Another explanation may be that the client experiences only a limited influence of external factors (for example, legislation) in their environment.

As a result, innovation has a limited influence on our provider's organization. With regard to flexibility we found that uncertainty in the client's political environment caused various IT projects to be pending for some time, following which they needed to be executed immediately. Due to the adaptive strategy of our provider under study the client experienced a high degree of flexibility. Moreover, the client has the opinion that flexibility is required to offer continuous and predictable IT services to end-users independent of the prevailing political circumstances.

> *During the sourcing period we recognized all sorts of developments that will take place in client's environment. We addressed these developments with the*

client that were confirmed. The client suggested initiating a branch platform to discuss business developments regularly. This creates the opportunity to discuss developments upfront to assess their impact on IT services. (Source: an account manager)

Reflecting our findings in light of the Interaction Approach we found that the client operates in a monopolistic market. This is important as the provider has to determine the extent to which uncertainty exists in order to cater to changing client circumstances. With regard to the variable 'atmosphere', behavioural dimensions are perceived as key determinants. In particular, interpersonal relationships between the client and the provider's employees contribute to the success of an outsourcing arrangement. Our study reveals that the proactive attitude and willingness of the provider's employees to adapt to changing client circumstances contributed to the success of the relationship. Previous research recognizes the importance of cooperation, as cultural adaptations need to be mutually initiated to smooth the transition to a working (that is, normative) relationship (Klepper and Jones, 1998).

Sourcing capabilities

The interviews with provider representatives revealed that various sourcing capabilities were affected. During the transition phase, as described in episode 1, discussions about the contract influenced the sourcing capability *planning and contracting* of our provider. Furthermore, the fact that the roles and responsibilities are unclear affected the *governance* capability of the provider. The organization change (see episode 2) affected the sourcing capability *organizational design* related to the relationship competence. In response, the provider decided to improve their soft skills such as relation management and client-oriented behaviour in order to achieve customer satisfaction. The provider conducted a client satisfaction survey to measure these items which showed that there had indeed been an improvement in soft skills. As discussed during the first episode, the provider's sourcing competence *transition* was stressed. The provider built a programme to cope with the issues regarding mutual interfaces and boundaries of the IT landscape. The programme consists of application architects and technical consultants who took the initiative to define the boundaries of IT services in close cooperation with the client's engineers. These provider roles are examples of the sourcing capabilities *process re-engineering* and *technology exploitation.*

Capabilities are key and conditional to deliver IT services as agreed. Without proper sourcing capabilities it is not possible to offer a good performance.

Besides that, a clear defined governance structure is required to cater to client developments adequate. (Source: a service delivery manager)

With regard to the sourcing competence *delivery* we found that the provider had to bring in various sourcing capabilities. Two major client episodes influenced the delivery competence of the provider. First, the client's reorganization towards a central sourcing management organization affected the provider's sourcing capabilities as *leadership, programme management* and *governance.* The provider's delivery of integral IT services is an important topic. Multiple IT services are delivered by various business units. As the client required a single point of contact and end-to-end delivery of IT services, the provider appointed the overall responsibility to a single business unit. This business unit, Managed Services, became responsible for the delivery and support of IT services as agreed. This example appeals to the provider's *leadership* capability. This integrated delivery model fits with the client's central sourcing management organization. The second client episode is related to the need for the establishment of a close relationship with the provider's employees. At the same time the client demanded 24*7 support for their applications and IT infrastructure. In response, the provider offered offshore support via an offshore partner in Indonesia. This resulted in a more complex delivery structure in which sourcing capabilities are key. Problem solving in relation to IT services, for example, consists of multiple IT elements that are supported both domestically and in offshore locations. The interviews with the provider's respondents show that the change with onsite employees and 24*7 support are related to sourcing capabilities such as *business management, governance,* and *domain expertise.*

The resource-based view (RBV) argues that some capabilities can only be developed over long periods of time, because it may not always be clear how these capabilities should be developed in the short to medium term, and because some capabilities cannot be bought (Roy and Aubert, 2002). In our case we found at the start of the arrangement that the provider under study lacked the necessary capabilities to support the proper provisioning of IT services. Studying the interviews revealed a lack of the sourcing capabilities *leadership, governance* and *organizational design.* All of these sourcing capabilities refer to the relationship competence based on the sourcing capability model developed by Feeny et al. (2005). Furthermore, we found evidence that during the first half of the outsourcing arrangement the provider struggled to develop these sourcing capabilities in the short to medium term. One explanation for this can be found in the limited client base and related outsourcing experience of the domestic provider. Since the provider introduced outsourcing services in 2001, fewer than ten client outsourcing arrangements have been supported. Hence, they have only limited knowledge and experience in relation to how to develop capabilities. However, we found that during the second half of the outsourcing arrangement the provider developed their sourcing capabilities, including aspects like cooperation and behaviour, to improve the levels of client satisfaction.

The RBV underpins the importance of intangible assets (for example, sourcing capabilities), arguing that they contribute to the firm's outperformance. The type of processes applied by the provider to support capability building is also important. In our case we found that the provider applies rather simple processes to strengthen sourcing capabilities. Based on their type, simple processes versus complex interdependent processes, capabilities require more or less modification when compared to other providers. This is consistent with the competence theory. Our longitudinal study confirms a shift from rather simple towards complex interdependent processes as applied by the domestic provider. An explanation can be found as casual ambiguity developed over time when recognizing that processes are essential to decrease client uncertainty.

Organizational structure

In general, the interviews with various participants revealed a significant difference between the situations before and after the client's organizational change (episode 2). Before the change the provider applied an organizational structure which is based on a leveraged model to support multiple clients. This leveraged model can be characterized as having a high level of decision-making and many layers in the hierarchy. However, after the client's change a new organizational structure was developed by the provider to assure customer orientation. Based on the interviews with the provider's representatives we observe a mixed view of decision-making. Some have the opinion that the locus of decision-making is perceived as high in the organization while others argue that this can be ranked as low in the organization. This can be explained as some participants combine both management roles (for example, delivery manager) and content-specific roles (for example, business consultant) while others focus on just one role (senior manager). Based on this finding we may conclude that some of the participants who are directly involved in the decision-making process (for example, senior managers) perceive the locus of decision-making to be low in the organization, while others who are less involved perceive it as being high in the organization. However, we found that the client-oriented team, which is responsible for day-to-day delivery, has the mandate to take many operational decisions that are necessary to support the client, with the exception of commercial decisions. When new commercial IT services are offered, this decision is made high in the organization.

With regard to the number of layers in the hierarchy, all providers' representatives that are involved in the outsourcing arrangement consider this dimension to be low. The fit of this organizational dimension with the client's demand is important. A limited number of layers in the hierarchy creates the opportunity to speed up decision-making and communication. With regard to the level of horizontal integration the majority of respondents charted this subdimension as moderate. The interviews revealed that several representatives of the provider combine different roles in one person, which may explain this finding. The IT service coordinator, for example, is also responsible for more technical consulting tasks. This can be explained by the fact that some resources are scarce and that, therefore, client-oriented teams are limited with regard to team members. This case study shows that team members combine multiple roles in order to achieve an efficient organization and, therefore, stay competitive in the market. Furthermore, when compared with other service providers in the market, our provider under study is relatively small. Given these facts, the level of horizontal integration combines several roles into one function.

> *After the centralized Sourcing Management department of the client was implemented, we reorganized our governance structure. We reorganized the delivery process, built new relationships, lower decision making and most important, faster the communication. This new governance structure fits well with the client's organization which creates a higher effectiveness. (Source: a delivery manager)*

We found that at the start of the arrangement our provider under study lacked the required experience to organize the adequate delivery of IT services. The struggle over how to cope with the organizational change on the client side (episode 2) demonstrated the provider's lack of attention to adapting their organizational dimensions. This reflects the RBV's causal ambiguity that can be applied to a discussion of the adaptiaton of the organizational structure. Furthermore, previous research identified that if organizational theory is to be relevant for practitioners, emphasis should be placed on organizational effectiveness and its determinants.

Governance mechanism

As a result of the client episodes both provider and client implemented an adjusted governance structure to achieve a sound arrangement. A three-layer model was developed to ensure fast decision-making and meet the need for a low level of hierarchy. For example, at a tactical level the contract management process and the service management process are managed in combination. On a strategic level the client and the provider-determined strategic service-oriented processes (SSO) relate to long-term contractual agreements. The executive management of the provider and the client discusses these aspects on a quarterly basis. On a tactical level both parties defined contractual obligations as well as service management agreements, which facilitated a high level of horizontal integration. These agreements are described as tactical service-oriented processes (TSO). Finally, at an operational level both parties apply operational service-oriented processes (OSO), aligning service management and operational support processes. We found that the provider's client-oriented team was responsible for managing the tactical and operational processes, while executive management manages the strategic processes. This governance structure is illustrated in Figure 4.1.

The introduction of the provider's dedicated client-oriented team caused higher transaction costs as more employees became involved in the integration of the end-to-end service. On the other hand, this team adds value as there is an increase in the effectiveness in delivering services towards the client. Moreover, we found that there was a decrease in uncertainty with regard to changes in client circumstances. Furthermore, we found that at the time of the organizational change on the client side, the provider applied an organizational structure that refers to the structure of a diversified organization (Mintzberg, 1983). The IT services as agreed were provided by different business units that were operating autonomously. Other researchers label this structure as a *funnel* (Oshri et al., 2007). This type of structure relies on single points of contact and control between provider and client. Following the change in the client's organization the structure changed into the structure of a professional organization. The characteristics of a professional organization indicate highly educated professionals organized in separate operational cores that require a certain degree of autonomy. This is consistent with our findings of the client-oriented team. Moreover, this fits with organizational theory which suggests that organizations that operate with a high degree of environmental uncertainty may decentralize decision-making, rely less on formal rules and policies and flatten their hierarchies.

Dynamic fit

Studying our provider under research we found empirical evidence for a sound relationship between sourcing capabilities and organizational structure. The influence on the fit between both constructs is perceptible when

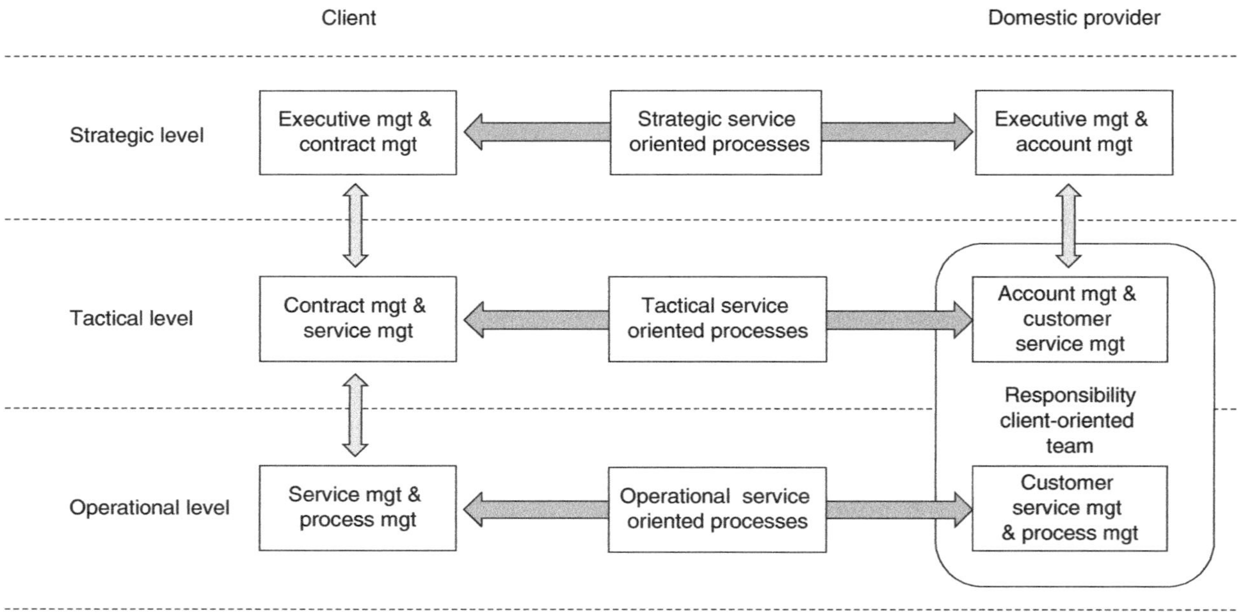

Figure 4.1 Governance structure

critical episodes occur in the client firm, resulting in fierce discussions with the provider. Based on our retrospective approach, in particular we identified two episodes that led to an adaptation of the service provider's fit: the transition struggle (episode 1) and the organizational change on the client side (episode 2). To illustrate the existence of a fit, during the second episode the provider intervened at an executive level. First, the provider suggested to the client that they should initiate mutual meetings where multiple provider employees need to attend, representing various sourcing capabilities. From the client side, multiple representatives also need to be present in order to ensure their capabilities. As a result, there was a decrease in the time in which projects were completed while there was an increase in the level of efficiency. Furthermore, this initiative contributed to the strengthening of the interpersonal relationships of both provider and client employees. Secondly, based on the client-oriented team, the provider adapted their organizational dimensions to meet the client's need for more dedication.

> *During the start of our service provisioning towards the client we experienced to adjust the fit between capabilities and organizational dimensions more unconsciously. Later on, we deliberately paid more attention to this form of alignment by also involving the client in our regular discussions. (Source: an account manager)*

However, we found that no formal process was applied to recondition the fit. This can be explained in part by the fact that the absence of a formal process to recover the fit is caused by the provider's organization being relatively small and flat (few layers in the hierarchy). This means that decisions related to clients can be made quickly. Analysis of the interview reports pointed out that the *governance capability* plays an important role as an initiator to adapt the fit between sourcing capabilities and organizational structure. In practice, we found that the client-oriented team is responsible for monitoring client developments and initiating actions to adapt the fit. Various developments are discussed in meetings with the client to determine the impact on the provider's services. Fit is important, which is shown by a respondent indicating that a fit is required to achieve a sustainable performance.

> *An example of applying and sustaining the fit at our client is to organize mutual meetings were different roles (capabilities) from our firm are represented. For instance, technical specialists, service managers and project managers are discussing client developments at the same time and interpret the influence on our*

IT services and organization. This approach results in a faster implementation, an increase of the effectiveness and an increase of client satisfaction. (Source: a service delivery manager)

Sourcing performance

With regard to the construct performance we found that the client perceives this topic to be the most important. As a result of the client's first outsourcing experience, the arrangement with the provider was deliberately discontinued as a result of poor performance. The interviews demonstrated that the presence of a fit is strongly related to the performance of the organization. We found that strongly developed sourcing capabilities are key to delivering a sound performance. Various client episodes showed that the provider deployed its capabilities to improve the performance. In particular, the way in which the provider arranged its organizational dimensions with a client-oriented delivery team had a positive influence on performance. Recovering the fit between sourcing capabilities and organizational structure contributed to the realization of a more balanced performance.

Whilst the client was reorganizing their sourcing management organization, first we were not able to cater to this changing circumstance. We discovered that our performance is capability driven. In fact, capabilities determine the success of delivering IT services. (Source: a transition manager)

Analyzing the interviews and accompanying documents, we found evidence that capabilities were strengthened further during the outsourcing arrangement (that is, causal ambiguity). Provider's experience of how to develop capabilities increased over time. As a result, the performance increased significantly. The RBV suggests that the variability in an organization's performance can be attributed to heterogeneity in the distinct bundles of resources. Consistent with this perspective, the RBV recognizes knowledge as a key intangible resource that is recognized as the provider developed their sourcing capabilities. We argue that the provider requires distinctive sourcing capabilities in order to perform as agreed. We find these capabilities both in existing expertise and processes. Based on the RBV, we argue that distinctive capabilities are those processes that contain both physical and human resources resulting in a responsibility for the organizations' tacit and explicit knowledge. This also contributes to the sustainability of provider's performance. Strategic resources that satisfy the conditions for a sustainable performance are superior assets and capabilities and distinctive core competences (Prahalad and Hamel, 1990).

Based on the interviews we found that offering a sustainable performance is not a formal policy that is extracted from the provider's business strategy. Analyzing the client satisfaction surveys, as completed by client representatives, we found that the stability of delivered IT services before the organizational change showed regular deviations. Annual client satisfaction surveys are conducted to measure the performance of service delivery on a scale of 1 to 5. Over the past four years the performance has increased, reaching an average score of 4 over the past two years. A significant improvement was achieved by paying attention to capabilities and organizational structure. The performance can now be regarded as sustainable. Furthermore, we found that the service levels as agreed with the client are met. In spite of this, when analyzing the client case under study we recognized that performance is also related to client perception. Proactive behaviour on the part of the provider's employees contributes to a better perception of the sourcing performance.

Conclusion

This case study demonstrated that client episodes have a significant effect on both sourcing capabilities and organizational structure. We found that establishing a fit between both core constructs is essential to the delivery of sound performance. We may conclude that the domestic IT provider paid unconscious attention to strengthening their sourcing capabilities and adapting their organizational dimensions, which are based on an ad hoc approach. The provider's congruent customer intimacy approach contributes to a more adequate response to client episodes and their subsequent adaptability. During the transition phase of the outsourcing arrangement, the provider struggled with their performance which underpins the necessity to focus continuously on adaptability. Despite a lack of a formal process at the start of the delivery phase to establish a fit between sourcing capabilities and organizational structure, the provider gradually succeeded in achieving an ad hoc fit. One important landmark was the introduction of a client-oriented team to ensure dedication to the client, to recognize client demands and to cope with changing circumstances. At the same time, organizational dimensions were adapted to improve the team's decisiveness. As a result of the provider's willingness to adapt to client episodes we found evidence that their sourcing performance improved over time. During the last two years of the arrangement the provider achieved a performance which was durable over time and which can be characterized as sustainable.

5
Case Study: Offshore Provider

> *Offshore Supplier: The customer is always talking about the win–win. To us that means the customer wins twice!*
>
> *(Joseph Rottman)*

In this chapter we describe our second case study, which is an offshore provider located in India. We first outline the context of the provider under study and this is followed by a client case. Similar to our first case study we study various client episodes to determine the provider's response. We then analyze the findings of the case study which are also clustered around the defined constructs. The chapter ends with a section of the conclusions that we have drawn.

Context of the case study

The offshore provider under study is a leading Indian enterprise. As a 'top five' player it concentrates on Information Technology. In 2008 the company had approximately 47,000 professionals of diverse nationalities, operating in 17 countries. Its range of offerings spans Infrastructure Services, Technology and Application Services, Systems Integration, and Business Process Outsourcing (BPO). The company's business strategy rests on three pillars: customer intimacy, strategic partnerships with clients and technology partners and a focus on market segmentation. Customer intimacy leads to a strong focus on the client's needs and a willingness to adapt to changing circumstances. This also drives process and technology innovation. One area of the business strategy is to establish strategic partnerships with technological providers, such as Microsoft and Cisco, which, in turn, strengthen their technological capabilities. These partnerships are also explored to increase the company's value added. Market segmentation is the third and final pillar. It is their strategy to differentiate the market into segments as each segment requires other business needs. As a result, the provider has developed specific services that fit with the specific business needs. Building on the described strategic objectives, the company is able to grow very rapidly.

The company's main goal is to reposition itself in the market as a transformation company. Supporting their clients to transform their businesses with innovative IT solutions, they are adding value to the clients' market position. For example, the provider focuses on transforming legacy IT environments into state-of-the-art e-environment solutions, integrating multiple market channels (for example, web portals, offices, call centres). Their concept of transformation is reflected in the slogan 'from running client's business to changing client's business'.

Since all Indian providers struggle with a high attrition rate, our provider under study introduced a specific programme called 'Employee First'. By supporting their employees with various facilities, the provider's executive management argues that there will be a decline in the the attrition rate of their staff, while there is an increase in the company's continuity in providing IT services. Examples of additional employee facilities refer to talent transformation sabbaticals, expert guidance or fast track growth, inner peace or democratic empowerment. Through offering additional services, the executive management believes that there will be an increase in the personnel's loyalty to the company. Practice shows that this approach works as the attrition rate, which is approximately 20 per cent in India, had decreased by around 4 per cent.

In addition to the business-driven approach to becoming a strong global player in the field of outsourcing, the company initiated various platforms that are related to its social commitments. As a part of their corporate identity, Corporate Social Responsibility forms a bundle of initiatives. One example is the SSN Institution which provides world-class research-oriented quality education at an affordable price in India. Another example is the Community Support Programs which works together with the NGO Udayan to campaign for the social advancement of underprivileged children. Thus a proportion of the company's earned revenue is carried back to the Indian population as an investment to develop the country and stimulate the economy.

Client object of case study

The object of our case study is a major Dutch bank and insurance company, which is offshoring its back-office applications. The company gained its first experience with outsourcing in 1998, when part of applications and IT infrastructure were provided through external providers. The banking and insurance industry has become extremely competitive, as the business is oriented internationally. Moreover, at present customers increasingly choose their own channel to do business with the company. As a result, the banking and insurance company has to adapt to their customers and develop into a multi-channel firm (a so-called 'clicks and mortar' company). The company emphasises that providing high-quality and competitive services is a main strategy. As IT is closely linked to the business strategy, applications that support the business processes must also be adapted to customers' needs.

In 2002, the Dutch bank and insurance company faced intensive market dynamism and adapted their business strategy to become more agile. To stimulate this agility, a selective sourcing strategy was developed in the area of application development and maintenance (ADM). The objective of the selective sourcing strategy is to encourage a competitive environment and gain a maximum value of each provider. As a result of their selective sourcing strategy, the company decided to divide its IT landscape into various application domains. Based on this strategy three service providers were selected. The first provider, our service provider under study, was selected for the development of back-office applications for three reasons: the quality of delivered services, a competitive price performance ratio and a business strategy that is based on customer intimacy. The second provider is responsible for the maintenance of a specific financial business application. The third provider acts as an intermediary between the Dutch bank and insurance firm and other selected service providers, fulfilling the role of application integrator. The integrator has subcontracted the services offered by the other two service providers. The playing field for all three providers is very competitive as the client applied no preferred provider role for additional application projects.

Our provider under study applies a blended site approach to support their client from on-site, onshore and offshore locations. In the Netherlands approximately 55 employees are located on-site divided over two main offices in Leeuwarden and The Hague. In total 10 employees are located onshore, while in India approximately 280 employees are involved in delivering the services. Proportionally the relation between onshore and offshore teams is about 20 per cent versus 80 per cent, which fits well referred to this client case.

Episodes

The provider–client outsourcing arrangement is studied in an attempt to determine how client developments influence the provider organization. In doing so, we applied a longitudinal study that revealed multiple episodes. Similar to the domestic case study, each critical episode describes a situation that highlights a client development and the provider's response to this development. By studying these episodes we were able to determine the effect on the provider's fit and sourcing performance.

Episode 1: Online banking

Two years after the start of the outsourcing arrangement, the banking and insurance company decided to launch a new programme which it called 'Run and Change the Bank'. The objective of this programme was twofold. First, existing banking applications had to be upgraded in order to process increased numbers of business transactions. Second, the bank needed to adapt as a result of intense market dynamism within the banking industry with customer demand for new distribution channels to do business. New web-enabled applications had to meet these increasing customer demands. This resulted in application development projects that required both sufficient resources and specific capabilities. At the same time, based on reviews of finalized projects, the need arose to forecast how many resources would be required to staff new application development projects taking the need for specific capabilities into account. Our service provider under study responded to this client episode by managing the business demand effectively through the mechanism of forecasting and backcasting. The service provider put itself in the position of the client and defined the impact of the programme on the required resources. They were able to make precise calculations of how many resources were needed within a specific timeframe, including their required capabilities. They introduced a resource and capability reporting tool that charted the resources very accurately (forecasting). When changes occurred during the execution of the programme (for example, more or less application development activities), the reporting tool automatically adjusted the planning, required resources and capabilities for the next six months. Subsequently, the implemented tool reported the performance regarding resources, capabilities and time spent (backcasting) over the past three months. This innovative reporting tool increased the effectiveness of the application development processes that were implemented. Hence, the time-to-market of new business applications improved significantly while the upgrades of existing applications were managed in a better way (that is, on time and on budget).

> *We have obtained a lot of knowledge and experience in the financial sector. In India we built our own bank that is used by our employees. By running our business including financial processes we empathise with the business needs of our customer's. (Source: an account manager)*

Interestingly, this innovation reporting tool introduced by the service provider appears to present a competitive advantage over the other providers engaged in the sourcing arrangement. Since the provider has a strong presence in the market segment financial services they obtained extensive knowledge and experience in this sector. The choice to be present in this market segment was made deliberately.

Episode 2: Human flexibility

As a consequence of the 'Run and Change the Bank' programme, the client embarked on various projects. These Application Development and Maintenance (ADM) projects were aligned with the business departments of the client because of their dependency on the scope and complexity of business needs. As the programming of applications is relatively labour-intensive, a flexible approach was required of our service provider under study with regard to the application of both resources and capabilities. In practice, some major projects had to start within a period of two months due to their dependency on market circumstances, with approximately fifty employees supporting various capabilities. In reaction to the required flexibility, in 2005 the service provider proposed two options. First, they could support the client by searching for the required resources and capabilities within the organization, based on a 'best-efforts' approach. This option was free of charge. Second, the service provider offered a professional service with output-based service-level agreements. To support the client with this latter option, the service provider had already organized a global resource pool. Resources that form a part of a global resource pool are inducted to the client's business and the corresponding IT environment before their formal deployment. At each moment in time, available resources could be allocated based on the required capabilities.

> *Recently, a client asked us to start up a global application project that requires 200 FTE's within one month. Due to our flexibility strategy we were able to organize those resources adequately. (Source: a service delivery manager)*

Hence, the service provider is able to comply with their client's request by ramping up a software programme team within a period of eight weeks. In order to offer efficient support for the client the resources are divided between on-site and offshore locations. Within this ramp-up period, the resources are allocated and trained. Collaboration between on-site and offshore employees is essential for the exchange of knowledge. Research (Kotlarsky and Oshri, 2008) underpins this form of exchange by arguing that knowledge sharing is associated with successful collaboration. This approach fits with the flexibility demand as required by the client. The way in which the service provider responds to this client episode underpins the coordination mechanism 'partnering flexibility' (Tan and Sia, 2006).

Episode 3: IT continuity

The execution of various application-oriented projects required many resources and related capabilities. As the client organization is operating in a dynamic market, goals must be achieved through managing the projects within the time schedule and on budget. Achieving these goals requires continuity from the perspective of the service provider. However, as the attrition rate of personnel of the Indian provider is comparatively higher than in the West, the provider has developed a resource overlay model. The objective of this overlay model is to ensure the continuity of services for the client, providing sufficient resources at any time. The expected number of resources is defined, based on the forecast for application projects. On top of the required number of resources, an overhead of up to 30 per cent is deployed. When original resources withdraw from projects, due to holidays, sickness or resignation, the substitute resource is deployed. On-site, the provider applies a model of primary and secondary responsibilities for each application or functional domain. Employees share the responsibility and arrange for replacement in the case of absence, leave and attrition. Offshore, the provider applies a model of so-called 'shadow-resources'. With these 'shadow-resources', the resource overlay model assures the continuity of the project. This approach applies to both the onshore locations in the Netherlands and the offshore locations in India.

Since multiple provider employees built relationships with client employees in order to discuss the progress of IT projects, there was a significant increase in the mutual exchange of information and IT services. This includes both content and commercially related information for IT specialists and executive management. The exchange of information and IT services caused a dispersed overview with the client with regard to all ongoing initiatives.

Consequently, the client required a single point of contact from the provider under study. In response, the provider introduced a client-oriented team that integrates the provider's communication and the delivery of IT services. The provider's team has a mandate for decision-making in relation to the provisioning of all operational IT services. Furthermore, the provider implemented governance procedures in order to ensure a coherent approach and, therefore, business continuity.

> *We found that multiple employees of both our client and our own organization are involved in the exchange of multiple documents, plans, planning schedules and of course operational IT services. This led to confusion at client's executive management level as they lack an integral view on the progress of agreed services. Moreover, it hindered their business continuity. Or as the client put it in other words: in the end it's all about continuity. (Source: a business development manager)*

We observed that the provider's response met the client's expectations of ensuring IT continuity. Meeting the client's expectations strengthened the satisfaction with regard to the provider's behaviour.

Episode 4: Service integration

It is a governance policy of the banking and insurance company to review their service providers regularly with regard to price/performance, quality and value added. Interviews with five respondents of the on-site client-oriented team revealed that the governance structure between client and service integrator (third provider: see box client object of case study) was viewed as ineffective. As the service integrator was responsible for the operational management of two subcontractors, the respondents argue that the value added of the service provider was limited. The throughput of initiated application projects expanded while simultaneously the costs increased. In our interviews we found that the governance structure between the various service providers showed that the service integration provider was responsible for both application developments tasks as well as reviewing the two subcontractors. This dual role is ambiguous when managing the interdependent processes.

> *Unclear distinctions regarding the different roles amongst the three service providers resulted in many fierce discussions on the client side. Indistinctness about who needs to initiate application work packages and unclear agreements about*

> *the different responsibilities were underlying causes for an ineffective process between the providers. (Source: a service delivery manager)*

As a result, the client decided to discontinue the task of the service integration provider, changing their role to one of review partner. Because there was fierce competition between the three service providers, the service provider under study positioned itself as a specialist in application development. The predictable operational performance, sustainable high quality and capabilities that they had demonstrated over the last three years convinced the client to rearrange the application development domain. The researched service provider had won this additional business at the expense of their competitors.

> *An important reason why we won additional business at the cost of our competitors is related to performance. The predictability of our sourcing performance and costs are a decisive success factor. (Source: a service delivery manager)*

The service provider under study developed a new governance structure in which they could interact directly with the client organization. This resulted in an adaptation of the delivery model.

> *We are quite eager to extend our businesses at our client. As we are focused on fulfilling client's demand and apply strong capabilities, we won new business while our main competitor lost most of their business. (Source: an account manager)*

Episode 5: Transformation

The client emphasizes that the provision of high qualitative and competitive services is a main strategy. Recently, the client decided to choose their own service channel to do business as a result of which existing business processes and supporting IT platforms needed to be adapted. This led to the development of a more complex multi-channel banking platform. The provider under study monitored these changing client circumstances and identified that specific technical capabilities (SAP application) needs to be increased. The provider assessed the client's business need and determined that their own technical capabilities were insufficient. This assessment was conducted globally, indicating that these capabilities were also needed for other clients. As a response, the provider decided to strengthen their capabilities and acquired a specialized firm. This would definitely accelerate the ability of the company to prepare for more complex projects in the future. Finally, the service provider searched the market and found a suitable company that possessed the required capability. This SAP consultancy company was acquired in 2008 which shows clearly that the service provider is proactively adapting to changing client circumstances. Moreover, one of the provider interviewees stated that to support the client's multichannel banking transactions, new payment transaction technologies needed to be developed to comply with international standards. Accordingly, the provider started a payment transformation programme in order to support the client.

> *We observed that the market of payment transactions is transforming nowadays. Technologies that are presently applied to support the existing payment services have to transform towards a Single European Payment Area (SEPA). When this new standard is introduced, there will be no distinctions between domestic and foreign payment transactions anymore. We make this transformation happen. (Source: a business development manager)*

Our finding seems to indicate that our provider under study is committed to cater to this episode which has a positive influence on the mutual level of trust.

The described episodes and related responses of the service provider under study is summarized in Table 5.1.

Table 5.1 Episode overview

Year	Event	Event description	Service provider response
2004	1	Start of the programme 'Run and change the Bank' including the initiation of various IT projects	Introduction of an innovative reporting tool (forecasting and backcasting)
2005	2	Strong demand of flexibility	Initiation of a global resource pool; Improvement programe to strenghten their sourcing capabilities
2006	3	Demand for IT programme continuity	Initiation of a new service called 'on-site shadow resources'
2007	4	Insufficient value add of service integrator	Offshore provider won additional business at the cost of their competetors; adaptation of the delivery governance structure
2008	5	Start of a transformation programme 'multichannel'	Provider strenghtened their sourcing capabilities by the acquisition of a SAP consultancy firm

Analyses

Referring to our research model, we will focus on the following areas: client developments, sourcing competences, organizational structure, fit and sourcing performance.

Client developments

Analyzing our case study we found evidence that the observed five episodes have had an impact on the provider's skills and sourcing competences. We found that the provider's sourcing strategy has an impact on the ability to adapt to client episodes. Derived from the sourcing strategy, the provider applies a client-oriented team to ensure the continuity of IT services and to sustain the long-term relationship towards the client. This finding is congruent with the provider's business strategy to focus on customer intimacy. In particular, when studying the interviews we found that the provider under study pays attention to behavioural aspects in their relationship with client representatives, strengthening their long-term relationship. For example, when the client initiated a new project to develop a multi-channel portal, our provider was selected because of their business mindset, a proven willingness to adapt and predictable performance in delivering services. We found clear evidence for this decision through a study of the client satisfaction reports. This finding seems to indicate that it is those providers who are able and willing to adapt to client developments that are more likely to gain additional business. With regard to the client's need for innovation we found that the customer intimacy policy of the provider fitted with this need. As a result, new business processes were designed and technologies adapted or acquired to fulfill the client's need. The strong customer focus resulted in a shared risk and reward mechanism that is applied regularly, resulting in advantages for both the client and the provider. The flexibility requirements of the client have a strong effect on the provider's sourcing capabilities. We found clear evidence that the provider used internal best practices to align their organizational structure with that of the client organization.

Studying the client developments as observed, the findings relate to various variables of the Interaction Approach, which is based on the Inter-Organizational Relationship theory (IOR). First, we recognize the influence of market dynamism on the client's firm, which relates to the 'environmental' variable of the Interaction Approach. We found evidence that the provider's business strategy to focus on client developments and adapt when necessary contributes to a strong relationship. For example, we determined that the offshore provider had gained additional business at the expense of their competitors. Secondly, we found that the provider's attention to behaviour dimensions was crucial as these were necessary to deal with the changing client circumstances. Our interviewees indicated that the behaviour dimensions commitment, cooperation and satisfaction were important. Moreover, previous research reveals that mutual commitment in outsourcing relationships is crucial as greater commitment leads to greater trust and vice versa (Kern and Willcocks, 2002). The commitment of the provider to the relationship is an indication that they are serious about achieving success and willing to exert considerable effort on behalf of the relationship (Mohr and Spekman, 1996). The behaviour dimension of power/dependency was not recognized in this case study.

Sourcing capabilities

Studying the sourcing capability model of Feeny et al. (2005) we found that all three competence areas were influenced. Taking the relationship competence area as a starting point, the customer intimacy approach of the provider contributes to the adaptation of sourcing capabilities (for example, governance, organizational design, leadership). Studying the sourcing competences of the service provider under study we found that their attention was focused in particular on skills, resources and capabilities. Moreover, the business strategy of the provider also includes building strategic partnerships with their clients. The strategic relationship between client and provider is affirmed by the shared risk and reward mechanism. As the provider offers a wide range of IT services we argue that the development of a broad portfolio will only be sustainable with a dedicated market orientation. It might take a long time to acquire or develop market-specific capabilities that are required to deliver IT services as agreed with clients (Barney, 1991).

Studying documents of the provider's market approach, we found evidence that the provider does indeed show market dedication since only five market segments are supported (Financial Services, Retail and Consumer, Life Sciences and Healthcare, Manufacturing, Telecom and Media). To retain a customer-oriented approach the provider needs to monitor client circumstances constantly and prove their willingness to adapt if necessary.

> *To support our client in delivering services we established an Operational Delivery Center (ODC) both on-site, onshore and offshore. The ODC forms a single-point-of-contact between the client and our organization. By aligning their demand and supply organization with our ODC we are able to improve the efficiency and the client satisfaction at the same time. (Source: a service delivery manager)*

Studying the *transformation* competence area, we found evidence that client developments were monitored and assessed regularly and decisions were made to adapt sourcing capabilities and organizational structure. A specific process was designed to monitor client developments and to weight their impact. According to the outcome any necessary actions were taken. This refers to the sourcing capability *process re-engineering*, one of the transformational competences.

Studying the *delivery* competence area we found that as the location in which IT services are delivered can be either on-site or offshore, knowledge management becomes more important. The provider acknowledges that there needs to be improvement in the exchange of knowledge between front-end and back-office employees. Interviews with representatives of the provider illustrate that the provider is struggling with this topic. Knowledge of the business market in which the client is acting, is present on the on-site locations of the provider in the Netherlands, but the offshore employees do not have that knowledge and experience as their focus is more on the areas of delivery and maintenance. As knowledge about business needs can differ, this leads to differences of understanding between on-site and offshore employees when prioritizing activities. The importance of knowledge management is also indicated by other researchers (see, for example, Oshri et al., 2007; Rottman, 2008) who argue that as a result of changing client needs, internal resources and capabilities are upgraded on a regular basis. We found that employees' knowledge was strengthened through the provision of training and the coaching of skills. The sourcing capabilities *domain expertise,* with regard to technology, and *behaviour management* were strengthened in this way.

We found evidence that the provider under study developed their capabilities and organizational structure regularly in order to adapt to changes in client circumstances. This refers to path dependency as part of the RBV. Moreover, the provider disposes knowledge of how to develop their capabilities over time. This relates to causal ambiguity. We argue that our findings can be explained with reference to two aspects. First, the number of clients as supported by the provider and their broad experience over the last ten years will have a positive influence on capability development. Secondly, the interviews showed that the provider regularly shares knowledge related to capabilities within the company. Sharing 'lessons learned' will accelerate the development of sourcing capabilities. Another possibility that would explain the conscious development of capabilities is the provider's attention to behavioural dimensions. This aspect protects the provider's resources from competitive imitation. We found that the provider invested constantly in building a sound relationship with their client. As a result, the behavioural dimension of trust and reputation was strengthened. These intangible assets refer to socially complex resources, as trust and good reputation are time-consuming and expensive to imitate (Dierickx and Cool, 1989; Barney, 1991).

Organizational structure

When observing the provider's responses, all client episodes lead to an adaptation of the provider's organizational structure. At first, they implemented a standard delivery model. This approach was based on a small team of provider representatives on-site and a leveraged team offshore delivering services for multiple clients. After considering the first episode 'online banking' and the second episode 'human flexibility' we found that the provider's organizational structure was adapted to a more dedicated client approach introducing a client-oriented team on-site. Due to the client episodes, the service provider decentralized their decision-making processes and flattened their hierarchies. This had a considerable impact on the organization. This finding is consistent with previous research (Ruekert et al., 1985) which found that firms that operate with a high degree of environmental uncertainty may decentralize their decision-making process. This contributed to both the efficiency and effectiveness in respect of delivering IT services.

Regarding the business strategy of the provider, we found that the choice for customer intimacy and flexibility has a positive effect on decision-making, one of the organizational dimensions. From the perspective of the studied client we observed that the provider adopted a business point of view in both episodes. The combination of a business focus and solid relationship between both parties contributed to faster decision-making. The provider allocated the level of decision-making at a low organizational level. In particular, the client-oriented team became responsible for operational decision-making. On the one hand, this resulted in a more adaptive organizational design, accelerating both relationship and delivery processes. On the other hand, the impact on the organization as a whole is extensive due to a hand-over of responsibilities to employees acting at an operational level. Moreover, the governance capability needs to be strengthened and expanded while enabling processes must be redefined. With regard to the level of hierarchy, in our client case the provider mirrored their delivery organization to the client organization in order to establish an effective operation. Moreover, we identified a few levels that also improve decision-making.

> *As the number of levels in hierarchy in our organization is only a few, this directly influences our decision-making process towards the client. As we have*

introduced a client-oriented team, this contributes to lower the levels in hierarchy for our client. (Source: a service delivery manager)

In order to support an effective organizational structure the provider and the client developed a governance mechanism. Governance agreements that form a part of this mechanism must ensure a coherent view on both communication and the delivery of services. Table 5.2 illustrates the most important agreements that refer to roles and responsibilities and communication.

With regard to the level of horizontal integration we found that interviewees assess this dimension as high. This can be explained by the finding that the provider's on-site employees perform various roles within their team. For example, as a consequence of the provider's continuity approach, employees need to fulfil various roles in order to ensure the continuity of services. This forms a part of the resource overlay model. Moreover, we found that the provider's offshore employees focus on dedicated capabilities (for example, hardware, software) that lead to a low level of horizontal integration. This

Table 5.2 Governance mechanism

Level	Members	Topics	Communication
Strategic	Client: CIO Provider: Sales director	Governance agreements Contracts High-level implementation plan	Meets twice a year
Strategic	Client: Programme manager Provider: Engagement manager	Architecture Service contracts Process improvement Standards, templates, tools	Meet once a quarter
Tactical	Client: Service center manager Provider: Service delivery manager	Planning and management Performance and status monitoring Productivity improvement	Meet once a quarter
Tactical	Client: Application manager Provider: Service delivery manager	Multiple releases in a service center Release planning and management SLA's and budgets	Meets every month
Operational	Client: Release manager Provider: On-site coordinator Provider: Offshore project manager	Release level operational decisions Coordination between teams of multiple entities	Meets every week

finding illustrates that a combined approach contributes to effectiveness in service provisioning.

Relating our findings to the organizational theory, interestingly, our results provide clear support that the provider's organization corresponds with a mix of organizational structures. First, during the start of the arrangement, we found evidence for the professional organization type (Mintzberg, 1983). Highly educated professionals form a relatively autonomous professional group to support the client. Their work is complex while the client's environment is relatively stable. The dimension of decision-making is expected to be bottom-up while specializations are horizontally integrated. We find support for both of the dimensions that were predominantly present in our provider's organization. Secondly, after the adaptation of the organizational structure (for example, the introduction of a client-oriented team) our results also reveal the presence of an adhocracy or innovation style of organizational structure (Mintzberg, 1983). By consciously applying a more dynamic governance model, the provider is more capable of handling environmental uncertainty. This appeals to the organic paradigm as discussed by other researchers (Zammuto and O'Conner, 1992; Daft, 1995). Because of the formation of temporary project teams of experts, their tasks and skills are not standardized. This kind of structure is able to respond quickly to complex and changing client circumstances. One example is the episode of human flexibility (episode 2). Furthermore, the combination of offshore expert teams and on-site provider representatives contributes to a mitigation of the level of client uncertainty.

Dynamic fit

In studying our provider under research we found a strong relationship between sourcing capabilities and organizational structure. The influence of client developments on the fit between capabilities and organizational structure appears strong when client episodes had a major business impact on the client firm. Applying a retrospective approach, we identified two factors which had a major influence the service provider fit: changing business priorities (episode 1) and changing business timelines (episode 2).

> *The relation between both capabilities and structure is strong. The initiator for a fit is the governance capability. When changing client circumstances affect the capabilities that relate to organizational structure, the governance capability is the link to restore the fit. (Source: a service delivery manager)*

Consequently, the provider has to adapt to the changing client circumstances in order to repair their fit between capabilities and structure. Since the provider's organizational structure is complex (for example, on-site, onshore, offshore) and technical skills and capabilities are dispersed, it is necessary to establish a structural alignment between both adaptability aspects. During the interviews various participants pointed out that the presence of the *governance capability* is the initiator in achieving a fit between both capabilities and organizational structure. Our analysis revealed that the provider under study consciously applies procedures to guide the fit adaptability process. Initially, the client-oriented team carries out regularly monitoring of client developments. Subsequently, after monitoring the developments the client-oriented team chart and categorize various types of client developments that are confirmed in meetings with client representatives. When the client confirmed the developments the client-oriented team assesses the impact of these client developments on their sourcing capabilities. Where necessary, the provider's sourcing capabilities are strengthened or renewed. We did not expect to find procedures to guide the adaptability process as previous research encountered severe problems with regard to the provider's ability to adapt (Kern and Willcocks, 2001). Furthermore, interview analysis confirms that applying a proactive adaptability strategy positively contributes to customer intimacy.

Remarkably, our interviewees indicated that the provider's client-oriented team were the first to observe changes in their client circumstances. This can be explained from the direct relationship with the client's sourcing management organization that is responsible for managing the operational relationship. Later the provider's executive management will be informed of developments by the client's executive management, marking the part of the process at which extensive developments are addressed in a more formal way. Important client developments are discussed by executive management of both parties on a regular basis. One of the most important findings of this study is that the provider consciously applies processes to create a fit which, in turn, has a positive effect on sourcing performance. This result suggests that establishing a fit is a well-considered choice, which contributes to outperformance. Applying processes to change capabilities fits with competence theory where firm-specific competences are managed from a holistic approach. In particular, this applies to these capabilities that form a part of the client-oriented team. As intermediary between changing client circumstances and provider core competences, dynamic sourcing capabilities help the provider to adjust its resource mix and maintain a sustainable performance. In this way, the provider stands out when compared to competitors.

Sourcing performance

Discussing the topic of fit in our interviews, multiple respondents indicate that the presence of a fit has an effect on the performance of the organization.

In the studied client case we found that the client selected the provider under study consciously. Strong capabilities and a customer intimacy approach were the main criteria that resulted in satisfactory organizational performance. The interviews with the respondents revealed that both sourcing capabilities and organizational structure affect the performance towards the client. We found that specific actions were applied to meet the performance objectives as agreed. For instance, the introduction of shadow resources (episode 3) is a valuable example of how the provider assures their operational performance. Delivering the performance as agreed in the contract concerns all providers' employees that are directly related to the client organization.

In addition to IT service performance, overall client satisfaction is reported from a number of ten client representatives randomly and anonymously. In an effort to ensure independence, the client satisfaction is measured by an external firm. Each quarter the performance is benchmarked to previous reports so that trends can be identified. Based on the latest insights an estimated performance model is established that is used to manage the ongoing results. This model highlights both the number and type of resources and necessary capabilities. Each week running IT projects are assessed to establish if they are still on track. However, there are some factors that affect the sustainability of the delivered performance. First, we found that the client must be explicit in describing their functional need. Insufficient functional demands lead to discussions which will increase the lead time. Secondly, the service provider needs to deploy sufficient own resources with relevant knowledge, to assure the continuity of services for the client.

Moreover, we found sufficient evidence that sustainability with regard to performance is possible. After fine-tuning the performance during the first two years of the sourcing arrangement, a sustainable performance level was achieved. Despite the fact that during the latter years many client developments took place, the observed performance remained the same. From the performance reports we found that zero faults were identified in the launch of 11 new software releases. This performance was confirmed by the project satisfaction reports. The project performance is measured each quarter based on recurring items. In a questionnaire, each quarter end-users rate questions and statements. Over the course of the past three years the provider's performance was rated at 4.

> *Yes we are able to deliver a sustainable performance over the last couple of years. Each quarter the customer satisfaction is measured on a scale of 1 to 5. During the last two years our score is 4 or above. In an exceptional situation when the score drops below 4, all internal signals become red. Immediately,*

> *we will start improvements projects to establish the performance. (Source: an engagement manager)*

Strikingly, we observed that, independent of their role or function, all employees behave as if they are personally responsible for achieving the performance as agreed. Analyzing the construct of sourcing performance we found evidence that the provider under study built their strategy of path-dependent, causally ambiguous, and intangible assets. As a result of this strategy the provider is able to outperform other providers. This is consistent with the resource-based view which argues that firms exploit their valuable, rare, and costly to imitate capabilities to generate economic rents (Barney, 2001: 648).

Conclusion

In this chapter we explored how an offshore IT outsourcing provider deals with the aspect of adaptability. Our case study shows that increasing market dynamism forces the banking and insurance company to adapt in order to meet customer demands. Because of this need the offshore service provider also had to adapt in order to meet the demands of their client. Our findings provide evidence that the provider under study is able to adapt to changes in client circumstances. This had a positive effect on client decision-making and, in contrast to service providers that did not adapt, the provider did not lose market share. We may conclude that the offshore provider consciously developed procedures to guide the adaptability process in order to deal with the client's uncertainties. This demonstrates that the provider under study realizes the value add of adaptability. As such, adaptability can be viewed as a competitive and strategic capability. Adaptability might easily result in organizational change and the redesign of facilitating processes. Therefore, our results suggest that mutual cooperation is mandatory. This finding is entirely consistent with previous researchers, who have argued that sourcing relationships require continuous attention (Kern and Willcocks, 2002). Derived from establishing a fit, adaptive capabilities are concerned in particular with behavioural dimensions as part of the relationship. We argue that the relationship dimensions of trust and cooperation are conditional for the provider to implement and apply a proactive adaptability strategy. As sourcing is a people business, the attitude of executive management and employees is likely to be crucial in the achievement of a sustainable performance. Our results provide clear support that strategic decision-making by executive management is required to ensure a fit in order to achieve a sustainable performance.

6
Case Study: Global Provider

Contrary to myth, Indian offshore firms do little Follow-The-Sun.
(Erran Carmel)

In this chapter we describe our fourth case study, which is a global provider. First, we introduce the context of the provider under study. In this section we also describe a selected client case. In the following paragraphs we study various client episodes to determine the provider's response. As a result of these findings, we analyze the case study that are also clustered around the defined constructs. Finally, we present the overall conclusion of this case study.

Context of the case study

Our provider under study is a leading global company for consulting, systems integration and outsourcing. The provider's mission is to be a global leader in providing technology-enabled business solutions and services while maintaining a focus on delivering innovative and practical results. As a result of this mission three major strategic objectives are stated. First, outsourcing services must form at least 50 per cent of the annual revenue. The company argues that a more sustainable revenue stream will underpin their solid financial state. Second, customers in industry and government have to be supported with solutions crafted to meet their strategic goals and enable them to profit from the advanced use of technology. Third, additional revenues have to be made by the introduction of outsourcing services towards the small and medium-sized enterprises (SME) market. The company employs more than 90,000 persons, in 80 countries worldwide. The provider classifies its key capabilities and solutions in the global market as Business Process Outsourcing (BPO), Applications Outsourcing, Enterprise

Resource Planning (ERP), Infrastructure Outsourcing, Managed Hosting, System Integration and Consulting.

As stated in their business strategy, the provider focuses on creating customer intimacy and offering flexible solutions. Previously, the company made a strategic choice to apply a selective customer approach. As a global company the provider supports large client organizations with a global reach. Subsequently, the provider focuses on customer intimacy to achieve customer satisfaction. The provider is organized in business units representing vertical industry groups, horizontal lines of service and geographies. Most of their clients are served directly by the industry vertical business units. These organizations are responsible for integrating all of the company's capabilities to deliver business results and industry process expertise to their clients. The horizontal lines of service provide basic building blocks of technology expertise such as scaled infrastructure management (Managed Services), application outsourcing and consulting consistently across industries and geographies. The horizontal service groups employ the standard processes and procedures that allow the company to quickly deploy resources wherever they are needed, and, because the company is global, provide economies of scale. The conundrum of being global is that the actual delivery of services must take place in local contexts, including concerns related to language, culture and local business practices. Geographies perform the vital task of maintaining customer intimacy, which is a company's defining characteristic. Their geographical (local) organizations provides understanding of the cultures and markets in which they operate and providing a channel for developing long-term relationships with local clients. The provider divides the geographic operations in: the Americas, EMEA (Europe, Middle East & Africa), Asia and Australia.

In order to determine our research objective, studying the provider's fit, an outsourcing arrangement with a client needs to be studied over time (longitudinal study). We selected a client case that meets the selection criteria. The selected client operates globally and acts in a dynamic market. We assume that client developments will have a significant influence on the sourcing capabilities and organizational structures of the provider. As a result, we are able to study the provider's effort to establish a fit.

Client object of study

The object of our case study is a global diversified resources company. This global company holds significant positions in major commodity businesses, including aluminum and coal. The company consists of 41,000 employees working in over 100 operations in 25 countries. Because of the limited number of competitors the resources market as a whole is static. However, the pressure to deliver the resources globally towards customers is dynamic. Being a global company and distributing the resources to customers all over the world demands a flexible mindset. Therefore, the company must be able to adapt to their customers and meet their demands.

Acting in a dynamic and complex global market delivering various types of resources, the global resources company decided to focus on flexibility in an attempt to achieve their business goals. In 2000 they decided to outsource a significant part of their IT landscape to various service providers. The global resources company divided their IT landscape into three main plots: (1) IT infrastructure and global application maintenance; (2) local application support; and (3) networks (data and telecommunications). The company's sourcing strategy is based on a multi-vendor policy, to select providers that best fits the specific defined IT plots. Our provider under study was selected for the IT infrastructure domain which constitutes 65 per cent of all IT activities. The seven-year, $700 million outsourcing contract included the transfer of the customer's IT staff to the provider under study. In 2007, the contract was extended for a period of two years.

All selected service providers have an extensive track record in their own area of expertise. Our provider was selected for three reasons: their reputation in the market with regard to flexibility; their proven high quality of delivered services; and their willingness to adapt to client needs by offering a customer intimacy approach. The second provider, a specialist in application maintenance, became globally responsible for the support of business and office applications. The third provider, which is globally managing networks, became responsible for the fixed and mobile communication services. The resources company applies a global central operating sourcing management organization employing 150 FTEs. This sourcing management department is responsible for both demand management towards their internal business units as well as supply management towards the service providers. The company indicated that our service provider was to have a direct relationship with the central sourcing management organization and it was therefore not allowed to interact directly with the business departments.

The global resources company is supported by our provider, based in three regions: Europe, Asia and Australia. Each region is headed by an account team that is led by an account executive.

In creating alignment between the three regions, all account teams report to a global account team that is located in Melbourne, Australia.

Episodes

We have conducted an empirical study on the provider–client outsourcing arrangement from a retrospective approach. In this way, we are able to determine the extent to which client developments have affected the provider organization. We identified a number of critical episodes, around which our findings have subsequently been clustered. Each episode is described with the client development and the provider's response. Studying these episodes we were able to determine the effect on the provider's fit and sourcing performance.

Episode 1: Delivery struggle

After our provider under study was selected by the client in 2001, a formal transition programme was initiated. Our provider developed a transition scheme to insource the infrastructure as originally managed by the customer.

> *In general, it is our believe that the transformation phase has the strongest influence on performance. We have the opinion that completing the transition phase successfully; we have created the required starting point for a stable delivery phase. Subsequently, we experienced that a sound performance will be the result. (Source: a delivery director)*

Following the completion of the transition programme the formal delivery phase started. Although a thorough and in-depth delivery model was developed and discussed extensively, a major disruption occurred. The provider applied a leveraged delivery model, meaning that all necessary operational capabilities, such as the number of available resources deployed and technical assets, were shared with other clients. We observed that the client experienced an increase in the lead times of IT services, while the communication between provider and client was slow because of the formal internal communication procedures put in place by the provider. Moreover, decision-making on the provider's side was slow as a result of the multiple layers in the hierarchy. As a result, business departments within the client's organization experienced difficulties in operational businesses such as the processing of customer orders and their confirmation. Following the start of the delivery phase there was a substantial decrease in the level of client satisfaction, as measured by the provider.

However, to assure business operational performance the client demanded dedicated operational support. To meet the business demands of the client, the provider announced the introduction of a client-oriented team. Based on the perspective of customer intimacy, this client-oriented team offered a dedicated approach in that they are responsible for the delivery of services. The introduction of a client-oriented team contributes to achieving flexible solutions that are proactive and adaptive. As a result, a handover of decision-making was effectuated towards the client-oriented team while shorter internal communication lines were also achieved. This dedicated customer approach was effected towards each geographical customer location. Applying a client-oriented team approach had a definite improvement in client satisfaction as shown in the client satisfaction reports.

Episode 2: Business needs for 'on-demand' support

As the business of the client under study can be characterized as dynamic and demanding, the same dynamic attitude is required from the provider. However, the client's experience was that the provider was not meeting their expectations. Our interviews with the provider's respondents revealed that client employees were dissatisfied about the quality of the service desk when they reported incidents or initiated changes. Long queues and undefined contact persons resulted in negative satisfaction reports. Additionally, when delivery issues occurred the provider was unable to bring additional resources into action. When the employees of the client's business departments experienced disruptions, or even failures, in their IT systems, these problems had to be solved immediately as IT outage would result in immediate financial losses. Following an assessment, the provider concluded that the existing service-level agreements did not fit with the high business demands of the client. The client stated the need for the on-demand support of their provider. The provider was incapable of meeting the client's need for on-demand support as a result of the limited number of resources available at the on-site locations. Responding to the identified business needs, the client-oriented team developed a new service (the so-called 'floorwalker' concept).

This concept is based on the principle that whenever there is an incident or when business employees experience any IT problems, they immediately contact one of the provider's available on-site service agents. Such incidents or problems might involve IT applications, for instance, or hardware such as desktops and printers. When a client business employee beckons the provider's service agent, the providers offer immediate support. Since the provider's service agent is present 'on the floor', the nickname 'floorwalker' was introduced. Only after the problem has been solved the problem will the corresponding administration and financial settlement be processed. By developing this new on-demand service, service levels became increasingly differentiated. Moreover, the client is willing to pay for this additional service. The floorwalker concept offers flexibility and meets the client's business needs and this new service has made a positive contribution to levels of client satisfaction.

> *The more demanding a client is, the more capabilities and organizational structure will affect each other. For instance, by supporting our demanding client it is crucial to apply a flexible behaviour. That's why our floorwalkers solve the client's issue's first and register the issues latter. (Source: a service delivery manager)*

Episode 3: Business needs for innovation

Acting in dynamic global resources businesses, the client needs to maintain their leading market position. To interact successfully in an environment of changing business circumstances, the client believes that innovation from a business perspective is a prerequisite to sustaining their market position. Moreover, the need for innovative solutions increases each year. The range of innovation covers both technology and processes. As a result, the provider under study is challenged to develop and regularly discuss innovative solutions that contribute to the client's market position. In addition to standard innovative IT solutions, such as storage area network solutions and virtualization, which are developed for all clients our provider is asked to develop specific client solutions, as is illustrated by the following. In response to the client's need to become more efficient in the field of office automation the provider developed specific electronic whiteboards. Following some business discussions, using the electronic whiteboard, the data on the whiteboard are transformed into digital data, which is then sent automatically to an email box. This solution definitely speeds up the process of handling information.

> *As innovation is one of our core values, clients expect new developments. We proclaimed 2007 as the year of innovation. Based on business needs of a client acting in the transportation industry we developed a camera solution that is able to register speed above 180 mph. A condition to produce the camera solution is dependent on a minimum volume. (Source: a service delivery manager)*

The introduction of new services requires effective support within the provider's organization. Therefore, new processes and tools have to be developed and implemented. As ad hoc innovation has made an insufficient contribution to client's businesses, a global innovation board was established to ensure continuous innovation. Here, new ideas can be discussed more concretely while an innovation calendar is defined. This strategy results in various innovative solutions – for example, a web portal that depicts the roles and responsibilities of the client's employees. This contributes to department governance processes, with the aim of achieving clear mutual communication.

Episode 4: Integrating IT services

Based on the sourcing strategy of the client, three service providers were selected to support the main IT activities. Since the beginning of the sourcing arrangements, the client has experienced that managing the three providers has become increasingly complex. On the one hand, the main object of the sourcing management organization of the client was to deliver end-to-end services towards their business departments and end-users. On the other hand, the service providers all delivered single services that still needed to be integrated by the sourcing management organization of the client. This integration required not only ample effort but also sufficient technical knowledge, which had been outsourced as a result of the sourcing arrangement. This resulted in increasing lead times for delivery to business departments. Therefore, the client informally requested our provider under study to integrate the various technical services of all three providers. The provider agreed to do so and since 2007, our provider has acted as a service integrator, managing their own services as well as those of the other contractors. However, in practice this integration activity has not been formally agreed and included in the contract. As a result, there is a serious tension in the relationship with the client and other service providers. The interviews demonstrate that the client expects to receive an end-to-end service which was not delivered. The cause of this underperformance is that the other providers will not cooperate with the integrator since they are not formally informed by the client. The interviews with respondents of our provider under study show a lack of formal agreements and responsibilities. Additionally, as this integration role has not been formally agreed in a contract our provider does not receive any financial contributions. This item is still subject to negotiation.

> *The subcontractors won't cooperate to integrate the various single services. Their motivation is clear: since there is no contract that mentions the integration*

aspect, they are also not paid. As we are not paid either, but still deliver an integral service this issue causes a lot of tension in the relationship to both the client and other providers. (Source: a sales manager)

Episode 5: Client sourcing strategy

The executive management of the client's global organization experienced that market dynamism increases over time. In order to respond quickly to the changing customer needs the company also needs to change accordingly. As a result of the clients adapting their organization to the changing market circumstances, IT providers need to align with their clients' business approach. In order to achieve increased flexibility, IT providers need to be adaptable enough to respond to their client's goals. The client announced that they developed a new sourcing strategy, changing their IT organization into a federative model. In this approach the central IT department becomes globally responsible for devising policies and related standards. In the federative model each business unit becomes responsible for managing the IT providers once they have been selected. Each business unit needs to select an IT service integrator that will be responsible for the operational management of the various subcontractors. The provider responded to this new client sourcing strategy through the introduction of a sourcing integration model supported by various processes such as service management and contract management. According to the provider this new service adds value to the client organization, relieving them of the burden of operationally managing subcontractors. The provider's experience with managing subcontracts can be formalized in a new arrangement. Consequently, the provider is both developing new capabilities and strengthening existing capabilities, managing subcontractors and developing integral process management. Moreover, organizational structures needed to be redesigned to offer adequate support for the delivery of end-to-end IT services.

We noticed that our client developed a new sourcing strategy that will have a very important effect on our business. Their decision change towards a fully decentralized multi-vendor approach means that each business unit becomes responsible for managing multiple providers. This will cost us money as we globally have a share-of-wallet of 65 per cent in delivering IT services. That's why we are developing a new dynamic integration service to position our self as an integration partner. (Source: a senior manager)

The episodes and related responses of the service provider under study are summarized in Table 6.1.

Table 6.1 Episode overview

Year	Event	Event description	Response service provider
2002	1	Delivery struggle: the need for a more customer-driven approach	Introduction of a client-oriented team (dedicated client attention)
2003	2	Business needs for 'on-demand' support	Introduction of the 'floorwalker' concept
2005	3	Business needs for innovation	Introduction of a continuous innovation programme
2006	4	Stronger demand for integrating IT services	Integral delivery of IT services
2007	5	Design and development of a new sourcing strategy	Development of a dynamic service integration model

Analyses

As the next step in our research, we will analyse the case based on the following research constructs: client developments, sourcing competences, organizational structure, fit and sourcing performance.

Client developments

The impact of client developments on the provider's organization is studied from the perspective of sourcing strategy, innovation and required flexibility. With regard to the sourcing strategy we found that our provider was selected because of their strong IT capabilities and their willingness to adapt to changing circumstances. The episodes mentioned in the previous sections underpin this choice. At the same time, our provider needed to demonstrate a proactive attitude with regard to the competition. Hence, our provider was requested to play an integration role, which was a confirmation of their customer intimacy approach. Recent client developments will have a strong impact as the client changes its sourcing management organization towards a decentralized approach in which each business unit builds its own sourcing management organization, becoming responsible for managing multiple providers. At the same time the overall contract will expire and the client will start reorienting on the existing sourcing strategy. This change will have an impact on both the capabilities and the organizational structure of our provider. The interviewed respondents have the opinion that the client's focus on 'innovation' has a strong impact on the provider's organization. In addition to the need for innovative solutions, the time to market of these solutions will also increase. For example, the introduction of BlackBerry devices for all employees had to be completed within a period of just two months. As the global IT landscape is a complex one, the provider required many additional resources with various sourcing capabilities, (for example, domain expertise, organizational design and planning and contracting).

> *The client's demand for flexibility is intense. When we want to answer client proposals for new projects, this requires sufficient resources and capabilities from our side. If we can't respond adequately, it becomes a serious problem. Therefore, we introduced 'forecasting' in our Client Focus Team so that we can prepare ourselves and prevent some surprises. (Source: a programme delivery manager)*

Since the client operates in a dynamic environment, flexibility is a requirement in order to cater with uncertainties on the client side. As flexibility is one of our provider's strategic pillars, the provider's respondents indicate that their organization is capable of dealing with this demand. The interviews show that the organization is supported by many processes and procedures to handle projects in a flexible way. To facilitate major projects with a global reach, rapid response teams become responsible for the execution of these projects. These rapid response teams dispose of various capabilities and operate directly at the client on behalf of the provider. This ensures direct decision-making and rapid communication.

Relating our findings to the Interaction Approach (Hakansson, 1982) we address the environmental variable of 'dynamism'. The client episodes show how our provider coped with dynamism and encouraged employees to change their behaviour in response to these developments. The interviews also revealed a lack with regard to the business mindset of the provider's employees. This view arose at the start of the outsourcing arrangement. As a result, employees are struggling to fathom the changing client circumstances and to translate these into the required IT services. This finding relates to the 'environment' variable of the Interaction Approach that addresses the social system. The existing social system surrounding the relationship between client and provider defines ways of behaviour amongst other matters. The provider's strategic choice to focus on flexibility enables the employees to cope with environmental uncertainty. This relates to the behavioural dimension of cooperation. Previous research indicates that flexibility is fundamental, since adjustments, changes and investments are not foreseeable at the start of an outsourcing arrangement (Gietzman, 1996). Moreover, we find that to ensure sufficient communication between client and provider the applied management process consists of regular communications and meetings. The latter correspond to the 'social exchange' variable as part of the Interaction Approach. Social exchanges help to reduce uncertainty, especially in situations of cultural or special disparity (Cunningham, 1980).

Remarkably, we find that the aspect of Power/Dependence, as part of the 'atmosphere' variable, was skewed in favour of the client. A good example is episode 4 (for example, integrating IT services) that underpins the client's power play towards the provider. Based on the selective outsourcing sourcing strategy of the client, this is in contrast with existing research (Kern and Willcocks, 2000) which observes that such an approach leads to a more balanced relationship between client and provider. The provider may have found himself dependent on the client for remuneration for the provided IT services. We argue that client dependency may relate to the provider's sourcing capability of leadership. We are of the opinion that the provider's leadership capability is immature. Moreover, the imbalance between power and dependency may lead to serious discussions and conflicts over time.

Sourcing capabilities

We found evidence that sourcing competences were adapted regularly as a result of both interaction with the client and also internal circumstances. This process of adaption is initiated by the client-oriented team. In particular, the service delivery manager is responsible for initiating the adaptation process for capabilities. Provider respondents involved in the client arrangement pointed out that based on input such as regular client meetings, client satisfaction reports and the monitoring of client developments, an assessment was made of their impact on sourcing competences. However, internal circumstances, such as the turnaround to vertical markets instead of a country-driven approach, also exert an influence on the adaptation of capabilities. We found that the provider applies a process to regularly adapt capabilities. This process, which is initiated by the client-oriented team, describes the various procedures to be followed. Examples of such procedure steps include: the involvement of relevant stakeholders; a description of the impact of adaptabilities on sourcing capabilities and organizational structure; and the expected timetable for the execution of these steps. This process is illustrated in Figure 6.1.

Some parts of the process are the result of annual plans whereas others result from monthly management team meetings or weekly operational meetings. In addition, the adaptation also takes into account personal development plans (such as training) for each employee.

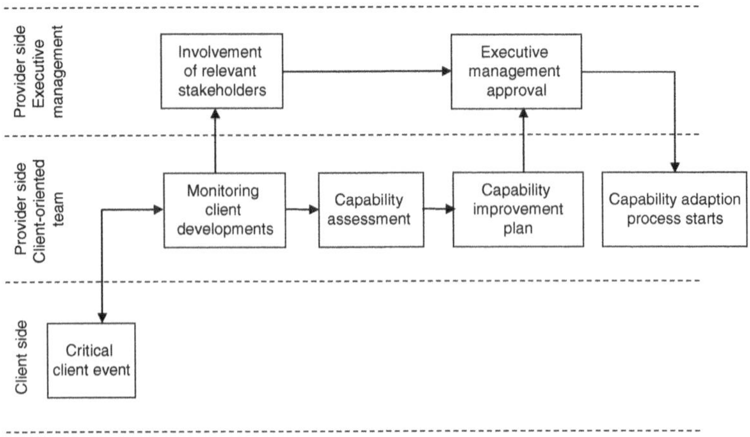

Figure 6.1 Capability adaptability process

Addressing the sourcing capability model of Feeny et al. (2005), we will discuss the three main sourcing competence areas related to our studied provider case. First, we found that sourcing capabilities directly related to the *relationship* competency area are adapted or strengthened from the perspective of soft skills. Sourcing capabilities that refer to this competence area, such as *organizational design, customer development* and *leadership*, were strengthened by focusing on client satisfaction. The main goal of the provider is to sustain the customer intimacy approach which, as mentioned earlier in section 6.1, is a strategic objective of the provider. However, the interviews revealed that client developments from a business perspective were not recognized by our provider. Multiple respondents affirmed that the capability *'business knowledge'* is absent. For instance, we found a lack of business knowledge of the client's diversified resources market. Respondents further announced that the internal change towards vertical markets will strengthen the need to acquire more business knowledge. Based on the interviews we found that business market knowledge is strongly related to business applications that support client business processes. With regard to the sourcing capability model, this *business knowledge* capability can be assessed as new.

> *Yes it's true that our business knowledge capability is weak. We are not capable in thinking from a business perspective; we are too focused on technology. Often our clients demand that we develop business knowledge to understand what is going on in their businesses. (Source: a delivery director)*

We found that the *transformation* competency area is affected by the role of the provider, which has changed towards being more of a service integrator. Based on the business needs of the client the provider experienced that managing several subcontractors requires existing capabilities to be strengthened. In particular, the sourcing capability *process re-engineering* needs improvement, as it is applied to establish efficient and effective processes. This is recognized as the client requires an end-to-end service and our provider needs to integrate various IT services. Furthermore, the respondents identify a lack to the sourcing capability *programme management*, required to manage integral programmes. A new challenge will rise as the client recently decided to change the governance structure from a central IT organization into a decentralized IT sourcing management organization. This change will influence all of the competence areas affecting sourcing capabilities as *leadership, governance, organizational design* and *customer development* (for example, account management).

Addressing the *delivery* competence area we found that the provider invests in regular training and workshop sessions to strengthen the technical capabilities of the employees. In particular, the interviews show that the introduction of new IT services as Storage Area Networks, virtualization and a dynamic workplace are facilitated by training and additional information sessions. Background information on these services is distributed by means of electronic (Intranet) and paper (hardcopy material) modes. Moreover, investments are made to support these services through tools and electronic guidelines. As well as developments that are initiated internally, the client under study will initiate developments that influence the provider's capabilities. Examples such as the 'floorwalker' concept will affect the provider's capabilities organizational design, process re-engineering, and behaviour management. The latter is important as the provider's employees need to think and operate from a client perspective, instead of displaying a typical provider's mentality. We found that the initiator to affect these types of changes is the client-oriented team.

The provider's choice to regularly strengthen their sourcing capabilities reflects the resource-based view (RBV). The interviews with the provider's respondents show various examples in which capabilities were adapted from a knowledge perspective (for example, training, transfer). Moreover, this finding is consistent with previous research (Feeny et al., 2005), which argues that adapting capabilities require regular investments. Referring to the RBV, knowledge management contributes to the achievement of a competitive advantage based on capabilities that are valuable, rare, imitable and not substitutable (Barney, 2001). Moreover, the conscious choice to adapt capabilities is in accordance with the key message of the RBV that strategic assets are essentially intangible. Especially in relationships where intangible assets are important, the development of soft skills (for example, capabilities) is key. The behaviour of the provider's employees is essential to the achievement of success. Specifically, in addition to the provider's attention it refers to the capability to motivate and manage people in order to deliver services with a 'front-office' culture (Feeny et al., 2005). Both interview analyses and the additional documents that we studied revealed the presence of processes to guide the adaptability of capabilities. The existence of these processes refers to dynamic capabilities that enable firms to change routines and services over time. We find that the provider's sourcing capabilities were developed and strengthened over time. Specifically, we found evidence that the provider developed in a number of areas: technical capabilities, organizational capabilities and relationship capabilities. This reflects the RBV were capabilities and competences are a combination of tangible and intangible assets. Since the provider is willing and able to adapt to client developments, this finding also reflects the competence theory assumption that achieving organizational competences requires an effective integration of internal organizational and external competitive dynamics. Constantly developing or strengthening capabilities in a dynamic environment requires dynamic capabilities.

Organizational structure

With respect to the episodes described earlier we found that the delivery struggle (episode 1) was perceived by the interviewees as a turning point. Strikingly, we did not expect to find that the provider's strategy was based on a leverage delivery model for a client that is operating in a dynamic and global market. As the provider is experienced in supporting multiple clients globally, their decision to neglect a more client-oriented approach caused severe problems that could have been prevented.

To improve the performance the provider introduced a client-oriented team. The aim of the client-oriented team is to strengthen the relationship with the client, applying a customer intimacy approach. The organizational structure of the client-oriented team, including their dimensions, is closely aligned to the client organization in order to facilitate the delivery of IT services.

The locus of decision-making is perceived by the client-team representatives as twofold. The representatives have the opinion that they are authorized to make decisions that are directly related to their client. The interviewed participants involved in the client-oriented team argue that with respect to decision-making, their team operates almost independently of the global organization. On the one hand, they are able to focus completely on the client side, which is congruent with the provider's strategy to create customer intimacy. Firms had experienced previously that when operating in an environment that can be characterized by a high degree of environmental uncertainty or changing client circumstances they may decentralize their decision-making process. On the other hand, the participants argue that this approach creates a difference between their team and the global delivery organization, which leads to regular tensions. Furthermore, we found that more strategically and commercially oriented decisions are made by executive management.

Although the provider is organized globally, the representatives experienced limited hindrance with regard to the number of layers in the hierarchy. This can be explained by the fact that the client-oriented team holds the responsibility for acting at a local level. In each country where the global provider is present a local organization is built. This local organization becomes responsible for supporting both local and global clients. In this way the organization can be considered to be flat. Moreover, we found that the limited numbers in hierarchy stimulates the process of decision-making in a positive way. Discussing the dimension of the level of horizontal integration, we found that the boundaries of the representative's function were defined clearly. All of the functions contain explicit single roles in order to create a maximum focus on the client organization. One example is the function of sales manager that is strictly related to sales and client satisfaction. Similarly, the technical functions were also based on a single role. Interviews show that approximately 10 to 15 employees are involved in the client-oriented team, depending on the specific programmes that are executed. When other functions are required in supporting the client, several employees with specific knowledge and experience will be involved. In this case we found that the extent to which additional expertise was required by the client fits with the provider's approach of lowering the level of horizontal integration.

Dynamic fit

The interviewed respondents revealed that they experience a strong relationship between sourcing capabilities and organizational structure. They have the opinion that the sourcing capability *organizational design* determines *what* organizational dimensions (for example, decision-making, level of horizontal integration) of the client-oriented team are required. The sourcing capability *organizational design* is considered by respondents to be the driver for organizational change. The client environment and related episodes determine *how* the organizational dimensions can be established on the provider's site. However, the provider's representatives perceive the sourcing capability *organizational design* to establish the organizational dimensions as a 'soft skill' that is also context-specific. This refers to the resource-based view that argues that tacit knowledge is difficult to capture, codify and imitate. The organizational dimensions, as applied by the client-oriented team, are discussed regularly. From a client perspective this requires the capability to recognize and value the actions taken by the provider to adapt to the client's needs. On the other hand, we observed that the effect of a well-aligned organizational structure also depends on the maturity of the client. The client in this case has stated clear sourcing objectives that are derived from their sourcing strategy. As a result, the provider is able to manage their own organizational dimensions based on their client's need.

The interviewed respondents indicate that the extent to which the fit is realized is also influenced by the global governance structure as applied by the provider. The provider facilitates IT services that are delivered from both on-site and offshore locations. In doing so, the provider's on-site client team is responsible for identifying client developments, managing the relationship, and verifying the delivery of IT services as agreed. The provider's offshore sites are responsible for the delivery of IT services. We observed that the alignment between the on-site and offshore sites seems to be difficult, creating a serious tension. The interviews show that unclear responsibilities – who will initiate actions and start work packages – result in underperformance. This may suggest that the sourcing capability *governance* is weak. Subsequently, the relation between sourcing capabilities and organizational structure became unbalanced. During the outsourcing arrangement with the client the provider decided to reconsider the organizational structure for the delivery of their IT services (episode 1). In order to prevent increased organizational costs for IT services, the provider decided to focus on domestic delivery. This refers to *ex post* costs as part of the TCE that encompass monitoring and adaptation costs (Wigand et al., 1997). As a result, a domestic client-oriented team was dedicated to the provision of IT services. We observed that following the redesign of the organizational structure the fit was restored.

> *There is definitely a relationship between sourcing capabilities and organizational structure. We experience this relationship when there is a strong customer demand. The more demanding a customer is, the stronger is the influence on the fit between capabilities and organizational structure. (Source: a service delivery manager)*

The client can be considered to be a demanding customer who requires constant attention and adaptation on the part of the provider if necessary.

To identify changing client circumstances, provider representatives are required on client locations to discuss business needs directly. Applying this approach, we found that the fit between provider's sourcing capabilities and organizational structure remains constant.

Sourcing performance

Analyzing the performance of the IT services delivered towards the client, the interviews revealed two important factors. First, the sourcing capabilities affect the delivery of the performance. The respondents of the client-oriented team express the opinion that well-implemented provider processes increase team maturity. A mature team encourages flexibility and handling speed. The capability to organize and build a mature team will increase levels of client satisfaction. Furthermore, based on the interviews we observed that involving employees in a client-oriented team for several years also contributes to the improvement of performance. Secondly, the organizational structure as applied also influences the performance. One important organizational dimension as perceived by the respondents is that decision-making must be applied at a relatively low level within the provider organization (that is, the client-oriented team). Studying the client case we found evidence that the organizational structure of the client-oriented team was redesigned after the transition phase. In order to achieve a closer alignment with the client organization to obtain more effectiveness, the organizational subdimension decision-making was adapted specifically. Based on this outcome, there was an increase in performance.

Discussing the topic of sustainable performance we observed that the achievement of this goal derives from the provider's business policy. In fact, the respondents of the client-oriented team experienced that after the adaptation of their organizational dimensions, there was a significant improvement in the performance towards the client. The provider implemented a performance process within their organization that monitors the actual performance. The client-oriented team is responsible for monitoring the performance process and initiate improvement plans. When the performance unexpectedly develops negatively, improvement plans are applied immediately, according to predefined procedures. A client satisfaction survey process collects the client's monthly ratings of the IT services. This performance process consists of the following steps: monitoring and indicating individual client performance ratings, bringing together all identified client ratings, making an assessment according to performance metrics, communicating performance reports and initiating and developing an improvement plan when necessary. However, we observed that the client plays an important role in providing a sustainable performance. Interviews with provider representatives show that when a client is used to a sustainable performance, there will be an effect of 'raising the bar'. A single incident may influence the perception of the client. We found that the client-oriented team caters for this effect by involving the client in establishing improvement plans to ensure sustainability. At the same time the provider pays more attention by motivating their personnel and improving customer-oriented behaviour.

Furthermore, we found that the provisioning of a sustainable performance is influenced by the provider's international delivery structure. In this client case the provider's data centre is located in Canada, while the service desk is located in Spain. So, the various delivery processes involving the client-oriented team need to be aligned in order to ensure a sound performance and meet the service levels as agreed. Providing IT services to globally operating clients has a significant influence on the provider's flexibility.

In addition, we found that the delivery of a sustainable performance forms part of the personal target of each of the client-oriented team members. Performance sustainability is weighted at 10 per cent in an annual personal assessment, with a financial bonus. Reviewing the performance reports of our provider under study over the last two years show that the target performance has been exceeded constantly. This outcome shows that the ability of the provider to strengthen their capabilities and organizational structure results in a sustainable sourcing performance. This is confirmed by the RBV which argues that firms build their strategies on path-dependent, causally ambiguous, socially complex and intangible assets outperform firms that build their strategies only on tangible assets (Barney, 2001).

Conclusion

In this chapter we explored how a global IT outsourcing provider deals with the aspect of adaptability. This case study indicates that all three client developments, as identified in our preliminary research, have an influence on the sourcing capabilities and the organizational structure of the provider. We may conclude that the global IT outsourcing provider applies a formal process to adapt their sourcing capabilities on a regular basis. This adaptability process ensures regular monitoring and strengthening of providers' sourcing capabilities and organizational structure dimensions. With regard to the sourcing capabilities, we observed a lack of business market knowledge with the provider. This lack was revealed when the client required a fast response to deliver IT services to support the client to act adequately in their dynamic market. We may conclude that the significance of business market knowledge increases as IT services that are provided are more related to business processes, for example, business applications, CRM. We found a strong relationship between sourcing capabilities and organizational structure in achieving a fit. At the start of the delivery phase we determined that several situations occurred, resulting in a fit that was out of balance. The provider initiated actions to repair the balance. A client-oriented team was established which had a positive influence on both the relationship and the fit. Interviews showed that the organizational design capability was identified as the initiator to achieve a fit. Our research revealed that establishing a fit is influenced by an additional attribute: customer intimacy. The provider's response to episodes illustrates that adaptation is an effect of their customer intimacy approach. Furthermore, we found evidence that business processes were implemented to achieve a sustainable performance.

7
Cross-case Analysis

> *Customers have no reservations when it comes to complaining about suppliers. But suppliers will never publicly complain about customers. If suppliers could speak openly, they would tell customers to stop harping on price and instead focus on value. Rarely will the low cost supplier also be the supplier with the best quality, best service, and best overall value.*
>
> *(Mary Lacity)*

Having outlined the empirical descriptive case studies, in this chapter we will analyse their implications for our research model. First, we relate our findings to the core constructs as mentioned in Chapter 2. We will discuss our findings based on the principle of concept mapping. In addition, we found another construct that is perceived as important, the provider's sourcing strategy. This construct is discussed and also explained. Secondly, we analyse our findings and relate them to our research model. Finally, we will summarize our findings and describe our conclusions.

Findings

Client developments

The starting point for our research is related to the client developments that were identified in our preliminary research: sourcing strategy, innovation and required flexibility. Comparing the concept map client developments which we developed with our conceptual research model, we found both similarities and differences. From a client perspective, our empirical research indicated similarities related to all three client development types. From a provider's perspective, we recognized the competence areas as mentioned earlier in our conceptual model: relationship, transformation and delivery.

Table 7.1 Client developments

Source concept	Type of relationship	Target concept
Sourcing strategy	Has impact on	Relationship competence
Sourcing strategy	Has impact on	Transformation competence
Sourcing strategy	Has impact on	Delivery competence
Sourcing strategy	Is cause of	Provider's value proposition
Sourcing strategy	Has impact on	Provider's portfolio
Provider's value proposition	Has impact on	Provider's portfolio
Provider's value proposition	Has impact on	Relationship competence
Innovation	Has impact on	Relationship competence
Innovation	Is cause of	Transformation competence
Innovation	Has impact on	Delivery competence
Required flexibility	Has impact on	Relationship competence
Required flexibility	Has strong impact on	Delivery competence

In addition, we also identified two new concepts on the providers' side. These new concepts relate to the providers *value proposition* and their present *share-of-wallet*. Table 7.1 shows an overview of the core concepts found including their relationships.

Analysis

Interestingly, our analysis reveals two related concepts. First, we identified the concept *value proposition* from the perspective of the provider. This concept is influenced by the client development *sourcing strategy*.

> *The sourcing strategy of our client, which applies a limited multi-vendor policy, definitely influences our sourcing capabilities. In general, we recognize three elements that are quite important: the delivery of sufficient resources related to projects, relationship management (e.g. domestic, regional and global support), and transition management (multiple smaller transition projects). (Source: a programme delivery manager)*

The concept *value proposition* can be described as the IT service proposition that is provided by a service provider including value-added services. Interviews revealed various value propositions including strong innovation capabilities and an integration capability. For example, the global provider developed an integrator service to act as a broker between customer and multiple subcontractors. Managing the subcontractors adds value while the customer utilizes a single point of contact. We observed that providers perceive the provisioning of a sustainable performance as a differentiator that adds value to the integral IT proposition.

> *An example of our value proposition is the development of our recent introduced dynamic sourcing service. This service relieves our customer by managing several providers and instead doing business with one single front end provider. In fact, we are the integrator. In return, we will manage the other providers by managing their operational services towards the customer. (Source: an engagement manager)*

Defining a strong value proposition enables providers to distinguish themselves from other providers as this can increase their opportunity to win new business and increase their share-of-wallet. This *share-of-wallet* is the second concept that we found to be influenced by the provider's value proposition. The *share-of-wallet* concept is also affected by the client's sourcing strategy. Providers define the concept *share-of-wallet* as their share of the total set of IT services that are delivered to clients, including IT services provided by competitors. Providers develop new IT solutions to achieve a competitive advantage and in doing so increase their share-of-wallet in their clients' businesses. We argue that the type of client's sourcing strategy influences providers share-of-wallet. It can be explained that when a client applies a multi-vendor strategy, the provider focuses more on adding value to their proposition in order to be able to provide more IT services when compared with their competitors. Our research provides evidence that underpins this claim.

Relating our findings to the Interaction Approach (Hakansson, 1982), three conspicuous aspects attract attention. First, the case studies show that the providers' respondents perceive their client's innovation need as the cause for transformation. However, the Interaction Approach provides no evidence for innovation as a specific determinant of one of the variables. The fact that innovation is primarily perceived as a content-driven aspect of outsourcing relationships might explain why this is not reflected by the Interaction Approach. Moreover, the fact that innovation appeals to change and renewal might be a partial explanation why the provider's transformation competence is affected. Transformation leads to an adaptive state affecting both the capabilities and the organizational structure of a firm. Moreover, the clients' need for innovation arise from market dynamics. It is a key determinant in the achievement of a competitive advantage (Linder, 2004). Second, as a result of client developments (for example, market, organization), we indicated the need for flexible behaviour on the part of the providers' employees. This finding is consistent with the 'environment' variable of the Interaction Approach which addresses the social system. The existing social system surrounding the relationship between client and provider defines patterns of behaviour. Previous research indicates that flexibility is fundamental, since adjustments, changes and investments are not foreseeable at the start of an outsourcing arrangement (Gietzman, 1996).

Finally, our research shows that the value proposition has been shown to be a critical determinant of a provider's sourcing strategy as a response to the client's sourcing strategy. Addressing the concept of *value proposition*, the Interaction Approach does not reflect on this importance. An explanation can be found in the more general method of approach of Hakansson's Interaction Approach, which is more holistic in nature. Since we particularize the Interaction Approach to outsourcing relationships, previous research (Levina and Ross, 2003) indicates that providers who want to increase the value proposition to their clients need to be able to develop a complementary set of core competences.

Provider's sourcing strategy

Studying the core concept *client developments,* our analysis revealed another related concept namely 'Provider's sourcing strategy'. Based on this core concept complementary concepts were identified. Table 7.2 shows the source concepts and target concepts and their relationships.

Analysis

We found that the provider's sourcing strategy relates to two main concepts. First, we identified that the provider's business strategy has an impact on the provider's sourcing strategy. Two strategic business aspects that affect provider's business strategy are customer intimacy and offshoring. The finding of customer intimacy is consistent with our desk research, which reveals

Table 7.2 Provider's sourcing strategy

Source concept	Type of relationship	Target concept
Provider's business strategy	Has strong impact on	Customer intimacy
Provider's business strategy	Has strong impact on	Offshoring
Offshoring	Has impact on	Provider's sourcing strategy
Provider's business strategy	Has impact on	Provider's sourcing strategy
Provider's sourcing strategy	Has strong impact on	Sourcing competences
Provider's sourcing strategy	Has impact on	Market segmentation
Provider's sourcing strategy	Has impact on	Provider's strategic objectives
Provider's strategic objectives	Is cause of	Strategic effects
Market segmentation	Is cause of	Segmentation approach

that all three providers apply a customer intimacy approach as part of their business strategy. All providers stated that customer intimacy is a discriminating factor that, when applied well, can lead to a competitive advantage in the market. This could be explained by studying the interviews in which the providers' respondents indicated that the driver for new business arises from client business needs and related requirements. Furthermore, applying an offshore component is perceived as a 'need-to-have' business strategy. The analysis of the offshore component tends to support the provider's blended sourcing strategy, integrating onshore and offshore components. Based on our interviews with the provider's executive management the rationale to execute operations offshore were based on reducing the cost level of IT services.

Secondly, we identified a relationship between the provider's sourcing strategy and market segmentation. The cases showed that providers apply a strategy of selective market segmentation. Their approach is to focus on a limited number of market segments, a maximum of four, so that they are able to create in-depth knowledge and experience in their customer's businesses. Doing so, they can distinguish themselves from their competitors.

Finally, as indicated earlier, we identified a relationship between providers' sourcing strategy and their sourcing competences. Referring to the sourcing capability *leadership*, we found that the provider's executive management, which forms a part of the Performance Prism facet *stakeholders*, can be considered as an initiator in the development of a sourcing strategy. The construct providers' sourcing strategy relates to the construct sourcing competences. The latter refer to the Prism facet capabilities. Since both constructs are interlinked, this provides evidence for the multivariate aspect of the Performance Prism.

Sourcing competences

As mentioned earlier, client developments are related to the provider's sourcing competences. Taking the sourcing competences as a starting point, we identified the relationships with relevant concepts. Table 7.3 shows the source concepts, the target concepts and their relationships.

Analysis

Interestingly, our results provide clear support for a new concept – the topic of adaptability. Interviews with provider's respondents show that monitoring client developments usually forms the starting point to adapt to changing client circumstances. Doing so, providers chart and categorize various

Table 7.3 Sourcing competences

Source concept	Type of relationship	Target concept
Provider sourcing strategy	Has strong impact on	Sourcing competences
Provider sourcing strategy	Has impact on	Adaptability
Adaptability	Is cause of	Achieving adaptability
Adaptability	Has impact on	Sourcing competences
Sourcing competences	Has impact on	SC influence on performance
Sourcing competences	Has strong impact on	Relationship competence
Sourcing competences	Has strong impact on	Delivery competence
Sourcing competences	Has strong impact on	Transformation competence
Relationship competence	Has impact on	SC influence on performance
Relationship competence	Has impact on	Business market knowledge
Transformation competence	Has impact on	SC influence on performance
Delivery competence	Has impact on	SC influence on performance

types of client developments. Subsequently, providers assess the impact of these client developments on their sourcing competences.

> *In recent years, our sourcing capabilities are adapted regularly as they were affected due to client developments. The process for this adaptation is initiated by our dedicated client team. (Source: a service delivery manager)*

Based on an analysis of the interviews we found that the concept of adaptability has an impact on changing client circumstances, provider's technology capabilities and their organizational structure. This is consistent with the findings of previous research (Charkravarthy, 1992). Interviews showed that the offshore provider designed and implemented procedures to guide the adaptability process. The authors did not expect to find these procedures as previous research encountered severe problems with regard to the provider's ability to adapt (Kern and Willcocks, 2001). One possible explanation could be that since the conducting of this research in 2001 the market has become much more mature and providers have invested in the development of their capabilities. Furthermore, interview analysis confirms that applying a proactive adaptability strategy has a positive impact on the development of customer intimacy. Analysis of the list of client episodes and the response of the service providers show clearly that managing change in IT outsourcing relationships encompasses adaptation both throughout the period of the arrangement and of the context in which change is required. The latter shows that capabilities are often context specific, as mentioned earlier in Chapter 2.

On the one hand, when referred to the RBV, capabilities are required to respond to environmental changes (Gosain et al., 2005; Tan and Sia, 2006). On the other hand, the RBV does not specifically address the determinant of adaptability, although aspects that contribute to adaptability are present. The case studies provide sufficient evidence that the providers developed both the processes and content of their capabilities over time which has implications in the area of path dependency. Specifically, we found that the global provider paid attention to strengthening the behaviour of their employees so that they are more aware of client need. The behaviour dimension refers to the RBV aspect of social complexity. However, we argue that the RBV in part lacks a motivation in respect of how capabilities can be adapted as a result of external circumstances. Our study contributes to the RBV by strengthening the empirical base research and, in particular, how resources and capabilities evolve over time (Porter, 1991; Lieberman and Montgomery, 1998).

Our findings with regard to the importance of sourcing capabilities add strength to the core competency approach to outsourcing. The case study findings reveal that providers who developed their sourcing capabilities regularly increased the value of their capabilities while simultaneously making them harder to imitate. Furthermore, the interviews demonstrated that the relationship competence as a whole has an impact on the business market knowledge of the provider, which, as a concept, is a new aspect. In particular, the case study of the global provider identified that clients experience a lack of business market knowledge within the provider's set of sourcing competences. Reflecting our findings to the Inter Organizational Relationship Theory (IOR), previous research (Kern and Willcocks, 2002) indicate that understanding the client's business is the only successful way for providers to adjust. This research underpins our finding with regard to the presence of business market knowledge.

Organizational structure

Analysing the concept organizational structure we found various variables and we identified the relationships with relevant concepts. Table 7.4 shows the relationship between the concept variables.

Analysis

In Table 7.4 we recognize the most important variables in relation to organizational structure. The analysed data all relate to the concept of organizational structure as a whole and not to the specific dimensions as mentioned earlier. The results of our research provide strong evidence that the concept

Table 7.4 Organizational structure

Source concept	**Type of relationship**	**Target concept**
Sourcing competences	Has impact on	Organizational structure
Offshoring	Has impact on	Organizational structure
Customer intimacy	Has impact on	Organizational structure
Provider sourcing strategy	Has impact on	Organizational structure
Organizational structure	Has strong impact on	Fit of sourcing capabilities and organizational structure
Organizational structure	Has impact on	OS influence on performance

offshoring has an impact on the organizational structure as applied by a provider. Based on our interviews with the providers' respondents we found that implementing an organizational structure that contains both on-site and offshore teams increases the complexity. Tasks and accompanying responsibilities of employees requires regular alignment between various teams. As assumed, the offshore provider applies the most extensive blended organizational form, deploying teams on-site, onshore and offshore. When compared with the domestic provider, the offshore provider and the global provider applies a more process-oriented approach. However, organizational structure processes are socially embedded and complex. Moreover, our study shows that the concept of organizational structure has a strong impact on the concept of fit.

Derived from the organizational structure, the offshore provider applies a client-oriented team to ensure the continuity of IT services and to sustain the long-term relationship towards the client. This finding is congruent with the provider's business strategy of focusing on customer intimacy. In particular, we found in three case studies that the client-oriented team have a decision-making responsibility. Consequently, this team is able to communicate directly with their client counterparts. The finding of the decision-making responsibility is contradictory to specific literature on services outsourcing which rely on formal, top-down, systematic decision-making (Dibbern et al., 2004; Cohen and Young, 2006). More generic literature shows that organizations that operate with a high degree of environmental uncertainty may decentralize decision-making, may rely less on formal rules and policies and may also flatten their hierarchies. Reflecting our findings in the light of Transaction Cost Economics (TCE) we found an interesting tension. Providers focus on lowering their transaction costs in order to stay competitive. However, because of their struggle during the transition phase, investments in specific assets were made that increased the transaction costs (for example, implementing a client-oriented team, offshore approach).

> *The importance of the organizational structure is significant. Just after the deal was signed, the transition period started. During that period, dimensions like decision-making and communication were not aligned properly with the client organization. When the formal delivery phase began, our organizational dimensions were rearranged which improved the performance towards our client. (Source: a programme delivery manager)*

This is consistent with the transaction cost reasoning that as there is an increase in asset specificity, more complex governance structures are required to attenuate costly bargaining over profits from specialized assets (Dyer, 1997). Since asset specificity refers to the degree of customization (Williamson, 1979) providers seek the promise from their clients before they actually make their investment. This is consistent with the findings in our case studies as the outsourcing arrangements studied are based on a long contract period. The tensions reveal itself in the fact that if the transaction costs are too high, it is more appropriate to conduct the transaction in-house (that is, the client side).

Fit

Addressing the research construct of fit, we have identified how providers are both willing and able to achieve a fit between sourcing competences and their organizational structure. Table 7.5 depicts the fit variables, together with their relationships.

Table 7.5 Fit

Source concept	Type of relationship	Target concept
Sourcing competences	Has strong impact on	Fit of sourcing capabilities and organizational structure
Organizational structure	Has strong impact on	Fit of sourcing capabilities and organizational structure
Fit initiator	Has strong impact on	Fit of sourcing capabilities and organizational structure
Fit limitations	Has impact on	Fit of sourcing capabilities and organizational structure
Sourcing competences	Has impact on	Organizational structure

Analysis

Our study provides evidence that both sourcing competences and organizational structure have a strong impact on the establishment of a fit. Analysing the process to realize a fit we determined that the governance capability, which is related to both the relationship competence and the delivery competence, can be seen as the initiator for the fit. On the one hand, the governance capability defines what type of provider sourcing capabilities needs to be adapted or strengthened. On the other hand, the governance capability affects the organizational design capability. The latter defines to what extent organizational dimensions have to be restructured, in relation to aspects such as the locus of decision-making and the level of hierarchy. Furthermore, our findings seem to indicate that the provider's client-oriented team is responsible for the initiation of an adaptation of the fit. An example of the position of a provider's client-oriented team, which specifically coordinates the demand management and supply management, is illustrated in Figure 7.1.

This team is able to interpret client developments and assess if adaptation is necessary. Based on the interviews we have built an example of roles and their locations that we recognized. This overview is show in Table 7.6.

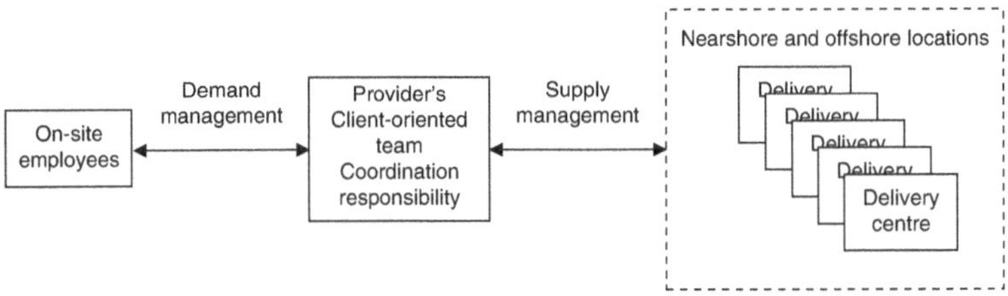

Figure 7.1 Position and role client-oriented team

Table 7.6 Example of client-oriented team roles

Client-oriented team roles	**Location**
Engagement manager	Onshore
IT architect	Onshore
Financial architect	Onshore
Compliance & security manager	Onshore
Demand manager	On-site
(IT) Business consultant	On-site
Service manager	Onshore
Delivery manager	Offshore
Subject Matter Experts	Offshore

We found that changing client developments has a significant effect on the extent to which a fit can be established. For instance, the change from a decentralized client organization towards a centralized client organization influences both the provider's sourcing capabilities and also the organizational structure.

We definitely recognize the relationship between sourcing capabilities and organizational structure. We perceive this relationship as strong, when we support a demanding customer. The more demanding customers needs are, the stronger the impact on the relationship between capabilities and their structure. (Source: an account manager)

We also found that when providers have no perception of their client's vision and sourcing strategy, there is an increased chance that the client's sourcing objectives will shift regularly. Consequently, providers will experience difficulties in the deployment of capabilities, which could in turn lead to the bringing in of other types of sourcing capabilities (for example, internally or externally). Furthermore, we found that establishing a fit requires a certain period of time. When too many changes occur in the client environment within a short period, the provider is unable to adapt quickly enough. This means that when there is increased uncertainty at the client, there will be less opportunity for providers to establish a fit. This was found, for instance, in the case of the domestic provider which at the beginning of their arrangement struggled to achieve a fit. This finding can be considered as a fit limitation. Huber (1984) argues that when the client environment is more dynamic and unstable, information acquisition needs to be more continuous, variant and wide-ranging. In this sense, analysing the interviews we found that the providers' executive management needs to be strategically oriented and able to apply an adaptive strategy. When relating the results of our study to the perspective of fit as a moderation, we find that the strength of the moderation is influenced by the extent in which capabilities and organizational structure are applied. Some of the literature (see, for example, Venkatraman, 1989) reviews this aspect.

From the perspective of the provider we also found that applying an offshore component in the client proposition will increase the complexity, which will in turn complicate the attempt to establish a fit. As the client, the provider's on-site team and the offshore delivery unit are all involved in the arrangement, they will influence both the sourcing capabilities and organizational structure, and thus the fit. Alignment between the organizational structure on-site and offshore requires continuous attention of the provider's management. Moreover, we found that aspects such as geography, language and time zone increase the complexity for achieving a fit. The application of offshoring has a considerable impact on the achievement of a fit. We relate this finding as an extension to fit as a moderation. Therefore, we argue that to establish a fit the provider needs to manage the chain of influencing factors. Aspects such as the client's need, the provider's sourcing capabilities and organizational dimensions, including offshore delivery, should be viewed and managed form a more holistic perspective. Managing the chain of influencing factors should be embedded in the provider's sourcing strategy. This approach contributes to achieving a sustainable performance over time.

Sourcing performance

As defined in the conceptual research framework we argue that sourcing competences and organizational structure have an effect on the sourcing performance. Applying the principle of concept mapping we identified relevant relationships that relate to sourcing performance. Table 7.7 shows the relationships between the source and target concepts.

Table 7.7 Sourcing performance

Source concept	**Type of relationship**	**Target concept**
Sourcing competences	Has a strong impact on	Sourcing performance
Organizational structure	Has impact on	Sourcing performance
Sourcing competences	Has a strong impact on	Fit of sourcing capabilities and organizational structure
Organizational structure	Has a strong impact on	Fit of sourcing capabilities and organizational structure
Fit of sourcing capabilities and organizational structure	Has impact on	Sourcing performance
Sourcing competences	Has a strong impact on	Sustainable performance
Organizational structure	Has impact on	Sustainable performance
Fit of sourcing capabilities and organizational structure	Has impact on	Sustainable performance
Requirements for sustainability	Has impact on	Sustainable performance
Sustainability limitations	Has impact on	Sustainable performance

Analysis

Since our research focuses on achieving a sustainable performance, we observed that this construct is influenced by various determinants. Based on our empirical research studying four provider cases, we found proof that sourcing performance needs to be assessed based on a multidimensional approach. As shown in Table 7.7, various concepts have a direct influence on providers' sourcing performance. These concepts relate to the Performance Prism facets *capabilities* (for example, sourcing capabilities), *processes* (for example, organizational structure) and *strategy* (for example, fit). Indirectly we found that the Prism facet *stakeholders* refer to providers' executive management who play an important role in developing a sourcing strategy. This was explained at the start of this chapter. Our findings underpin the existence of interlinked relationships between various constructs that reflects multiple dimensions.

When compared, the relationship between sourcing competences and sustainable performance is stronger than the relationship between organizational structure and sustainable performance. Interviewees consider sustainability to be a particularization of sourcing performance. For example, a temporary lack of fit might result in a decrease in sustainability whereas the level of sourcing performance is still acceptable. The analysis of the interview reports would tend to support this possibility. One explanation for this finding might be the weight of individual sourcing capabilities. When providers bring their sourcing capabilities into action, clients experience their real knowledge and experience. In this way the providers' sourcing capabilities have a strong influence on their performance.

Our findings provide evidence that the design of the applied organizational structure at the three providers under study varies in their ability to facilitate the exchange of IT services. As a result, different performance results were identified. We observed attributes such as the locus of decision-making, and the level of hierarchy in the organization that influences the sourcing performance in particular. As a result, decision-making is perceived as slow while multiple stakeholders are involved in the creation of additional costs. This clearly supports the transaction cost theory, which argues that the need for coordination and the likelihood of behaviour may be affected by the level of the market (that is, client organization) or complexity in the exchange process (Leiblein, 2003). From the perspective of the TCE, we indicate a tension between transaction-specific investments (for example, client-oriented team) and firm-like structures. When environmental uncertainty increases, the coordination cost will also increase, reducing the attractiveness to provide IT services. On the other hand, we observed that the providers' intention to provide a client specific organizational structure contributes to a more sustainable performance. This tension could be observed with all three providers. To reduce the total cost, providers consciously apply an offshore strategy – as wages are lower in developing countries – while retaining their sustainable performance.

Analysing our results along the lines of the RBV, various aspects were recognized. We found evidence that when sourcing capabilities were adapted and strengthened over time, the sourcing performance increased while the level of performance became sustainable. The findings indicate a positive relationship between path dependency and firm performance. This is consistent with previous research (King and Zeithaml, 2001). Interestingly, we found that the governance capability and the organizational design capability depend strongly on knowledge. As this type of knowledge is causally ambiguous it is very difficult, if not impossible to transfer knowledge within the firm. This might explain why all providers struggled to implement an effective organizational structure during the start of their arrangement and meet the performance as agreed. In addition, case study analyses indicate that capability robustness and repeatability are perceived by the interviewees as conditional for performance sustainability. This contributes to the value of resources and capabilities in which they become inelastic in supply. The RBV asserts that firms that follow this line of reasoning gain and sustain a competitive advantage.

Overall analysis

Studying the outcome of our qualitative analysis we found the core concepts as addressed in our theory as well as additional concepts. A partial explanation can be found from a consideration of the data gathered in the course of the interviews we conducted. Due to the distinction between the three case studies additional concepts and relationships were found. Moreover, the additional concepts can be explained in part by a lack in the literature, as these aspects have not been researched before. This has also been observed by certain studies (see, for example, Currie and Seltsikas, 2001; Gonzalez et al., 2006), underlining the point that the provider's side is underresearched. The research model, as shown in Figure 7.2, provides insights into relevant concepts and their interrelationships in developing a fit between sourcing capabilities and organizational structure. The constructs in *italic* as depicted in Figure 7.2 are considered to be additional concepts. Based on our qualitative analysis the core concepts as addressed in our theory are validated and even extended.

The findings from our research have important theoretical implications. Both the RBV and TCE approaches affect the constructs as mentioned earlier.

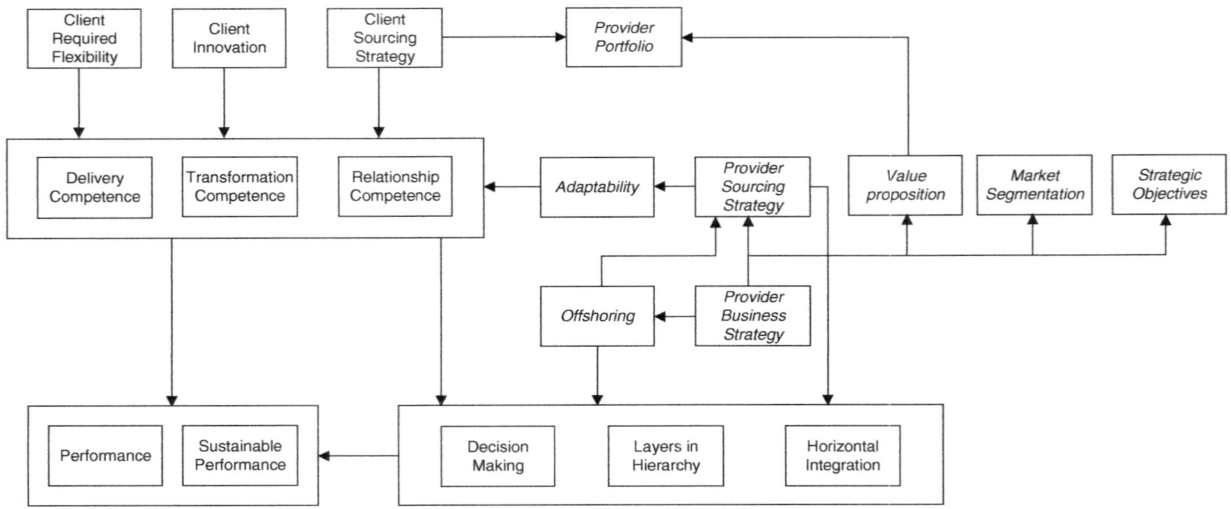

Figure 7.2 Adjusted research model

RBV variables address three important aspects that were identified in all four case studies: path dependency; causal ambiguity; and social complexity. First, all providers in the study experienced that they need to make a conscious effort to develop their sourcing capabilities over time to meet client's business needs. As an example, since the domestic provider was less experienced in providing outsourcing services they struggled with the development of their sourcing capabilities. This relates to the area of path dependency. So indeed history does matter. Although sourcing capabilities are developed over time, the importance of these capabilities in future may be influenced by internal or external effects. For instance, changes in the client's business environment that lead to provider adaptation may render the capabilities less valuable in future (Barney, 1995). This refers to the concept of dysfunctional resources. Resources that have created value in the past can become dysfunctional – that is to say, they prevent change and lead to a lack of adaptability capability instead. This has to be taken into account as an important consideration. Secondly, we found that it is not always clear to a provider how to develop capabilities to establish a fit with reference to causal ambiguity. Analyses of all three cases identifies that the influence of senior management is related to the willingness and ability to adapt to changing client circumstances. The willingness to adapt refers to an intangible capability of the firm whereas the ability to adapt refers to a tangible capability. We argue that establishing a fit assumes the existence of an adaptability capability that is causally ambiguous in nature. To achieve adaptability, the RBV variables path dependency and causal ambiguity form a prerequisite in order to adapt to both internal and external circumstances.

Third, our study demonstrates that the achievement of a sustainable performance is a reflection of social complexity. This capability cannot be bought since other providers in the market are unable to understand the relationship between the resources and sourcing capabilities controlled by the company possessing the capability. When a sustainable performance is based on a well-controlled fit that displays social complexity characteristics, it will be difficult for competitors to replace such an advantage. Therefore, the existence of a sustainable sourcing performance is influenced by the ability of a provider to invest in developing sourcing capabilities and an adequate adaptation process. This is consistent with our research that demonstrates the existence of the adaptability capability.

One important TCE variable that was found is the extent of asset specificity. Asset specificity refers to the level of customization which influences the transaction cost. Our analysis shows that all three providers started their outsourcing arrangement based on an organizational structure that can be identified as highly standardized, and therefore non-specific. Referring to this situation, the level of asset specificity can be considered as low, while transactions are relatively frequent. As the transaction costs are low, the activities to coordinate the IT services towards the providers' clients can be kept in-house. This is related to Williamson's (1975) 'Market form of coordination', explained in Chapter 2. This also means that the value add of a provider is low, which decreases their attractiveness in the market. However, in order to meet increasing client business needs, the providers adapted their organizational structure for their clients and became highly customized (idiosyncratic). For instance, the offshore provider implemented an on-site client-oriented team, an onshore team (the Netherlands) and an offshore delivery team (India) as an extension of their own organization. Moreover, we identified TCE variables as uncertainly and frequency. To cope with environmental uncertainty, providers established a client-oriented team (for example, physical asset specificity) to support the day-to-day delivery of IT service and, thus, decrease risks. Subsequently, when the level of client uncertainty is high the providers need to adapt their organizational structure on a regular basis. This will result in a high level of asset specificity that also increases knowledge transfer within the company (for instance, human specificity). When both of the transaction-type classifications – frequency of occurrence and asset specificity – are high, the coordination costs will increase significantly. This occasion refers to a 'Hierarchical form of coordination' (Williamson, 1975).

Based on our research we argue that providers require an organizational structure that is based on a certain degree of customization. Depending on the extent of client circumstances, the level of customization can be mixed or idiosyncratic. One example of a mixed form concerns providers who customize their client contact by means of a client-oriented team but who provide standardized IT services. This was the case in respect of the domestic provider in our research. An example of an idiosyncratic form is a provider who customizes both the client contact, through the creation of a client-oriented team, and the provisioning of value-adding IT services. This is reflected in our research by the cases of the offshore provider and the global provider.

As discussed in Chapter 2, the RBV and TCE apply different starting points, representing an inside-out perspective and an outside perspective accordingly. However, despite their differences the theories yielded complementary results. The findings have shown that both RBV and TCE are required to understand and explain the complexities of establishing a fit and achieve a sustainable sourcing performance. RBV and TCE variables were present in the cases studied and produced similar results. The RBV is an effective theory for understanding the relationship between capabilities and performance and providing a theoretical view for resource allocation decisions in a provider organization (McIvor, 2009). Moreover, the RBV can be applied to explain why and how sourcing capabilities need to be adapted as a result of client developments. Furthermore, applying a TCE perspective, we have highlighted the importance to the field of business improvement and organizational process re-design. The TCE is helpful in creating more insight into the tension between the uncertainty surrounding transactions and their accompanying coordination cost. After all, the higher the uncertainty, the higher the coordination cost. This is therefore related to the providers' organizational structure and organizational dimensions. However, in some instances the RBV and TCE theories can be contradictory. When providers invest in developing their sourcing capabilities and redesigning their organizational structure, asset specificity increases, which contributes to the added value of the organization. Contradictory, the transaction cost will increase that result in higher *ex post* costs. Consequently, the position of a provider will be less attractive when compared to competitors or even to a client whose rationale was to outsource its IT function in order to achieve cost reductions. Thus, our providers under study have to find a balance between the extent of asset specificity and their market attractiveness.

Conclusion

In this chapter, we applied a qualitative research analysis to the three providers in our study. We analysed how providers cope with changing client circumstances and the way they influenced provider's capabilities and organizational structure. In particular, we investigated if providers were able to achieve a sustainable performance despite environmental uncertainties. The case studies revealed additional concepts which resulted in an increased complexity of the relationships between the core concepts. This complexity may arise from the various factors that we found which all influence both sourcing capabilities and also the way they are organized. Specific concepts that were found concern the offshore strategy and adaptability capacity of a provider and their attention to strengthening their value proposition to clients. Moreover, a lack of scientific research on the provider side could explain why some constructs were not described in literature since they were not identified during previous research.

When analysing the case studies, we determined that the required sourcing capabilities and the way in which they are organized are related to the sourcing strategy of a provider. The case studies showed that all providers at the start of their arrangements applied an 'one-size-fits-all' approach. The provisioning of IT services for the client was standardized while neglecting specific client circumstances. As a result of client demands, sourcing capabilities and their organizational structure were later adapted to suit the required client situation. We did not expect to find a standard approach as some providers have long-standing experience in the field of providing IT outsourcing services. However, during the adaptability process a more customized approach was used to meet client's needs.

In particular, we found that the application of an offshore strategy increased the complexity, making it more difficult to establish a sound organizational structure. Alignment of both on-site and offshore teams required mutual and frequent communication while the decision-making responsibility needed to be determined and managed adequately (Rottman and Lacity, 2009). Moreover, our research demonstrated that the governance capability and the organizational design capability were identified as initiators in the establishment of a fit between sourcing capabilities and organizational structure. We argue that both sourcing capabilities need to be superior when compared with the other sourcing capabilities as they have a considerable influence on the presence of a fit. This shows that both sourcing capabilities and organizational structure are intertwined and affect the extent to which a fit can be established. We argue that the lower the value a provider places on its strategic resources, the more it ignores specific attention in establishing a fit. Maintaining resources with a low strategic value leads to an ineffective fit. On the other hand, the higher the value a provider places on their strategic resources, the more the firm is justified in establishing a fit internally. Therefore, we conclude that the provider's sourcing strategy forms the primary driver for existence of a fit.

To conclude, our case studies provided sufficient evidence that a fit between sourcing capabilities and organizational structure contributes to a positive sourcing performance. Our research revealed that those providers that are able to adapt to changing client circumstances, while simultaneously establishing a fit, are successful in achieving sustainable performance. Consequently, achieving a sustainable performance requires the consistent attention of providers' executive management as developing a sourcing strategy is a strategic choice.

8
Quantitative Results

The focus in outsourcing partnerships should be extended by introducing innovation in addition to flexibility and cost effectiveness.

(Erik Beulen)

This chapter describes the quantitative research that we conducted to test the relationships between the constructs outlined in Chapter 2.

This research consists of three steps. First, as no existing scales are available for the constructs in our research we developed new scales based on an Exploratory Factor Analysis (EFA). We used the scales representing the core constructs in analyses of variance (ANOVA) to illustrate differences between the different providers. Secondly, we conducted a Confirmatory Factor Analysis (CFA) to define the validity and reliability of the measures. Third, at the start of our main study we test the hypotheses that relate to the main constructs and their causal relationships. The main study consists of a Confirmatory Factor Analysis (CFA) to establish a measurement model. Subsequently, the structural model will be tested by applying LISREL to the responses.

The results of this quantitative research are based on three providers, namely: the domestic provider, the offshore provider, and the global provider. The outcomes of our Confirmatory Factor Analyses and the empirical testing of the hypothesized model are described subsequently. As a consequence, the results are discussed and finally the conclusions and limitations are described.

Method

Sample and data collection

Data were collected between June and September 2008 by means of an online questionnaire. This questionnaire was circulated among three providers via the Internet by means of Surveyworld, an online web-questionnaire tool. The survey was set up in two languages, Dutch and English, involving participants working with a domestic provider, an offshore provider and a global provider. The participants of the domestic provider and the global provider received a survey in Dutch, while an offshore provider received one in English. The survey consists of 11 parts divided into four main sections and it was accompanied by a short covering letter which explained the purposes of the study. The first section addressed the extent to which the respondents perceive changing client circumstances. The second section investigated how changing client circumstances affect the sourcing capabilities of the service provider. The third section studied how the capabilities are organized while the fourth section addressed the sourcing performance.

The questionnaire was refined during a pre-test and completed by ten respondents that represent both scientists and sourcing professionals. While a vast majority of the questions remained identical, minor modifications were made to the questionnaire to fit the particular departments, terminology and practices. These changes did not affect the basic intentions of the scales used, neither the reliability nor the validity of the construct. Moreover, considering the need for clarity, and preventing the terminology from being interpreted differently, a glossary of definitions was included. The questions were rated on 7-point Likert scales, or, when the questions were about the importance of specific issues, on a 5-point scale ranging from not important at all, to extremely important.

To make sure that only provider participants with relevant knowledge and experience would complete the questionnaire two profiles were sketched. Only participants that matched the profile were asked to complete the survey. The following profiles were set up:

- Management at executive level and middle management level that are actively involved in outsourcing arrangements – either, nationally and/or internationally.
- Provider employees that are involved in outsourcing arrangements from an organizational, technical or financial perspective.

A total of 248 invitations were distributed. The final sample contained 135 respondents from four different countries, resulting in a response rate of 54 per cent. At the domestic providers, a total of 87 invitations were sent out and 49 respondents completed their survey, resulting in a response rate of

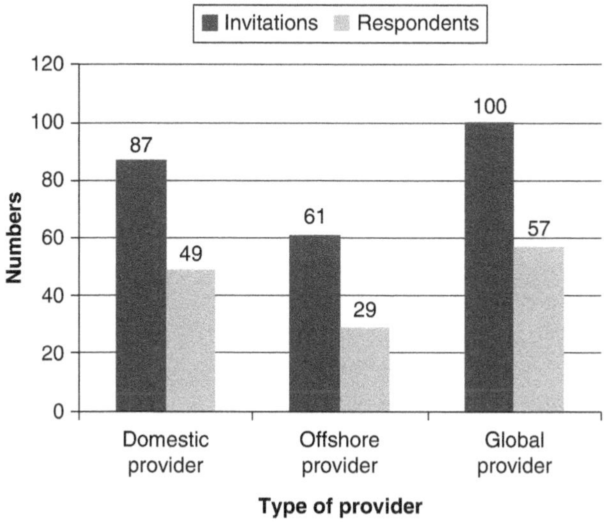

Figure 8.1 Overview providers and response rate

56 per cent. At the offshore provider, 61 invitations were sent out and 29 responses were received, resulting in a 47 per cent response rate. Finally, 100 invitations were sent to participants of the global provider from which 57 respondents submitted a complete questionnaire. This resulted in a response rate of 57 per cent. Figure 8.1 depicts an overview of the providers involved compared to the invitations and response rate. Countries included in the sample are the Netherlands (114 participants), the United Kingdom (10), Ireland (3 participants), and India (8 participants).

An analysis of the non-responsiveness provides two explanations. One group of participants responded that they are associated with another target group as determined in our survey. Another group of participants, which refused to fill out the survey, indicated that they are not primarily involved in outsourcing arrangements. The latter group referred to back-office functions such as internal services and HR processes.

Testing differences between subsamples

In order to control for bias between the three providers, we used analyses of variance to establish if bias towards one of the organization occurred for the used constructs (Plugge and Bouwman, 2009). The ANOVA analysis is making use of the structural model scores on the scales. We choose a post hoc test, making use of the Gabriel procedure as well as Games/Howell

Table 8.1 ANOVA of constructs across providers

Construct	Provider	N	Mean	SD	F	Sig.
Client developments	Global provider	53	−0.14	0.95	2.778	0.066
	Offshore provider	25	0.41	0.62		
	Domestic provider	46	−0.05	1.16		
Sourcing capabilities	Global provider	53	−0.42	0.87	26.09	0
	Offshore provider	25	1.04	0.7		
	Domestic provider	46	−0.078	0.87		
Organizational structure: Decision-making	Global provider	53	0.077	0.94	7.083	0.001
	Offshore provider	25	0.5	0.84		
	Domestic provider	46	−0.36	1.01		
Organizational structure: Level of hierarchy	Global provider	53	−0.1	0.89	0.657	0.52
	Offshore provider	25	−0.021	1.22		
	Domestic provider	46	0.12	0.99		
Influenced performance	Global provider	53	−0.16	0.95	1.432	0.243
	Offshore provider	25	0.02	0.93		
	Domestic provider	46	0.17	1.07		
Performance	Global provider	53	0.35	1.06	9.635	0
	Offshore provider	25	0.09	0.74		
	Domestic provider	46	−0.46	0.87		

options (Field, 2005), as the sample sizes for the three cases are different. The data in Table 8.1 show that there are differences with regard to the concepts sensitivity to change, and adaptability. There are no significant differences with regard to the clients' developments. Sourcing capabilities also show significant differences between the three companies. With regard to organizational structure concepts we see differences in decision-making and horizontal integration, but not with regard to levels of hierarchy. We also see differences with regard to performance.

Scales

To our knowledge, there are no existing standardized and validated scales available for the constructs that we use in our research approach. Therefore, we executed an Exploratory Factor Analysis, using SPSS 16.0. Due to the small number of respondents we checked the Kaiser–Meyer–Ohlin (KMO) measure of sampling adequacy as well as Bartlett's test of Sphericity. KMO was .91 and the analysis met the Bartlett criteria. We used principal component analysis with varimax rotation and Kaiser Normalization. All of the scales reach a reliability level of >.80, with the exception of the last scale related to Influenced Performance. As a two-item scale is used, the reliability reaches an acceptable level of .71. Based on the factor analysis we found relevant constructs that can be related to the research model. We also found constructs that are related to the decision-making style within the service provider, and the perception of the organizational structure (perceived levels of hierarchy), and finally, the sustainability of the sourcing performance, as well as the perceived influenced performance.

Measure development

Most researchers agree that common method variance is a potentially seriously biasing threat in behavioural research. We use several procedures to empirically examine the possibility that common method bias threatens the interpretation of our results: (1) the Harman one-factor test; (2) a confirmatory factor-analytic approach to Harman's one-factor test; and (3) the single method factor approach.

The rationale for the first test is that if common method bias poses a serious threat to the analysis and interpretation of the data, a single latent factor would account for all manifest variables or one general factor will account for the majority of the covariance among the measurements. In our case, the one-factor model obtained using principal components analysis revealed several factors in the unrotated factor solution. However, as suggested by Podsakoff et al. (2003), this is considered a weak test. More recently, some researchers using this technique have used Confirmatory Factor Analysis (CFA) as a more sophisticated test. A worse fit for the one-factor model would suggest that common method variance does not pose a serious threat. The fit was considerably worse for the unidimensional model than for the measurement model, suggesting that common method bias is not a serious threat in this study.

Despite its apparent appeal, there are several limitations with the previous procedure. Therefore, additional statistical remedies are recommended for this purpose. One of these approaches is the use of latent variable models (Podsakoff et al., 2003). This method involves adding a first-order factor with all of the measures as indicators to the researcher's theoretical model. The fit was considerably worse for the single method factor approach than for the measurement model, suggesting that common method bias is not a serious concern in the study. Overall, we can conclude that common method bias does not threaten the interpretation of our results.

Measurement model

To refine our measures, we conducted a Confirmatory Factor Analysis (CFA) using LISREL 8.8 to determine the validity and reliability of our measures. As observed from Table 8.2, the results of the ten-factor model provided an

Table 8.2 Measurement model

Construct code	Items and Questions	Description	SCR	AVE	Standardized λ
C 1	Item	Sensitivity to change	.88	.71	
	Q 2.1	Provider monitor changes in client circumstances			.90
	Q 2.3	Changing client circumstances are discussed with clients			.75
	Q 2.4	Assessment of changing client circumstances on IT service provisioning			.87
C 2	Item	Adaptability	.80	.58	
	Q 2.6	Provider encourage internal cooperation between working groups in different countries			.67
	Q 2.8	Provider encourages employees to take a proactive attitude			.69
	Q 2.12	Management stimulates employees to deal with customer requirements			.90
C 3	Item	Client developments on capabilities	.78	.54	
	Q 5.1	Sourcing strategy			.59
	Q 5.2	Innovation			.73
	Q 5.3	Required flexibility			.86
C 4	Item	Sourcing capabilities	.86	.67	
	Q 4.2	Continuous improvement			.74
	Q 4.4	Adaptability to changing clients needs			.79
	Q 4.6	Capability improvement by training			.61
C 5	Item	Decision-making	.80	.67	
	Q 7.1	Management is experienced in organizational change			.91
	Q 8.5	Activities are carried out by cross-functional teams			.64
C 6	Item	Level of hierarchy	.83	.62	
	Q 8.1	Provider is a lean organization			.84
	Q 8.2	Communication between different levels in hierarchy within our company is easy			.71

	Q 8.7	Hierarchical layers in the provider organization			.78
C 7	Item	Horizontal integration	.76	.70	
	Q 7.2	Provider facilitates employees with training to work in cross-functional teams			.70
	Q 8.9	Management has expertise to lead various cross-functional teams			.73
C 8	Item	Client developments on organizational structure	.83	.62	
	Q 9.1	Sourcing strategy			.78
	Q 9.2	Innovation			.79
	Q 9.3	Required flexibility			.81
C 9	Item	Performance monitoring	.85	.67	
	Q 11.1	Performance of IT services is monitored			.89
	Q 11.2	Performance of IT services is assessed			.93
	Q 11.6	Performance of the delivered IT services is durable over time			.55
C 10	Item	Client developments on performance	.82	.61	
	Q 12.1	Sourcing strategy			.74
	Q 12.2	Innovation			.76
	Q 12.3	Required flexibility			.84

X2 (305) = 443.22, CFI = .97, RMSEA = .05, RMSEA Range = (.04 to .06)
SCR = Scale Compose Reliability
AVE = Average Variance Extracted

acceptable fit ($\chi2(305) = 443.22$ CFI = .97 RMSEA = .05 RMSEA RANGE = (0.04 to 0.06). The factor loadings of each individual indicator on its respective construct were statistically significant ($p < .001$) establishing convergent validity. With regard to *'Service providers focus on client developments'* we used three separate scales. The items are identical; however, the framing of the three-item scales was different for the three separate scales. For the three scales the framing of the three-item scales was focused respectively on the effect of service providers focus on client developments directly on capabilities (items 5.1–5.3), on structure (items 9.1–9.3) and on performance (items 12.1–12.3).

Since our research contains several multi-item reflective scales, we investigated the psychometric properties of these measures through the composite reliability index (Bagozzi and Yi, 1988) and average variance extracted (Fornell and Larcker, 1981). Both indexes exceeded the recommended benchmarks of .60 and .50 respectively. Evidence of discriminant validity among the dimensions was provided by two different procedures recommended in the literature as follows. First, the 95% confidence interval constructed around the correlation estimate between two latent variables never includes value 1 (Anderson and Gerbing, 1988). Second, the comparison of the square root of the AVE, as shown on the diagonal in Table 8.3, with the correlations among constructs (that is, off-diagonal elements) reveals that the square root of the AVE for each component is greater than the correlation between components, in support of discriminant validity (Fornell and Larcker, 1981). Overall, these results provide adequate evidence of convergent and discriminant validity as well as reliability.

Results

The structural model

Having satisfied the requirements arising from measurement issues, we tested the structural model in Figure 8.2. The fit indices for the overall model were as follows: chi-square value (df = 339) = 598.88; comparative fit index (CFI) = .94, non-normed fit index (NNFI) = .94; standardized root mean square error of approximation (RMSEA) = .08. These values collectively indicate that the structural model has an acceptable fit. Most hypothesized effects are significant. The coefficient on the paths from construct *'Sensitivity to change'* and construct *'Adaptability'* to construct *'Sourcing capabilities'* is .55 ($t = 7.49$, $p < .01$) and .77 ($t = 6.97$, $p < .01$) respectively confirming hypothesis 1a and hypothesis 1b. Unfortunately, the path from construct *'Client developments'* to construct *'Sourcing capabilities'* was not significant

Table 8.3 Correlation matrix with AVE

Constructs		Mean	SD	C 1	C 2	C 3	C 4	C 5	C 6	C 7	C 8	C 9	C 10
C 1	Sensitivity to change	4.59	1.22	.84									
C 2	Adaptability	4.65	1.24	.64	.76								
C 3	Client developments	3.61	0.8	.29	.32	.73							
C 4	Sourcing capabilities	4.67	1.21	.72	.70	.33	.82						
C 5	Decision-making	4.31	1.35	.55	.72	.25	.58	.82					
C 6	Level of hierarchy	4.2	1.42	.30	.41	.13	.37	.34	.80				
C 7	Horizontal integration	4.1	1.36	.62	.75	.31	.70	.68	.33	.84			
C 8	Client developments	3.1	0.89	.40	.34	.47	.44	.30	.15	.36	.79		
C 9	Performance monitoring	5.09	1.14	.57	.55	.29	.55	.54	.35	.55	.27	.82	
C 10	Client developments	3.46	0.81	.15	.14	.44	.21	.08	.06	.12	.50	.27	.78

AVE = Average Variance Extracted. The numbers on the diagonal are the square root of the AVE. Off-diagonal elements are correlations among constructs.

.03 ($t = .03, p > .10$), and thus hypothesis 1c is not confirmed. The R^2 measure of construct *'Sourcing capabilities'* (.80), can be indicated as robust. Similarly, the paths from construct *'Sourcing capabilities'* to construct *'Decision-making'*, construct *'Level of hierarchy'* and construct *'Horizontal integration'* are .78 ($t = 8.19, p < .01$), .37 ($t = 3.66, p < .01$) and .77 ($t = 7.63, p < .01$) respectively. Thus, these positive relationships suggest that hypotheses 2a, 2b and 2c are supported.

Only one of the three hypothesized antecedents of construct *'Performance'* is significant. Thus, hypothesis 3c that relates construct *'Horizontal integration'* with construct *'Performance'* is significant .44 ($t = 2.66, p < .01$). The R^2 measure of construct *'Performance'* (.40) can be indicated as solid. However, the path coefficients from construct *'Decision-making'* and construct *'Level of hierarchy'* to construct *'Performance'* are .08 ($t = 0.53, p > .10$) and .12 ($t = 1.30, p > .10$), respectively, failing to support these relationships, which mean that hypotheses 3a and 3b are not supported. Furthermore, the path from construct *'Client developments'* to the set of constructs *'Decision-making'*, construct *'Level of hierarchy'* and construct *'Horizontal integration'* is indicated as insignificant.15 ($t = 1.31, p > .10$), which lead us to reject hypothesis 2d. These is a decrease in the R^2 values in general as one shift from left to right in our structural model. This is because the constructs *'Decision-making'*, construct *'Level of hierarchy'* and construct *'Horizontal integration'* are all factors that refer to organizational dimensions, which is the moderating variable in our structural model. As the relationship between construct *'Decision-making'*, construct *'Level of hierarchy'*, construct *'Client developments'* and construct *'Performance'* are not significant, this result might affect the R^2 value construct *'Performance'*. Finally, the path from construct *'Client developments'* to construct *'Performance'* is significant .26 ($t = 3.07, p < .01$) which supports hypothesis 3d.

The structural model explains 80 per cent of the variance in construct *'Sourcing capabilities'*. The structural model also explains 40 per cent of the variance in the final dependent variable, construct *'Performance'*. The results of the structural model, as illustrated in Figure 8.2, indicate that construct *'Sourcing capabilities'* fully mediate the relationship between the antecedents and consequences of construct *'Sourcing capabilities'*. In addition, the construct *'Horizontal integration'* help us to explain the indirect effect of construct *'Sourcing capabilities'* on construct *'Performance'*. This study meets the generally accepted tests of statistical rigour, while at the same time providing a parsimonious model.

In order to provide greater confidence in our model specification, we test our theoretical model (MT) against an alternative model specification (MA).

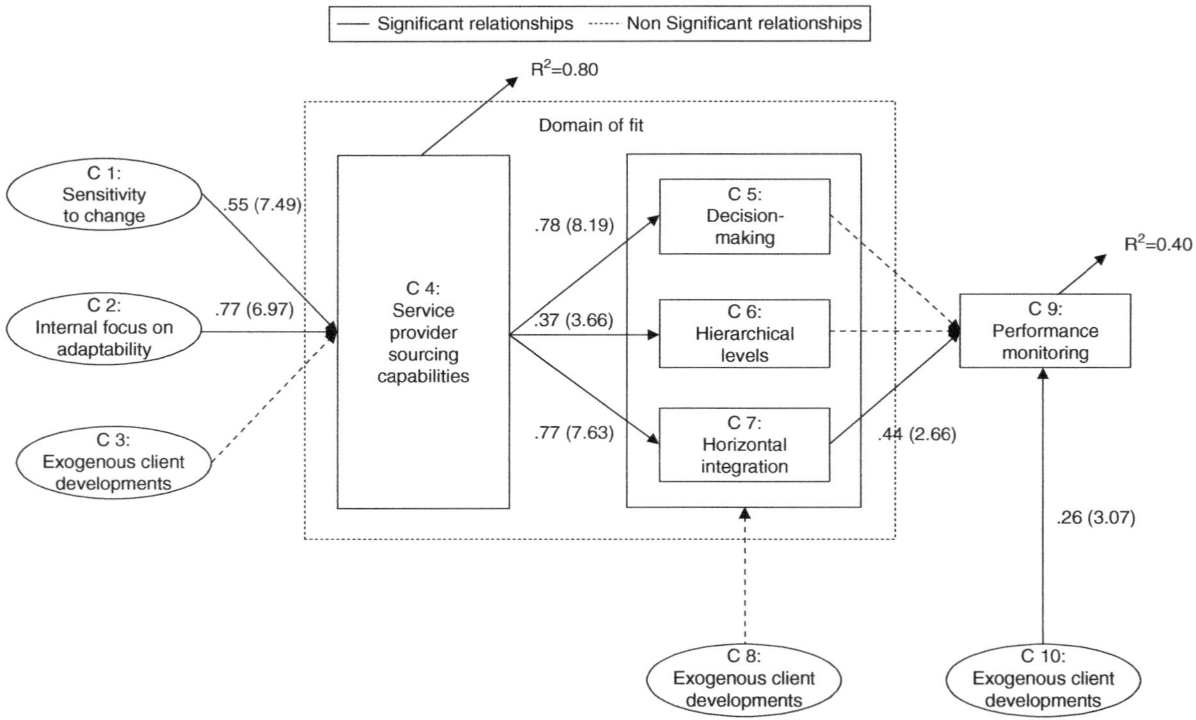

Figure 8.2 Main effect results

This procedure, suggested by Anderson and Gerbing (1988), was carried out considering the relationship between capabilities and performance as well as the direct path to performance from sensitivity to change, adaptability and client developments. However, the results suggest that these alternative paths do not improve the overall adjustment of the theoretical model significantly. Therefore, our results confirm the mediating role of capabilities and also the indirect effects discussed previously.

Discussion

The results of our study offer partial support for the research model. Based on the results and analyses of the providers under study, the findings of this study demonstrate that sourcing capabilities and organizational dimensions are perceived to be critical factors in achieving a sustainable performance. This finding is consistent with the existing literature (King and Zeithaml, 2001). The relationship between decision-making, level of hierarchy and performance were found to be non-significant. Moreover, the relationship of client developments to both capabilities and organizational structural dimensions is also non-significant. A summary of the findings is depicted in Table 8.4.

From an analysis of variance we saw that there is a fair degree of communality between the global and the domestic provider. Only the score of the offshore provider is clearly higher than the scores of the domestic provider and the global provider. A possible explanation is that the offshore provider is more able and willing to adapt their capabilities regularly and achieve continuous improvement. The offshore provider employees who participated in the survey underpinned these findings. In general, the offshore provider consciously applies processes and procedures. Therefore, it can be argued that the role of the provider's executive management plays an important role in adapting and strengthening sourcing capabilities. Another possible explanation could be that the provider's executive management stimulates employees to work in cross-functional teams to speed up decision-making. Executive management that encourages the cooperation between work teams has a positive influence on decision-making. This could be an explanation for why the performance of the offshore provider differs significantly when compared to the other providers.

Based on the quantitative results we argue that there is a direct, significant causal relationship between *'Sensitivity to change'* and *'Sourcing capabilities'* (H1a). This path is strong and statistically significant. The results demonstrate that the provider's attention to monitor and assess *'Sensitivity to change'* is important for obtaining insights into clients' business needs. These insights can be used to determine if specific sourcing capabilities need to be

Table 8.4 Summary of the results

Hypotheses	Results
H 1a: Outsourcing service provider's sensitivity to change and uncertainty a client has to deal with, will lead to adjustment in service provider sourcing capabilities.	Supported
H 1b: Outsourcing service provider's internal focus on adaptability will lead to adjustment in service provider sourcing capabilities.	Supported
H 1c: Exogenous client developments will lead to adjustment in service provider sourcing capabilities	Rejected
H 2a: Adjustment in service provider sourcing capabilities will have an effect on organizational decision-making.	Supported
H 2b: Adjustment in service provider sourcing capabilities will lead to a reduction of organizational hierarchy.	Supported
H 2c: Adjustment in service provider sourcing capabilities will lead to horizontal integration.	Supported
H 2d: Exogenous client developments will lead to adjustment in service provider organizational structure.	Rejected
H 3a: Decision-making is positively related to the monitoring of the performance of an outsourcing arrangement.	Rejected
H 3b: Level of hierarchy is positively related to the monitoring of the performance of an outsourcing arrangement.	Rejected
H 3c: Horizontal integration is positively related to the monitoring of the performance of an outsourcing arrangement.	Supported
H 3d: Client developments an outsourcing service provider has to deal with will be positively related to the monitoring of the performance of an outsourcing arrangement.	Supported

adapted. Interestingly, this finding is new when compared to the original conceptual research model that we developed. The findings are consistent with the empirical results of the three case studies. Moreover, discussing *'Sensitivity to change'* is a prerequisite for providers to initiate the adaptability process. Studying the *'Adaptability'* construct, we find strong evidence that providers are both willing and able to adapt their sourcing capabilities as a result of changing client circumstances. The results indicate that the path from *'Adaptability'* to *'Sourcing capabilities'* (H1b) is quite robust. Providers can create adaptability by developing their sourcing capabilities, specifically by managing relationships and developing procedures for dealing with change. The results indicate that executive management stimulates employees to cater for clients' requirements. By consciously applying an adaptability process, providers are more capable of handling environmental uncertainty.

This appeals to the organic paradigm as argued by Zammuto and O'Conner (1992) and Daft (1995). Our findings reveal that attention must be paid by the provider's executive management to encourage employees to take a proactive attitude. This refers to the aspect of behaviour. This finding demonstrates that 'soft skills' also need to be developed and strengthened in order to increase the ability to adapt. As adaptability is conditional, we argue that executive management needs to encourage the internal cooperation between onshore and offshore employees. This refers to the aspect of organizational dimensions. When we reflect on the qualitative research, our results are consistent with the evidence that we found in the three case studies. Moreover, the finding of this construct is an extension of our conceptual research model as developed earlier. In addition, in our analysis of the results of hypotheses 1a and hypothesis 1b we find that they form a coherent whole. The providers' willingness to assess client developments and their ability to adapt is key to the development and strengthening of their capabilities. This evidence underpins our finding that the existence of sound sourcing capabilities forms a prerequisite to establish a fit with organizational structure.

The result of hypothesis 1c, which reflects the causal relationship between constructs *'Client developments'* and *'Sourcing capabilities'*, is only marginally meaningful and therefore not significant. The findings show that the participants in the survey are of the opinion that the impact of the exogenous factor client developments on the endogenous factor capabilities is less important. However, this finding contradicts the results of the case studies. The findings of the case studies demonstrate that client developments do have a direct influence on sourcing capabilities. There may be a twofold explanation for these contradictory results. First, an underlying premise of the resource-based view is that firms outsource activities in order to obtain access to external capabilities (Gurbaxani, 1996; Quinn, 1999; Poppo and Zenger, 1998). It can be argued that provider employees do not feel that client developments will affect their sourcing capabilities. Even if they do adapt their capabilities, as indicated earlier, it is doubtful that employees perceive external developments to be the cause for adaptation. Secondly, the construct *'Client developments'* does not reflect individual developments within client organizations, and, therefore, underscores more specific client developments. The qualitative research, however, did study the independent factors: the applied sourcing strategy of clients, their innovation needs and the required need for flexibility. A possible explanation for the finding of the construct *'Client developments'* can be found in the way the questionnaire was set up.

The results of our study demonstrate that the causal relationship between *'Sourcing capabilities'* and *'Decision-making'* (H2a) is clearly supported. This finding is affirmed by our qualitative analyses. In particular, decision-making refers to the leadership capability that was identified to manage the fit between capabilities and organizational dimensions. We find that decision-making is an important aspect that relates to the willingness and ability of executive management to develop an effective relationship with clients. Our findings indicate that hypothesis 2b, which reflects a causal relationship between *'Sourcing capabilities'* and the *'Level of hierarchy'*, is supported positively. This relationship is also illustrated in the client cases under study. The level of hierarchy is dependent on the size and complexity of the provider organization. All case studies revealed that offshoring will further expand the organizational structure and increase the number of levels in the hierarchy. Initiated by the governance capability client-oriented teams were established to shield clients for the number of levels in hierarchy on the provider side. At the same time, the participants that responded to the survey perceive the communication between different levels in their organization as easy. One possible explanation can be found in the country-oriented approach that was applied by all providers. Moreover, providers have to watch the number of levels to prevent the organizational structure from becoming ineffective. The results indicate the existence of a causal relationship between *'Sourcing capabilities'* and *'Horizontal integration'* (H2c). Our findings show that the providers facilitate their employees with training to work in cross-functional teams. Literature already demonstrated that providers need to decide if employees are being brought together in autonomous work teams, cross-functional teams and taskforce (Doll and Vonderembse, 1991; Davenport and Nohria, 1994). Employees in service-oriented firms are usually cross-trained. In doing so, they have a better understanding of the overall processes and they are more able to respond quickly to changing business needs. Mechanistic organizations have a low level of horizontal integration and organic organizations have a high level of horizontal integration. Moreover, executive management has expertise to lead various cross-functional teams. This can be explained from the existence of the leadership capability. This finding reveals that horizontal integration is strongly related to the capabilities of departments and employees.

Empirical results indicate that there is support for causal relationships between *'Sourcing capabilities'* and *'Decision-making'*, *'Level of hierarchy'* and *'Horizontal integration'*. This provides evidence for the existence of a fit between the main constructs. We argue that the way in which the providers' organizational dimensions are applied depends on exogenous factors.

In particular, the clients' organizational structure (for example, centralized versus decentralized) and the market in which clients operate (for example, dynamic versus static) affect the establishment of the providers' organizational dimensions. For example, when clients operate in dynamic markets, providers need to lower their level of decision-making in order to respond to environmental uncertainty. This is consistent with previous research (Prescott et al., 1986) in which the authors argue that environments moderate the strengths of relationships, but not the form of the relationship. Therefore, we argue that in provider organizations there is a tight relationship between sourcing capabilities and the way in which they are organized. The results indicate that hypothesis 2d, which refers to the causal relationship between *'Client developments'* and *'Organizational structure'*, can be considered to be not significant. The outcome of the study demonstrates that the participants in the survey are of the opinion that client need is less important in influencing organizational structure. This contradicts the results that were found in the literature and in the case studies. In the case of IT outsourcing providers, the external environment is defined by the client organization and by market dynamics (Hakansson, 1982; Lawrence and Lorsch, 1967; Bourgeois et al., 1978). When contrasted with the results of our case studies, clarification could be twofold. First, insights into how client developments influence organizational dimensions are unavailable and/or not communicated to the participants of the surveys. One possible explanation could be that provider employees who are not directly related in outsourcing arrangements have less insight or are less involved in this type of effects.

Hypothesis 3a, which refers to the causal relationship between *'Decision-making'* and *'Performance'*, is also rejected. Since decision-making encompasses various items that could influence sourcing performance, our findings indicate two important elements: complexity and internal cooperation. The literature (Levina and Su, 2008) suggests that the organizational dimension decision-making becomes more complex as the chain of decision-making responsibilities expands (for example, on-site, onshore, offshore). The survey results, however, indicate that although provider management is experienced in organizational change, their effect on sourcing performance is limited. This means that the contribution of internal decision-making to establish a sound performance may not be overestimated. Moreover, we find that provider activities are carried out by cross-functional teams. This result indicates that the providers under study pay attention to internal cooperation. As the provisioning of outsourcing services can be defined as a multidisciplinary and complex business (Willcocks and Lacity, 2009), internal cooperation is a prerequisite to the achievement of success. An insignificant relationship between decision-making and performance among managers may reveal a tension with which executive management has to deal. Hypothesis 3b regarding the relationship between the *'Level of hierarchy'* and *'Performance'* can be perceived as not significant. Since further expansion of the organization through offshoring will increase the number of levels in the hierarchy, the results imply that participants perceive their organization as lean. As a result, the influence on performance is less important. The aspect of communication between different levels in hierarchy is indicated as easy. This is consistent with previous research (Walton, 1985), which argues that organizations operating with a high degree of environmental uncertainty may flatten their hierarchies. Explanations for this finding can be found in our qualitative research where interviews revealed that the providers under study all applied a country-oriented approach. We conclude that the level of hierarchy as an influencing factor on performance is less important.

The findings of our research show that the dimension *'Horizontal integration'* has a dominant influence on *'Performance'* (H3c) as this is strongly related to the capabilities of departments and employees. First, we find that providers facilitate their employees by training to work in cross-functional teams. This approach is consistent with previous research (Davenport and Nohria, 1994; Doll and Vonderembse, 1991) that indicates that employees in post-industrial firms are being brought together in autonomous cross-functional teams. Employees are trained to work in such teams to understand the integral process of service provisioning and to respond to changing client needs. Studying the dimension decision-making we indicated that provider activities are carried out by cross-functional teams. This finding is consistent with the extent to which employees are trained to work in cross-functional teams. Secondly, we find that participants of the survey have the opinion that management is experienced to lead various cross-functional teams. Since outsourcing services depends on multiple processes, which are based on information-intensive work, cross-functional management is required to guarantee coherence. Therefore, we argue that the level of horizontal integration must be high because of the interdependencies of different service provisioning processes. The aspect of horizontal integration refers directly to the content of providing IT services to clients. Hence, clients experience the results of these IT services and relate them to the delivered sourcing performance. This might be an explanation of why the results of our study identify a significant causal relationship between horizontal integration and performance. The results indicate that the causal relationship between *'Client developments'* and *'Performance'* (H3d) is significant. This finding shows that client developments do have a direct influence on the performance of providers in outsourcing relationships – a result that is consistent with our findings in the case studies. One explanation could be found in the importance of client developments. For instance, the client's need for required flexibility, such as additional project resources, can be measured by the providers' response. As a result, clients experience the effect of the providers' willingness and ability to fulfill these needs and relate the outcome to the providers' sourcing performance.

Conclusion

In this chapter we tested the hypotheses described in Chapter 2. We may conclude, based on empirical testing, that the dynamic fit model can be validated. Our research contributes to IS/IT research as there is currently little empirical work on the issue of fit. We may conclude that provider performance can be assessed by testing the relationships between the core constructs in the research model – for example, client development, sourcing capabilities, organizational structure and sourcing performance. The degree to which performance is attributed to performance monitoring is used as a proxy for high-level sustainable performance. This study, which is exploratory in nature, has important implications for research. Our results offer partial support for the research model and constitute a first valid theoretical foundation. The model focuses on the concept of fit and it seems promising in terms of its capacity to describe and explain the impact on sourcing performance. In particular, we paid attention to the development of a multidimensional measure of sourcing performance, and tested hypotheses empirically between the predictor variable – for example, capabilities – and criterion variable – for example, sourcing performance – by means of a moderation variable, such as organizational structure. The results of our analysis also show that the constructs can be used to analyse the differences between the three types of providers – domestic, offshore, and global. The findings provide evidence that the domestic provider and the global provider may achieve a fit when focusing on sourcing capabilities and organizational structure. Both capabilities and also the way in which they are organized are well balanced. However, the analysis of the data indicates that the offshore provider score is demonstrably higher if adaptability processes and procedures are applied consciously.

9
Conclusion

> *Successful outsourcing requires strong people skills, dogged determination, persuasive communications, consistent messages and plain hard work.*
>
> (Wendell Jones)

In this book we have argued that IT outsourcing providers who manage to establish a *dynamic fit* between *sourcing capabilities* and their own *organizational structure* are less susceptible to changes in their clients' environment. Adapting to changing client circumstances enable providers to achieve a sustainable performance. First, we address the key objectives as mentioned in the introduction. Then, we discuss the answers to the key objectives. Next, we address the research contributions for science and practitioners while recommendations for further research are described.

Key objectives

Remarkably, the provider's side of IT outsourcing arrangements is still under-researched whereas the importance of client–provider relationships has increased significantly over the past decade. Previous research has identified a recurring problem on the provider's side – namely, a lack of sustainability in service performance, for example, the continuous delivery over time of high-quality services. A lack of provider performance will result in failures on the client side. The quality of service delivery is decreasing while the costs to abrogate the lack of provider performance will increase. Furthermore, the lack of provider performance could also have a negative business impact on the client as the time-to-market of products and services increases. As a result, the client's satisfaction with the provider's performance decreases, which can lead to various disputes. On the other hand, market developments change over time, which will have an impact on client organizations. Hence, providers involved in IT outsourcing arrangements also have to be aware that this will impact on the provisioning of IT services. Therefore, clients need to hold regular discussions about their market developments and business needs with their providers in order to align outsourcing activities.

As stated in the introduction, various key objectives were mentioned that will be discussed. The objectives are highlighted below.

1 Monitor and assess changing client circumstances in IT outsourcing arrangements.
2 Assess the impact of key client developments on service providers' sourcing capabilities.
3 Assess the impact of key client developments on service providers' organizational structures.
4 Identify what aspects influences the performance of service providers towards their clients.
5 Develop a dynamic fit approach that provides insight in the interplay between client developments, sourcing capabilities and organizational structural dimensions, as well as create a deeper understanding of their effect on the provider's performance.

Answers to the key objectives

Monitor and assess changing client circumstances

Our first key objective was to monitor and assess how service providers deal with changing client circumstances in IT outsourcing arrangements. As mentioned, changes in the environment of the client will affect the provider's organization, and therefore these changes are also relevant for the provider's behaviour (Plugge et al., 2008). In response to our first objective, we conducted a preliminary exploratory research, investigating relevant client developments that occurred during IT outsourcing arrangements. As described in Chapter 3, this preliminary research is based on the Inter Organizational Relationship (IOR) theory applying Hakansson's 'Interaction Approach' for a more comprehensive and holistic view of the client environment. Three categories were studied, including environmental developments, atmosphere developments and developments that arise in the exchange of IT services. We have identified seven developments that, from a client perspective, have a significant impact on provider capabilities: globalization, market dynamics, legislation, sourcing strategy, innovation, architecture and required flexibility. Subsequently, we have decided to focus on client-related developments that are based on organizational aspects. As a result, we have identified *sourcing strategy, innovation* and *required flexibility* as client developments that will influence the providers' sourcing capabilities. These three key developments were applied in the selected case studies.

Assess the impact of key client developments on sourcing capabilities

Our second key objective was to assess the impact of key client developments on service providers' sourcing capabilities. Studying the sourcing capability model of Feeny et al. (2005) we found that all three competences areas were influenced. Taking the relationship competence area as a starting point, the interviews revealed a lack of the sourcing capabilities *leadership, governance* and *organizational design*. Interestingly, the interviews revealed that client developments from a business perspective were not recognized by our providers resulting in the absence of the capability *'business knowledge'*. Business market knowledge is strongly related to business applications that support client business processes. In respect of the sourcing capability model, this *business knowledge* capability can be assessed as new. Studying the *transformation* competence area, we found evidence that the offshore provider regularly monitored and assessed client developments and decisions were made to adapt sourcing capabilities. This refers to the sourcing capability *process re-engineering*. Moreover, during the transition phase discussions about the contract influenced the sourcing capability *planning and contracting* of the providers. Specifically, the domestic provider built a programme to cope with the issues regarding mutual interfaces and boundaries of the IT landscape. Furthermore, the fact that roles and responsibilities were unclear affected the sourcing capabilities *governance, process re-engineering* and *technology exploitation*. Studying the *delivery* competence area we found that the providers had to bring in various sourcing capabilities. As a result of the clients' reorganization the provider's sourcing capabilities *leadership, programme management* and *governance* are affected. Moreover, as the location in which IT services are delivered can be both on-site and offshore, knowledge management becomes more important. The providers acknowledge that the exchange of knowledge between front-end and back-office employees needs to improve. Knowledge of the business market in which the client is acting, is present on the on-site locations of the providers in the Netherlands, but the offshore employees do not have that knowledge and experience as they are more focused on delivery and maintenance. As knowledge about business needs can differ, this leads to differences of understanding between on-site and offshore employees when prioritizing activities. The providers under study developed their capabilities regularly in order to adapt to the changing client circumstances. In particular, we found that after the providers' struggle at the start of the arrangements, they invested constantly in building a sound relationship with their clients. Additionally, the providers decided to improve their soft skills like relationship management and client-oriented behaviour in order to achieve customer satisfaction. As a result, the behavioural dimension of trust and reputation was strengthened. Constantly developing or strengthening capabilities in a dynamic environment requires dynamic capabilities. This finding emphasizes the aspect of the firm's specificity and immobility of resources and capabilities.

Assess the impact of key client developments on organizational structures

Our third key objective was to assess the impact of key client developments on service providers' organizational structures. In general, the interviews with various participants revealed that the critical episodes described earlier related to the start of the delivery struggle for all providers were perceived as a turning point. Before the start of the delivery phase the providers applied an organizational structure which is based on a leveraged model to support multiple clients. This leveraged model can be characterized as having a high level of decision-making and many layers in the hierarchy. However, after the clients' changes a new organizational structure was developed by the provider to ensure customer orientation. The introduction of the provider's dedicated client-oriented team caused higher transaction costs as more employees are involved to integrate an end-to-end service. On the other hand, this team adds value as the effectiveness in delivering services towards the client increases. Moreover, we found that uncertainty with regard to changing client circumstances decreased. Based on the interviews with the provider's representatives we observe a mixed view on *decision-making*. Some have the opinion that the level of decision-making is perceived as high in the organization while others argue that this can be ranked as low in the organization. This can be explained as some participants combine both management roles and content-specific roles while others focus on just one role.

The representatives experienced limited hindrance with regard to the *number of layers in the hierarchy*. The fit of this organizational dimension with the client's demand is important. A limited number of layers in hierarchy create the opportunity to speed up decision-making and communication. With regard to the *level of horizontal integration* the majority of respondents charted this sub-dimension as moderate. The interviews revealed that several representatives of the providers combine different roles in one person, which may explain this finding. The IT service coordinator, for example, is also responsible for more technical consulting tasks. This can be explained by the fact that some resources are scarce and, therefore, client-oriented teams are limited with regard to team members. Our study shows that team members combine multiple roles to achieve an efficient organization and, therefore, stay competitive in the market. At the start of the arrangements the providers under study lacked the required experience to organize the delivery of IT services adequately. Their struggle how to cope with organizational changes on the client side demonstrated the provider's lack of attention to adapting their organizational dimensions.

Identify what aspects influence the performance of service providers towards their clients

Our fourth key objective was to identify what aspects influence the performance of service providers towards their clients. In addition to the influence of sourcing capabilities and organizational structure on provider's performance, we also found that the aspect of adaptability has an impact on changing client circumstances as well as the providers' performance. Our findings show that the providers under study in general were able to adapt to changing client circumstances. In particular, we may conclude that the domestic provider unconsciously paid attention to strengthening their sourcing capabilities and adapting their organizational dimensions. This can be explained by the absence of a formal adaptability process that proactively monitor and assess client developments. As a result, the provider shows reactive behaviour when it comes to adaptation. As the maturity of the domestic provider increased during the arrangement, they were more able to adapt to changing client circumstances. However, we may conclude that the offshore provider and the global provider designed and implemented procedures to guide the adaptability process. We did not expect to find these procedures as previous research encountered severe problems with regard to the provider's ability to adapt.

The adaptability mechanisms, as found in the offshore case study and the global case study, are fairly simple. Whereas complex mechanisms and IT support were expected, the main mechanism found in the cases consisted of having good relationships, spotting the need for adaptability and the application of procedures to guide the adaptability process. The needs that were spotted, often after having received indications from various sources, triggered the start of the adaptability process. Subsequently, the need for adaptability and the organizational implications were evaluated, which might in turn result in decisions and resulting actions to proactively deal with this need. The analyses of the provider's response to the client developments demonstrate that the 'adaptability myth' is all about the willingness and ability to manage change in IT outsourcing arrangements. As such, adaptability can be viewed as a competitive and strategic capability that is related to the provider's sourcing strategy. The role of the provider's executive management is essential in adapting and strengthening sourcing capabilities. Therefore, we conclude that the provider's sourcing strategy is the primary driver for the adaptability capacity. Adaptability might easily result in organizational change and the redesign of facilitating processes. Therefore, mutual cooperation with clients is mandatory.

Develop a dynamic fit approach

Our fifth key objective was to design a dynamic fit model that provides insight into the interplay between client developments, sourcing capabilities and organizational structural dimensions and to create a deeper understanding on their effect on the provider's performance. We found that establishing a dynamic fit has a positive effect on a provider's performance. IT providers, who monitor their client's developments, are expected to be able to adapt to changing client circumstances. Based on our empirical research studying three provider cases, we found evidence that sourcing performance needs to be monitored based on a multidimensional approach. Our findings underpin the existence of interlinked relationships between various aspects that reflects multiple dimensions. Based on client episodes and provider responses, over time sourcing capabilities were adapted and strengthened. As a result, the sourcing performance increased and the level of performance became sustainable. All providers under study experienced that they consciously need to develop their sourcing capabilities over time to meet client business needs.

An explanation for the identified lack of sustainable performance at the start of the arrangements is found in capabilities that are lacking on the provider side as well as in how these capabilities are organized. Clients need to gain access to relevant provider capabilities, while at the same time providers are not capable of performing on a sustainable high level. Consequently, this results in tension in the relationship with the outsourcing partners. Referring to provider's sourcing capabilities, our research demonstrated that on an organizational level the *governance capability* and the *organizational design capability* were identified as initiators to establish a fit between sourcing capabilities and organizational structure. Our findings show that the *governance capability* and the *organizational design capability* need to be superior when compared to the other sourcing capabilities as they influence the presence of a fit considerably. Empirical results indicate that there is support for relationships between *'Sourcing capabilities'* and the organizational dimensions *'Decision-making'*, *'Level of hierarchy'* and *'Horizontal integration'*. This finding demonstrates the existence of a fit between both aspects.

Consequently, sourcing capabilities as well as organizational structure are intertwined and affect the extent to which a fit can be established. The lower value a service provider places on its strategic resources, the more it ignores specific attention in establishing a fit. Maintaining resources with a low strategic value leads to an ineffective fit. On the other hand, the higher a provider values their strategic resources, the more a provider is justified in establishing a fit internally. Therefore, we conclude that the provider's sourcing strategy forms the primary driver for existence of a fit.

As a client's situation is subject to change, the supporting organizational structures of the IT provider also vary over time. Our research revealed that these providers, when establishing a fit at the same time, succeed in achieving a sustainable performance. Therefore, providers need to shift their client strategy from a supply-oriented perspective to a demand-oriented perspective. This fundamental paradigm shift requires consistent attention of the providers' executive management. Developing and maintaining a sustainable sourcing performance, however, is influenced by the ability and willingness of a provider to invest consciously in developing sourcing capabilities and an adequate adaptation process.

Additional findings

Additionally, our research reveals another interesting finding, which is how sourcing performance is monitored. Establishing a dynamic fit that aligns multiple dimensions – for example, client developments, capabilities, organizational structure, or performance – requires non-traditional evaluation methods. Practice shows that multiple providers apply a business scorecard (BSC) to measure their performance. However, the BSC method lacks the perspective of the client as a performance dimension. In our research we have applied the Performance Prism framework (Neely et al., 2002) that encompasses all relevant performance dimensions. The Performance Prism can be regarded as multidimensional, providing a balanced analysis of the environment in which IT services are provided while highlighting various stakeholders and measuring internal strategies, processes and capabilities. Mapping the Performance Prism framework to IT service providers enables us to measure the performance dimensions on an organizational level.

Research contributions

Contributions to science

Since the provider side of IT outsourcing arrangements is under-researched our study contributes to partially filling this gap. As the topic of a sustainable performance of IT providers has been hardly researched, our research shed some light on this important topic. This study, which is exploratory in nature, has important implications for research. Our results partially support the research model and constitute a first valid theoretical foundation. The model focuses on the concept of fit and it seems promising in its capacity to describe and explain the impact on sourcing performance. In particular, we paid attention to the development of a multidimensional measure of sourcing performance, and tested hypotheses empirically between the predictor variable (e.g. capabilities) and criterion variable (e.g. sourcing performance) by means of a mediation variable (e.g. organizational structure). The results from our analysis also show that the constructs can be used to analyse the differences between the three types of providers, i.e. domestic, offshore, and global.

Our study contributes to the RBV by strengthening the empirical base research – for instance, how resources and capabilities evolve over time (Porter, 1991; Lieberman and Montgomery, 1998). In particular, our research contributes to the approach of 'dynamic' capabilities in which a firm aims to achieve a competitive advantage (Teece et al., 1997). Moreover, our empirical research helps to understand the dynamic capabilities approach how providers are able to improve their performance by establishing a dynamic fit and that contributes to sustainability. Interestingly, the RBV does not specifically address the determinant of adaptability although aspects that contribute to adaptability are present. In particular, our qualitative research demonstrated that all three providers developed both the processes and content of their capabilities over time which refers to path dependency. As the RBV lacks a motivation with regard to the adaptiveness of capabilities, we argue that our finding adds strength to the RBV. In particular, our findings extents the RBV and core competence theory by providing support about how capabilities can be adapted as a result of client developments. Therefore, we claim that our study contributes to the RBV by strengthening the empirical base research, particularly how resources and capabilities evolve over time. This offers a partial answer to questions that were mentioned in previous research (Porter, 1991; Lieberman and Montgomery, 1998).

Another important contribution we add is the relationship between organizational dimensions and the Transaction Cost Economics (TCE). In order to stay competitive, providers focus on lowering their transaction cost. However, we find that investments in specific assets (for example, organizational structure) were made that increased the transaction costs. This is consistent with transaction cost reasoning that as asset specificity increases, more complex governance structures are required to attenuate costly bargaining over profits from specialized assets (Dyer, 1997). We also find that transaction characteristics, which are operationalized by the organizational dimension, may vary across different contexts. This is consistent with previous research (Williamson, 1975).

With regard to the RBV and the TCE we find that our results contribute to both theories; however, they focus on different aspects. We may conclude that a discussion of both theories as individual approaches only partially explain the existence of a dynamic fit and the relationship towards sourcing performance. Referring our results to the RBV and TCE we claim that both theories are necessary to explain and understand the presence of a dynamic fit and their influence on sourcing performance. Aspects of both theories were present in our findings and yielded complementary. Therefore, our results have important theoretical implications. The findings provide support for the growing body of literature arguing that the RBV and TCE are complementary (McIvor, 2009).

Since there is little empirical research on fit, our IS/IT approach to study a fit endeavours to explain if providers are able to achieve a sustainable performance. We studied various elements and relate the outcome to sourcing performance. This is contrary to previous research that studies each element separately and thus did not capture the simultaneity embedded in the multidimensionality of performance. In particular, our qualitative research revealed that adaptability can be viewed as a strategic resource that is value, rare and imitable. Therefore, we argue that the ability and willingness of providers to adapt to changing client circumstances enlarge the likelihood of a fit. Moreover, addressing fit as a moderation, we find that the strength of the moderation is influenced by the extent in which capabilities and organizational structure are applied. Our accumulation of empirical evidence means that our study contributes to the existing literature on fit (Venkatraman, 1989). This intra-organizational view on fit finds support for both the RBV (for example, capabilities) and TCE (for example, organizational structure) theories. Our results provide evidence that a dynamic fit has a positive relation to sourcing performance. In particular, providers who focus on establishing a fit are more able to achieve a sustainable performance that is durable over time than providers who pay less attention to a fit.

In addition, we have developed a measuring tool that enables us to measure the concept of fit which discusses the contribution of service providers in outsourcing arrangements. As a result, a structural model was developed using new scales to test the model and hypotheses. The structural model is now open for further testing. The structural model indicates significant relationships between the client developments, sourcing capabilities, their organizational structure, and performance. In particular, this measuring tool can be used to measure the extent in which a fit is present in provider organizations.

Contributions to practitioners

This study contributes to IT outsourcing providers in that it increases their awareness of the relevance of establishing a dynamic fit that will significantly improve their sourcing performance. Providers will benefit from the insights of this research by knowing which determinants affect their sourcing performance. As a consequence, providers have the opportunity to manage their performance towards clients. Therefore, we argue that within the boundaries of our research, providers are able to make a choice for delivering a sustainable performance.

The results of our research provide insights how providers may create a dynamic fit between their capabilities and organizational structure. By strengthening their sourcing capabilities they are able to respond to their clients' business needs. Moreover, developing an organizational structure that reflects the client's environment supports the establishment of a dynamic fit. The results of this study can be used by providers to increase their maturity in providing a sustainable performance. An important insight concerns the moment when the organizational structure needs to be implemented. In terms of practice the findings revealed that at the start of the transition phase of an arrangement, providers need to establish a proper organizational structure. In fact, a relatively clear understanding of effective organizational structures may encourage provider's managers to implement a client-oriented team that contributes to the achievement of a sustainable performance.

From a managerial perspective, our results suggest that monitoring and assessing changing client circumstances on a regular basis is a prerequisite for providers to become an agile organization. Regular evaluations with regard to their clients' developments allow IT providers to adapt to changing business needs by focusing on the way capabilities are organized and made available. In particular, provider's executive management play an important role with regard to the ability and willingness to adapt. Recent literature (Plugge and Janssen, 2009) suggests that provider capabilities must be adapted regularly to meet customer demand. Most fundamentally, our research demonstrates that providers need procedures and routines to enable the adaptability process. Provider's executive management have to implement these procedures to proactively monitor changes in the client environment and take appropriate measures for dealing with them. This might include training, but also the acquisition of external capabilities. This research also suggests that the provider's ability to adapt should be part of the sourcing decision process of clients. During both the sourcing strategy and the tender selection phase, clients can identify to what extent an outsourcing partner will cater for environmental uncertainty.

The findings of our study also contribute to consultancy firms when advising clients during the tender and selection process related to IT outsourcing providers. Previous research identified that the selection process of providers has been shown to be a critical determinant of outsourcing success (Levina and Su, 2008). IT outsourcing consultancy firms can benefit from our results by paying attention to the aspect of adaptability and sustainable performance. As clients are acting in dynamic markets, a more adaptive provider is required to quickly adapt to changing circumstances. Consultancy firms need to deepen their understanding of providers by studying the extent in which they are able to adapt. This will increase the value of consultancy firms in supporting clients related to the selection process of preferred providers. Moreover, consultancy firms that are involved in an IT outsourcing tendering process may use the aspects of adaptability and a sustainable performance as selection criteria. In doing so, providers perception can be managed by arguing the importance of clients' need. Finally, our research suggests that the provider's ability to adapt and achieve a sustainable performance should be part of the sourcing decision process of clients. During both the sourcing strategy and the tender selection phase, clients can identify to what extent an outsourcing partner will cater for environmental uncertainty.

Recommendations for further research

Studying the provider side of IT outsourcing arrangements is a relatively new line of research, and clearly, there is a need for further research. In particular, the research model and accompanying constructs can be refined.

As mentioned in our conclusions, the results of our research identified several issues that require further research. First, multiple case studies are recommended to obtain more insights to the variety of causes and effects of the identified relationships. Expanding the research by involving a substantial number of providers will provide more rigorous measurement that can be used to enhance and strengthen our results. Based on these findings, we recommend to statically generalize the findings. Future research could also examine the effect of contextual variables of provider organizations on our results such as size, culture, behaviour and experience in providing IT outsourcing services. Researchers could study the offshore dimension as a consequence of a provider's business strategy. Geographical dispersion that comprises more than one country and one culture may introduce a new dimension in establishing a dynamic fit. This element refers to previous research (Oshri et al., 2007) in which the authors argue that the offshore providers' ability to manage expertise within its organizations is an organizational challenge.

Second, further research is required to conduct a more extensive survey among provider organizations that will help us to develop our model further. Furthermore, our structural model could be tested by industry, taking environmental effects into account (i.e. dynamic, static).This analysis could reveal important insights how client developments by industry influences our main constructs. We hypothesize that client developments may vary by industry, and therefore have another effect on provider organizations. Future research should include the effect of the industry, which refers to environmental uncertainty.

Third, we recommend studying the perspective of provider's adaptability capability. Although our study focuses on the provider side, we acknowledge that the IT outsourcing relationship is dyadic. Hence, it is worthwhile to study client developments in more detail as these will change over time. Thus, we would suggest conducting longitudinal research to explore client developments on a wider scale. Subsequently, the extent in which providers are able to adapt to changing client developments can be explored more thoroughly. The results of this longitudinal research may provide new insights when compared to the causality effects in our research model. Therefore, we would encourage other researchers to explore this topic and enlarge the understanding of providers' strategic adaptability process. Moreover, expanding the view of providers how they adapt is valuable. Aspects like guiding processes, procedures and the role of executive management will deepen our insights.

Fourth, as our research specifically studied the existence of a sustainable outsourcing performance, further research at the provider side is required to investigate other factors. Further work needs to extend our understanding of how organizational dimensions influence a sustainable sourcing performance. It is worthwhile to examine how the locus of decision-making and levels in hierarchy affect a sustainable performance. Our research revealed that the extents to which providers are able to adapt, indirectly relate to performance and, in particular, in establishing a sustainable performance. Moreover, our findings reveal that providers who are managing the chain from client developments up to sustainability are more able to achieve a sustainable performance. Sustainability factors, however, may not be viewed as similar. These factors can be related to different orientations such as content, processes or contingency (Kettinger et al., 1994). Thus, in particular more longitudinal research could examine the effect of additional sustainability factors that are related to the environment of provider's organizations or within the provider organization. In this way, our research model can be expanded to a more comprehensive model identifying the relationships between sustainability factors and outsourcing performance.

Finally, our research design allowed us to combine an in-depth qualitative research with a quantitative empirical sample analysis. We do not claim that our results are definitive or conclusive, but instead we intend to open up new research questions such as: How can clients and providers collectively cater to new developments that arise within the organization or environment? Which specific provider capabilities are adapted as a result of client developments? In which way do provider organizational dimensions individually affect outsourcing performance?

In conclusion, our research made an attempt to take an initial step in creating a dynamic fit between sourcing capabilities and organizational dimensions and their effect on sourcing performance. We hope that the results of our study, in advocating the importance of conducting research on the provider side, will spur further research along these lines.

Appendix A: Research Methodology

Research perspective

Since empirical research on fit is limited, we conducted an empirical research study that is based on qualitative and quantitative exploratory research. Qualitative methods are instrumental in explaining causal relations, while quantitative methods are more suited to testing relationships on the basis of confirmed or disconfirmed predictions (Bacharach, 1989). This research perspective is consistent with previous literature (Kern and Willcocks, 2002), arguing that more exploratory research is necessary to understand the relationship between clients and providers involved in outsourcing arrangements.

The strength of a qualitative study is that it focuses on naturally occurring, ordinary events in natural settings, so that we have a strong grip on the nature of 'real life' (Miles and Huberman, 1994). As the performance of IT outsourcing providers can change over time, longitudinal research is required. By thoroughly investigating the period of an outsourcing arrangement, longitudinal research will provide reliable insights into how the performance during the arrangement is affected by the fit between capabilities and organizational structure. Because of longitudinal research we can determine if an IT provider is able to achieve a sustainable sourcing performance towards their customers. This leads to a more holistic view compared to taking 'snaphots' at a certain moment, meaning we can really understand what is going on. With regard to quantitative research, empirical data were used to test our developed hypotheses. It was argued that within IS research, the scientific empirical approach is based upon the high-level attributes of the research (Galliers, 1992). Scientific approaches may be defined as having arisen from the scientific tradition characterized by repeatability, reductionism and refutability. Moreover, scientific research assumes that observations of the phenomena under research can be made objectively and rigorously. Empirical research contributes to the relevance of research in general by creating more insight in the actual real-life situations (Benbasat and Zmud, 1999), and thus to the objectives of our research.

Research design

With regard to our key objectives, this study is based primarily on a multiple case study. We prefer the case study method as 'when, how or why'

Table A.1 Case study tactics for four design tests

Criteria	Case study tactics	Phase of research
Construct validity	Use multiple sources of evidence	Data collection
	Establish chain of evidence	Data collection
	Have informants review draft case study report	Composition
Internal validity	Do pattern matching	Data analysis
	Do explanation building	Data analysis
	Do time-series analysis	Data analysis
External validity	Use replication logics	Research design
Reliability	Use case study protocol	Data collection
	Develop case study data base	Data collection

questions are being posed, when the investigator has little control over events, and when the focus on a contemporary phenomenon within some real-life context (Yin 1984: 16). Addressing previous research (Herriott and Firestone, 1983), the authors argue that evidence from multiple case studies is often considered to be more compelling and more robust than the single case studies. This research is designed to make a thorough exploration of how the dynamic fit between sourcing capabilities and organizational structure within provider organizations is established. The case study method is well established in IS research, especially when it is used for 'sticky, practice-based problems' such as assessing the fit between capabilities and organizational structure. In setting up a research design several criteria must be taken into account to verify the quality. Yin (1984) has described four criteria, providing suggestions how to make case studies meet these criteria (see Table A.1). Several of these tactics are used in the case studies in this protocol.

All four quality criteria are explained in the data collection section and the data analysis section. It has often been questioned if case study results can be generalized since the number of entities that are described in case studies is too small for statistically justified generalization. However, our main objective is to expand and generalize theories (analytical generalization) and not to enumerate frequencies (statistical generalization) (Yin, 1994). So case studies can be generalized to situations that are sufficiently similar to the observed cases with regard to relevant variables. Moreover, we conducted a qualitative research to test the hypotheses which were derived from the theory. This latter refers to the aspect of analytic generalization. The results of our empirical research are generalized to the level of the organization as a whole.

Longitudinal approach

To determine if a provider demonstrates a sustainable performance over time, we will measure two important phases of an outsourcing arrangement. During our empirical research we applied a retrospective approach, to measure the segregated sourcing phases transformation and delivery. Following a longitudinal approach over time, we have decided to determine the scope of measuring for a period of five years, which corresponds with the average outsourcing contract term in the market. This means that starting our empirical research in 2008, the period from 2002 to early 2010 will form the boundary of our measuring period taking the various provider contract periods into account. This longitudinal approach reflects to our original research problem 'a lack of sustainability in service performance towards clients', as described in the introduction.

Case study protocol

In order to develop a formal plan for conducting the case studies, a case study protocol needs to be produced to provide guidance and to record the data. The case study protocol consists of the following elements:

- Information on provider organization.
- An interview protocol.
- A survey protocol.
- A case database.

With regard to the first element, multiple sources of providers' information are identified, which have a direct relationship to the methods (for example, desk research, interviews) used in our case studies. For each service provider information is gathered about their history, their mission, market position, strategic objectives and their sourcing strategy. The second element is the interview protocol that consists of information related to the preparation of the interview and the interview questions. Consequently, the protocol describes the execution of the interviews and the way in which the data are analysed. The generic interview protocol is provided in Appendix E. The survey protocol, which is the third element, reveals information that concerns our research constructs. Each questionnaire is accompanied by a short covering letter that explains the purpose of the study. The questionnaire is provided in Appendix G. Considering the need to create an overall picture of the results, a glossary of the terms used in the questionnaire defining each is also enclosed. As a result, the questionnaire will provide more insight to 'how' and 'what' questions. All of the collected data will be stored in a case study database, which is the fourth element of the case study protocol. The database establishes a structure to provide a comprehensive overview of relevant data, qualitative as well as quantitative. From the perspective of the case study analysis, first, we group the information as a result of the interviews and surveys into the format of the case study protocol. The questions of the interviews and surveys are identified by a number. We have developed a table with the different topics corresponding to a number applied on the interview form and survey form. Each topic is associated with the relevant data collection method.

However, as a result of the confidentiality requirements of the service providers and their customers, we have not disclosed the details of the service providers involved. Table A.2 shows the relationship between the research topic and the corresponding question label. The first column refers to the researched aspects such as client developments and fit. The second column describes the methodology that was used to gather the information: desk research (D), interviews (I) and survey (S). The third column refers to the number of interview questions that were used. The interview questions are detailed in Appendix E. The fourth column shows the number of the survey questions used. The survey questions are explained in more detail in Appendix G.

Case study selection

In case studies it is essential to select a proper unit of observation. The unit of observation reflects the coherence of sourcing capabilities and organizational structures dimensions, and the providers' performance in establishing a dynamic fit. We use a set of criteria to select appropriate case studies. First, regarding the sourcing capabilities of an IT provider, we identify aspects such as market dynamism and client developments. Depending on these aspects, the extent of sourcing capabilities may vary. We clustered the extent of depth to three categories: limited, average and extensive. Secondly, within the market we can distinguish between different portfolio strategies of IT providers. Some providers focus consciously on a limited number of IT services, while other providers apply a portfolio strategy that is based on an average of three IT services or even a wide or extensive) range of IT services. Both criteria – the extent and the portfolio – refer to the construct sourcing capabilities.

Third, the level of client demands, which can be clustered into the categories limited, average and extensive, is related to the construct organizational structure. Fourth, the same goes for the element of geography that is also

Table A.2 Relationship between research topics and questions

Information	Source	Interview question	Survey question
1. Information on provider organization			
A. Mission	D,I	A1A	
B. Market segments	D,I	A1B	
C. Importance of outsourcing	D,I	A1C	
D. Business strategy	D		
2. Position of the provider within the market			
A. Type of competitors	D		
B. Type of market dynamism	D		
C. Market strategy	D		
3. Changing client developments			
A. Sourcing strategy	S		B2.1
B. Innovation	S		B2.1
C. Required flexibility	S		B2.1
C. Additional	D		B2.1
4. Assessment of providers capabilities	S		B2.2
A. Relationship	S		B2.2
B. Transformation	S		B2.2
C. Delivery	S		B2.2
5. Assessment of providers organizational structure			
A. Decision-making	S		B2.3
B. Levels of hierarchy	S		B2.3
C. Horizontal integration	S		B2.3
D. Additional	D		
6. Fit between organizational structure and capabilities			
A. Existence	I	A3A	
B. Capability influence	I	A3B	
C. Organizational influence	I	A3C	
D. Additional	D		
7. Assessment of providers firm performance			
A. Client developments	I,S	A4A	B2.4
B. Sourcing capabilities		A4B	B2.4
C. Organizational structure	I,S	A4C	B2.4
8. Information background of the interviewees	I	A4D	B2.4
A.	I		
B.	I		
C.	I		

Table A.3 Applied criteria and suggested cases

Theoretical criteria	Practical citeria	Domestic provider	Offshore provider	Global provider
Sourcing capabilities	Extent	Limited	Average	Extensive
	Portfolio	Limited	Average	Extensive
Organizational structure	Level of demand	Limited	Average	Extensive
	Geography	Domestic	Regional	Global

related to the organizational structure as applied by an IT provider. All four aspects influence the capabilities and structure of providers' organizations and, therefore, can be used as criteria to select providers. Since we can differentiate between the various criteria, we have selected three cases that satisfy of all these criteria. We suggest that three provider organizations will be researched because of the researchability of our study: a domestic provider, an offshore provider and a global provider. Table A.3 shows the different criteria-related characteristics of the selected case studies. We selected these three companies on theoretical sampling arguments, assuming that there might be differences in focus between the providers.

We have chosen three different methods for gathering data: desk research, interviews, and a survey. As a result, both qualitative and quantitative research will be part of our study. This will lead to an approach in which the collection of both qualitative and quantitative data is continuously integrated. Miles and Huberman (1994: 41) describes this approach as design number 1.

Previous research (Rossman and Wilson, 1984, 1991) argue that there are three basic reasons to link qualitative and quantitative data: (1) to enable confirmation of each other via triangulation; (2) to elaborate or develop analysis, providing a richer detail; and (3) to initiate new lines of thinking through attention to surprises or paradoxes. Analysing variables and situational factors will establish a chain of evidence. By consulting multiple sources of evidence, and enabling confirmation of each other via triangulation of data, we are able to achieve construct validity. According to qualitative research, the issue of reliability tends to be more complex. To ensure reliability, we build and provide access to a research database so that it is possible for another researcher to repeat the operations of the case study, such as data collection procedures, with the same results (Yin, 1994). The method of desk research was applied to gather more general information with regard to the case studies. Background information includes the size of the company, geographical dispersion, type of services and a description of the markets in which the company acts. In addition, other relevant information such as documents and plans were analysed.

Case study interviews

To deepen our understanding of the constructs we interviewed different participants. To avoid 'elite bias' we interviewed multiple management and employee representatives. This is necessary because respondents express their personal opinion about how they perceive the behaviour of, for instance, the organizational structure. It is inevitable that their opinions contain a subjective account of the actual behaviour. We use two criteria for the selection of participants. First, the interviewees were selected from a strategic level as they are involved in decision-making. They are capable of discussing the relationship between capabilities, organizational structure and firm performance, so it was worthwhile discussing these topics with them. Secondly, due to their position they were able to look at their organization as a whole and identify the relationships between the researched topics and the processes that support them. The target groups who participated in the interviews were divided into three areas: sales, transformation and delivery.

Based on three providers, in-depth interviews were conducted with 23 participants who are directly involved in the case studies. This was to ensure internal consistency within each provider organization. The interviewed respondents have a minimum of four years' experience with regard to the outsourced IT services. All interviewees are located in the Netherlands. They are responsible for activities on different levels: executive, middle management and operational. Interviewee roles, as illustrated in Appendix D, are positioned across the firm. In this way we apply a cross-section within the organizations that yield to establish a holistic view. All of the respondents were interviewed in the period June 2008 to October 2008. Interviews varied in length between 90 minutes and 120 minutes and they were conducted via a semi-structured design with many open-ended questions. Applying a semi-structured interview method as a research instrument is useful to select data and information for exploratory-descriptive studies that may be extended later (Denzin, 1978).

Prior to each interview, the questions were adjusted to the participant's area of expertise – for instance, transition. All the interviews were then transcribed, and the text was confirmed by the respondents for approval to ensure accuracy and reliability. Any discrepancies that may have arisen can therefore be checked and thus we eliminate any interviewer bias. All cases and accompanying data were stored in a case study database. The database included interview transcripts and additional information such as annual reports, outsourcing documents and performance-related information. All documents were codified by a database number (see Table A.2). We developed a table with the different topics corresponding to the case study number applied on the interview form. Each topic is associated with the relevant data collection label.

Survey method

The survey method, which is part of the quantitative research stream, consists of a questionnaire, with questions that relate to our research constructs. The sample and data collection will be explained in more detail in Chapter 8. As Galliers (1991) argues: surveys are a good means of looking at a far greater number of variables and, therefore, they can provide a reasonably accurate description of real world situations from a variety of viewpoints. While a vast majority of the questions are identical, minor modifications were made to the questionnaire to fit the particular departments, terminology and practices. Considering the need for clarity, and given the fact that the terminology can be interpreted differently, a glossary of definitions was included. Each questionnaire was accompanied by a short covering letter which explained the purpose of the study (see Appendix G).

Data analysis

Yin (1984) describes two general strategies for analysing case study evidence: (1) developing a case description; and (2) relying on theoretical propositions. As we have based our study on exploratory research and our theory on various hypotheses, our research adopts both strategies.

In qualitative research coding data is an integral part of data analysis (Neman, 2000). The research questions and related constructs we have defined will guide the coding process. Our first attempt at theorization of the collected data is coding the interviews using the method of categorized subjects (Miles and Huberman, 1994). Our research was clustered around the defined constructs and the responses of all provider representatives were grouped together into subject categories that can be related to variables in the research model. As pointed out by Lincoln and Guba (1985), the validity of interpretive analysis defies quantification. We will include excerpts from the transcribed interviews (see Appendix F) to allow readers to judge for themselves the validity of our research. This process allows us to develop a qualitative, interpretative approach to construct case study research.

Concept mapping

When executing our qualitative research concept maps are used to guide us through the process of data analysis. Since knowledge is fairly nonlinear, concepts can be seen as organized networks. By selecting and organizing relevant information we are able to identify links between concepts, so that we can fathom the data. Concept mapping is a tool for fostering conceptual relationships. A concept map is a two-dimensional representation of information which illustrates the connections between and among individual concepts (Novak and Gowin, 1984). The technique was developed by Novak (1984) based on ideas from previous research (Ausubel, 1963). A concept map may be defined as 'a perceived regularity in events or objects, or records of events or objects, designated by a label' (Novak, 1990). The label for most concepts is a word. Together, nodes and labels or named links define propositions, assertions about a topic, domain or thing. Multiple linkages between concepts may depict how each concept is related to other concepts. Concept maps are particularly useful for representing networks of concepts, where links are not only connected to adjacent concepts, but are also often linked to concepts in different sections of the concept map (Tergan, 2005). On the one hand, creating links between concepts may indicate the ability to synthesize related statements of interviewed representatives. On the other hand, links may indicate an interpretation of the concepts. Concept maps can be applied to create a holistic representation of knowledge (van Dijk and Kintsch, 1983). The idea behind methods and tools is that cognitive processing of complex subject matter can be enhanced if the task-relevant knowledge is well organized and the structure behind ideas, knowledge and information are made explicit by means of visualization (Tergan, 2005).

Most articles related to concept mapping refer to Novak and Gowin (1984). However, other forms of concept maps were also developed. An improved method of concept mapping is a cyclic concept map (Safayeni et al., 2003). This type of map can be constructed in any way that is the best justified option. An embodiment of a concept map is a situational model that is appropriate to create insight into relationships between concepts. A situational model is a mental representation of the situation (Slotte and Lonka, 1999) and it is this model that is applied to analyse the text gathered from our interviews.

Based on the principle of concept mapping, tools can support the management of the data. A visualization of the concept mapping tool 'Webster' (Alpert and Gruenenberg, 2000) show examples of the representation of knowledge. The software programme Atlas.ti focuses on segmenting text into words and sentences that can be indexed with codes. The software visually represents selected concepts, codes and memos into diagrams together with their mutual relationships. When applying Atlas.ti all text obtained can be linked to concepts. New concepts, text, sentences and fragments can be added easily. As a result, text and concepts can be linked automatically. The concept maps can be represented in more detail or with a more generic character.

Atlas.ti v5.2 was used to code and combine the interview data of the 23 respondents into concept maps. The concept maps represent the information from three service providers. Concept mapping resulted in a total of 212 codes (concepts). We conducted seven rounds of concept aggregation. Over the course of four rounds a number of that are closely aligned to each other were aggregated into a single code. For example, the code 'providers value add' is closely aligned to the code 'providers value proposition'. Next in round five, we reduced the number of codes by ignoring concepts which are more general influencing factors. Some examples include the codes 'competitive advantage' and 'market segmentation influences'. Subsequently, during the sixth round we reduced those labels which were named as 'Is associated with'. During the seven round we left out those codes that were labelled as 'Is part of'. Finally, we identified 82 codes (concepts) that represent the most significant elements of our theoretical research model. Labelling the relationships between concepts we have used the following names: 'Has impact on', 'Has strong impact on', 'Is cause of'. As a result of the coding process, we were able to create more insight and identify relevant concepts and relationships.

Cross-case analysis

The cross-case analysis consists of a cross-case overview and the identification of fit patterns. All case studies are compared and assessed based on our research constructs. This will provide a comprehensive picture for the cross-case analysis. Based on the cross-case analysis we were able to draw conclusions as to how a dynamic fit can be improved to achieve a sustainable performance. The results of three case studies are expected to deliver a valuable contribution both to the scientific community and to practitioners.

Quantitative analysis

The stated hypotheses, as described in Chapter 2, help to focus attention on certain data and ignore irrelevant data. On the one hand, our hypotheses help us to organize the entire case study. On the other hand, hypotheses about causal relations answer the 'how' and 'why' questions and are useful in guiding case study analysis. As our research is based on an exploratory approach, pattern-matching is the most appropriate mode of analysis to apply. Pattern-matching compares an empirically established pattern with a predicted one (Yin, 1984). If the patterns coincide, the results can help our case study to strengthen its internal validity. In this research different hypotheses will be compared with the outcome of our research. The data analysis method applied is explained in more detail in Chapter 8. Because we apply a questionnaire method, it is important to establish whether any patterns to events, motivations and outcomes emerge. This allows us to establish differences in interpretation by respondents so that we can investigate possible explanations. To maximize external validity, the study will use replication logic to conduct and analyse the multiple case studies. All cases will use predetermined questions for analysis. Finally, we will compare the results to the selected various theories and treat them as a dataset for comparative analysis (Glaser and Strauss, 1967).

Appendix B: Preliminary Research: Overview of Interviewees

Case studies	Department	Date	Interview Duration	Job description
Company A Banking	IT	25-10-2006	1.5 hour	Group CIO (EVP)
		16-8-2006	1.5 hour	Global Head ADM (EVP)
		15-9-2006	1.5 hour	Manager Offshoring services (VP)
		21-8-2006	1.5 hour	Head of Architecture department (SVP)
Company B Retail	IT	13-7-2006	1 hour	CIO Europe
		18-7-2006	1 hour	IT Director Europe
		10-8-2006	2 hours	Head Architecture department
		18-7-2006	1.5 hour	Demand manager
Company C Chemicals	IT	20-10-2005	1 hour	CIO
		30-10-2006	1 hour	Global IM manager
		18-9-2006	1.5 hour	Global sourcing manager
		3-10-2006	1 hour	IT Director
		20-10-2006	1 hour	Vendor manager
		20-10-2006	1.5 hour	Vendor manager
Company D Telecom	IT	14-7-2006	1 hour	CIO
		18-8-2006	1 hour	Manager solution center
		21-9-2006	1.5 hour	Director IT Operations
		24-8-2006	1 hour	Demand manager
		14-8-2006	1 hour	Programme manager
Company E Manufacturing	IT	27-8-2006	1 hour	Group CIO
		6-10-2006	1.5 hour	CIO Europe
		6-10-2006	1.5 hour	CIO Asia
		15-9-2006	2 hours	Manager Telephony and networks

Appendix C: Preliminary Research: Interview Questions

The interview instrument is based upon Hakansson's Interaction Approach model which consists of three categories.

Category 1: Environment

Number	Question
Env 1	How does the environment affect your company?
Env 2	How do the market developments influence your company and which activities?
Env 3	How would you characterize the competitive climate in your industry and how is this related to IT?
Env 4	How does external legislation (e.g. Sarbanes-Oxley) affect your IT services?
Env 5	Do you review the 'environmental' developments with your IT provider on a regular basis?

Category 2: Atmosphere

Number	Question
Atm 1	How does the atmosphere affect the relationship between your company and your provider?
Atm 2	How does your outsourcing strategy (total, selective) affect your IT provider(s)?
Atm 3	How would you characterize your position toward the IT provider: power or dependency?
Atm 4	By what means does your company culture influence your IT provider?
Atm 5	Does innovation plays an important role within your company and if so, in what way will this influence the IT provider?

Category 3: Exchange

Number	Question
Exc 1	What are the relevant exchange processes?
Exc 2	What are the characteristics (e.g. regular vs ad-hoc, generic vs specific) of each of the exchange processes?
Exc 3	What were some of the recent management difficulties you encountered in the relationship with your provider?
Exc 4	How would you describe the flexibility requirements toward your IT provider related to the exchange process?
Exc 5	How important is the relation between the demand manager (customer) and the delivery manager (provider)?

Appendix D: Main Research: Overview of Interviewees

Organization	Date	Interview Duration	Job description
Domestic provider	1-5-2008	1,5 hour	Executive manager
	30-4-2008	1 hour	Sales director
	1-5-2008	1,5 hour	Account manager
	30-4-2008	1 hour	Transition manager
	30-4-2008	1 hour	HR manager
	28-4-2008	1 hour	Senior manager
	21-5-2008	1 hour	Service delivery manager
	21-5-2008	1 hour	Service delivery manager
Offshore provider	9-6-2008	2 hours	Sales director (Head Benelux)
	8-5-2008	1 hour	Account manager
	28-5-2008	2 hours	Business consultant
	28-5-2008	1,5 hour	Engagement manager
	26-5-2008	1 hour	Service delivery manager
	26-5-2008	1 hour	Service delivery manager
	27-5-2008	1 hour	Service delivery manager
Global provider	16-5-2008	1 hour	Executive director
	18-5-2008	1 hour	Senior director
	17-5-2008	1,5 hour	Delivery director
	17-5-2008	1 hour	Sales manager
	16-5-2008	1,5 hour	Service delivery manager
	20-5-2008	1,5 hour	Service delivery manager
	20-5-2008	1,5 hour	Programme delivery manager
	20-5-2008	1 hour	Team lead

Appendix E: Main Research: Interview Questions

The following questions will be a part of the in-depth interview sessions and will yield more profound information. Four topics will be investigated: strategy, assessment of client developments, fit between capabilities and organizational structure and firm performance.

Strategy

Number	Question
S 1	Mission of the company that is strived for, strategic objectives (market leadership or cost leadership, differentiation strategy)
S 2	Characteristics of the market segments involved in (static or dynamic markets, simple or complex services required)
S 3	Importance of the outsourcing service for the company (focus and priority of the service within the organization)

Client developments

Number	Question
CD 1	How are new client developments addressed that will influence the organization? How is this process established? Who is responsible within the organization to support this process? Who is discussing those developments with clients?
CD 2	How is the adaptability process developed? Who is responsible within the organization to adapt to client developments? Which parties are involved with this adaptation process?
CD 3	Which bottlenecks can be addressed that restrain the organization for adapting to client developments? Who is responsible for removing the bottlenecks and on what level is this taking place?

Fit between capabilities and organizational structure

Number	Question
F 1	Defining the fit. What is the definition of the fit? And how is the fit defined?
F 2	Decision-making. How is the decision-making organized to define the fit? And who is participating in the decision-making unit?
F 3	Who is responsible for achieving this fit? Process. Is a formal methodology used to achieve the fit between structure and capabilities?
F 4	Description of the process that is used to create the fit. Is the fit reviewed regularly and adapted when necessary?

Firm performance

Number	Question
P 1	Firm performance. In what way is the fit affecting firm performance? What actions are taken when the performance is decreasing as a result of an insufficient fit? Is the relationship between the fit and performance reviewed regularly? And if so, who is participating in the review process?
P 2	Responsibility. Who is responsible for the relationship between the fit and performance? Is the fit with regard to the performance measured, and if so, how is the performance determined?
P 3	Sustainable performance. Is achieving a sustainable performance part of the provider's strategy? If so, can you deliver some evidence that underpin this strategy? Is the relation between the fit and firm performance determined for each sourcing phase? Are the outcomes of the different phases compared to each other? Is it possible to achieve a sustainable performance?

Appendix F: Main Research: Interview Extracts

Domestic provider

Document ID	Code	Question ID	Information	Service provider's response	User ID
			Construct Fit		
Domestic provider	F	F01	To what extent do sourcing capabilities and organizational structure affect each other? Why?	Sure we experience a fit between capabilities and structure. After some transition struggles we adapted our organizational structure towards the client (e.g. decision-making related to the delivery team). Subsequently, the performance improved. Recently, we introduced a new IT service (workplace automation) as part of our portfolio. We cosiously invest in strenghthen our capabilities by means of people and assets.	DP 4
Domestic provider	F	F02	To what extent is the organizational structure aligned regularly with the present sourcing capabilities? Can you describe this process?	This certainly is true for our client. Our organizational structure is mirrored to the client organization while some specific capabilities were strenghtened (e.g. flexibility, process reenginereing). Also, we introduced a new way of working. Provider representatives need to work for several years on a client case by which experiece increases. This refer to sales, transition and deliviry. In particular, alingment procedures are applied when extensive changes are carried through.	DP 5

(continued)

Continued

Document ID	Code	Question ID	Information	Service provider's response	User ID
Domestic provider	F	F04	To what extent does a robust fit between sourcing capabilities and organizational structure enable you to deliver a sustainable performance to your client?	The effect of fit on performance is present. Our employees act as they are formerly working for the client organization in stead of our company. Also, our client experience our employees are their own. This helps to build a partnership and increases client satisfaction.	DP 3
Domestic provider	F	F04	To what extent does a robust fit between sourcing capabilities and organizational structure enable you to deliver a sustainable performance to your client?	Fit definitly lead to a stable performance. At the start of the arrangement we unconsiously paid attention to establish a fit between capabilities an structure. We learned that during the transition phase we have to pay attention to establish a fit. For instance, by positioning the delivery team at once. At the same time we can discuss organizational dimensions like communication. An impartant aspect remains the continuity of our own employees.	DP 6

Document ID	Code	Question ID	Information	Service provider's response	User ID
			Construct Performance		
Domestic provider	P	P02	To what extent do sourcing capabilities affect the sourcing performance towards your client? Why?	Quality is extreme important. Each client requires a certain level of customization at the front-end. The challenge is to organize the delivery of IT services at the back-end efficiently based on operational exellence. This requires the necessary capablities to do so. Our clients have the opinion that this approach is working fine and are satisfied about our flexibility (proactive behaviour, raising ideas, level of cooperation).	DP 1
Domestic provider	P	P02	To what extent do sourcing capabilities affect the sourcing performance towards your client? Why?	Applying sourcing capabilities is conditional for a sound performance. Without the proper an sufficient capabilities it isn't possible to achieve the performance as agreed. We also developed a govenance structure on strategic, tactical and operational level. This appraoch offers structure an continuity which from a relational perspective is strong.	DP 4
Domestic provider	P	P03	To what extent does the organizational structure in supporting sourcing capabilities affect the sourcing performance towards your client? Why?	We mirrored our organizational structure (delivery team) to the client situation. At the start we had a lot of discussions about decision-making and the interpretation of the contract that resulted in smaller adaptions. As a consequency of a client change from a decetralized structure to a centralized structure, we had some problems to adapt to this change. Finally, we rearranged our organizational structure too. We implemented a client team based on empoyees who are only working for one client, which improved the performance significantly. Right now, we experience the performance as good.	DP 2

Offshore provider

Document ID	Code	Question ID	Information	Service provider's response	User ID
			Construct Client Developments		
Offshore provider	CD	CD01	To what extent does your department perceive an increasing pressure of your client in delivering outsourcing services? Why?	At various moments we experience a client pressure to deliver a solution quickly. Internal client discussions take to long, which meand that a provider solution needs to be build fastly. This mostly results in unrealistic delivery time schedules and a very tight planning. Managing client expectations is crucial to achieve the agreed performance.	OP 5
Offshore provider	CD	CD01	To what extent does your department perceive an increasing pressure of your client in delivering outsourcing services? Why?	Our client definitly want to change regularly, however, they don't know want the really need. This leads to unclear specifications related to application functionality. as a reult, the pressure increases as the planning time frame is already decided. An appraoch could be that for all new client requests a clean order forms needs to be filled out and approved by us before we start building or changing a functionality.	OP 7

Offshore provider	CD	CD02	To what extent do you identify and monitor changing circumstances with your client?	From a delivery perspective, we experience client developments as on-going. New opportunities are sent internally to the right department. Applying a morre business oriented mindsetis necessary. We focus on building a 'Partnership' with our client which is a pro for our entire company. In some situations these changing circumstances are discussed with the client. for instance, the introduction of Lean Six Sigma result is an increase of goodwill, not in direct business spend. We also are willing to take some risks, for instance for ramp-up an offshore team on short notice while this team is ramped-down within two months.	OP 4
Offshore provider	CD	CD02	To what extent do you identify and monitor changing circumstances with your client?	Within our company we apply a specific department (programme team) that is monitoring client developments. As an example, they also discuss new developments from our company such as a new reporting system for legacy environments.	OP 6

Document ID	Code	Question ID	Information	Service provider's response	User ID
			Construct Performance		
Offshore provider	P	P02	To what extent do sourcing capabilities affect the sourcing performance towards your client? Why?	We experience the effect of sourcing capabilities to performance strongly. The client deliberatly has chosen our firm because of a strong mix of valuable capabilities (e.g. technological, governance, banking and insurrance knowledge, payment services). The extent to which we cooperate with our client is a significant impactfactor too.	OP 2
Offshore provider	P	P02	To what extent do sourcing capabilities affect the sourcing performance towards your client? Why?	From a technological perspective, we find that the relation between capabilities and performance as very strong. Capabilities form the basis for the relationship to our clients. Within our company we assess our capabilities as mature. For instance, to deal with uncertainty, we apply a 'shadow-resource' appraoch. This means that each client-team is extended with at least three additional employees that are fully involved in client businesses. When one of our employees is leaving, the shadow-resource will fulfill this place. At the end, it is all about continuity and achieve the targets as agreed.	OP 4
Offshore provider	P	P04	To what extent are you delivering a sustainable sourcing performance towards your client? Does your client agree with this statement?	The answer is YES. This is based on the client satisfaction that we measured during the past years. We measure the clients satisfaction monthly by means of an external company (independent) based on a scale from 1 to 5. On this scale, our score is an average of 4 for a period of three years. In some cases we achieve a 3.8. As a result, we develop an improvement plan (e.g. root cause analysis) to recover the score. In some cases it is hard to determine the real cause of a lower score.	OP 5

Global provider

Document ID	Code	Question ID	Information	Service provider's response	User ID
			Construct Sourcing Capabilities		
Global provider	SC	SC01	To what extent are the sourcing capabilities within your department influenced by client developments? How would you perceive the impact: low, medium of high?	Indeed, we notice the influence of client developments on our capabilities. For instance client x. The client strongly focuses on our capabilities when they have to decide to buy our application service offer. Our competition with provider y is fierce as both parties are able to offer the same type of IT service. The capabilities applied are the differentator. The performance offered strongly relates to the ability and availability of our capabilities (technology, offshoring).	GP 3
Global provider	SC	SC02	To what extent are the sourcing capabilities within your department influenced by the sourcing strategy of your client (e.g. sole sourcing, multi vendor sourcing)? How would you perceive the impact: low, medium of high?	The impact is high. Recent strategy decisions will lead to more and fierce competition in the market. This requiers a strong focus at each level in our organzaition, which will have consequences for our capabilities.	GP 4

(*continued*)

Continued

Document ID	Code	Question ID	Information	Service provider's response	User ID
Global provider	SC	SC02	To what extent are the sourcing capabilities within your department influenced by the sourcing strategy of your client (e.g. sole sourcing, multi vendor sourcing)? How would you perceive the impact: low, medium of high?	Capabilities are more and more affected by our client developments. By means of a recent change in our client strategy, from a fully centralized organziation towards a decentralized organzaition, each BU will have the right to develop their own sourcing strategy and accompanying policies. In practice, this means a change to a multivendor strategy. However, this will cost us business as we have a share-of-wallet of 65% related to the IT spend of our client. This new strategy definitly will have an impact on our capabilities and governance.	GP 6
Global provider	SC	SC02	To what extent are the sourcing capabilities within your department influenced by the sourcing strategy of your client (e.g. sole sourcing, multi vendor sourcing)? How would you perceive the impact: low, medium of high?	The sourcing strategy of our client will have a significant impact on our capabilities. This relates to (1) sufficient resources; (2) the size of the client within our firm(large/small); (3) relationship management (regional or central appraoch); (4) transition (more smaller transitions in stead of few large transitions).	GP 7

Document ID	Code	Question ID	Information	Service provider's response	User ID
				Construct Fit	
Global provider	F	F01	To what extent do sourcing capabilities and organizational structure affect each other? Why?	We sure notice the relation between capabilities and organzaitional structure. Most importantly, we observe this relationship at demanding clients. The more demanding a client, the stronger the relationship between capabilies and structure. For example, take the floorwalker concept. Both the necessary capabilities and adaptation to the required organizational structure (communication, decision-making) lead to a more on-demand delivery model. High flexibility means that first we solve the problem and create a trouble ticket later. As a result, we changed our organizational design to the client environment. (decision-making is low in our organzaition, direct communication).	GP 2
Global provider	F	F01	To what extent do sourcing capabilities and organizational structure affect each other? Why?	There is a strong relationship which is influenced by the type of delivery that is applied. Our global proposition in combination with offshoring services influneces the fit too. An other example is the fact that our client is quit demanding. Decision-making is low in our organization by means of the client-focus teams. The fit is also based on a mix between on-site and local (domestic) support and global delviery teams. Despite the fact that many activities can be executed remotly, local presence is still important. On the other hand, our choice to implement a dedicated client-focus team contributes to establish the fit between capabilities and structure. The fit remains constant while client circumstances changes often.	GP 6

(continued)

Continued

Document ID	Code	Question ID	Information	Service provider's response	User ID
Global provider	F	F01	To what extent do sourcing capabilities and organizational structure affect each other? Why?	Sure we notic the relation between both aspects. Our organizational design capability (clients WHAT question) decides our design and implementation of specific dimensions (decision-making, hierarchy). In particular, the client environment determines the organzaitional dimensions of our structure (HOW question). These dimensies can be seen as 'soft skills'. Remark: during the salesphase we discussed these governance aspects with the client (perception management). We noticed that this approach also requires to some extent the client appreciate this capabilities. Partly, it is about tacit knowledge, that is dependent on clients maturity. At the same time, building our capabilities need to be a regular activity.	GP 7

Appendix G: Survey Questions

Cover letter e-Survey

Are you experiencing an increasing pressure of your customers with regard to outsourcing services? Do the dynamics of the market also affect your daily activities in delivering IT services to your partners? Changes in market and relations between sourcing partners are assumed to change the way in which {provider} supports its customers. Sourcing capabilities will need to expand, gaining in width and in depth. Your company organizational structure might also need to be adapted in order to retain a satisfied customer.

Currently, the Delft University of Technology is conducting research on the supply side of outsourcing arrangements. The objective is to obtain insight in the consequences of client developments for outsourcing services of your company. As a result {provider} will have a deeper understanding of what affects sourcing relations and performance, and be better equipped to improve customer satisfaction.

As you are involved in supporting customers, you are invited to fill out a questionnaire. The following topics will be discussed: changing client circumstances that might affect your sourcing relation, capabilities of your organization, the way your organization is structured in order to be able to offer sourcing services, and of course the performance of your company. The questionnaire consists of approximately 50 questions which will take about 15 minutes of your time. Individual answers will remain confidential. Results will be presented on an aggregated level.

Please complete the questionnaire before September 20th. If you have any questions or remarks concerning the questionnaire, please contact Albert Plugge (a.g.plugge@tudelft.nl) for additional information.

We would like to thank you in advance for your kind co-operation.

On behalf of {provider} and Delft University of Technology,

Albert Plugge

Glossary

Topic: Changing client circumstances
Description: Changing client circumstances can be described as developments that arise within the client environment and the way these affect the provider organization.

Topic: Capabilities
Description: Capabilities refer to an assembly of skills, techniques, and know-how and can be related to three organizational areas: relationship, transformation and delivery.

Topic: Organizational structure
Description: An organizational structure is applied to support outsourcing arrangements and consists of various subdimensions including decision-making, number of layers in the hierarchy, and level of horizontal integration.

Topic: Performance
Description: Capabilities and organizational structure form a combination of both tangible and intangible assets and will contribute to improved firm performance.

Topic: Sustainable performance
Description: A sustainable sourcing performance arises from provider's ability to adapt to changing client circumstances, which result in a consistent high-quality service performance over time.

Topic: Sourcing strategy
Description: The sourcing strategy can be defined as the client's strategy to outsource their complete (for example, total outsourcing) IT function or just selective parts (selective outsourcing) of their IT function.

Topic: Innovation
Description: Client's increasing interest of developing new IT services of re-engineering processes that result in adding value to the organization.

Topic: Required flexibility
Description: Client's growing need for flexibility refers to a proactive attitude of providers to response to changing business needs.

Questionnaire

Section: Changing client circumstances

First we want to focus on the changing client circumstances like the impact of globalization, market dynamics, innovation and expanding legislation your sourcing client has to deal with. We are wondering how your company is dealing with these changing client circumstances. Changing client circumstances can be described as developments that arise within client environment and the way these affect your organization. Please, could you assess the statements as you perceive it on a seven-point scale.

Number	Question	Strongly disagree	Disagree	Slightly disagree	Neither agree nor disagree	Slightly agree	Agree	Strongly agree
2.1	{Provider} will monitor changes in client circumstances regularly.	○	○	○	○	○	○	○
2.2	{Provider} will identify changes in client circumstances regularly.	○	○	○	○	○	○	○
2.3	Important changing client circumstances are regularly discussed with the client.	○	○	○	○	○	○	○
2.4	Changing client circumstances are regularly assessed on their effect on IT services your company is providing.	○	○	○	○	○	○	○
2.5	Changing client circumstances affect {provider's} provisioning of services.	○	○	○	○	○	○	○
2.6	{Provider} encourage internal cooperation between working groups who are located in different countries.	○	○	○	○	○	○	○
2.7	{Provider's} business strategy is based on customer intimacy.	○	○	○	○	○	○	○
2.8	{Provider} encourages employees to take a proactive attitude.	○	○	○	○	○	○	○
2.9	{Provider} has mechanisms for developing new ideas to stimulate innovation.	○	○	○	○	○	○	○

2.10	Creating innovative IT services forms a part of our company's business strategy.	O	O	O	O	O	O	O
2.11	{Provider} is effectively organized in order to cater to flexibility requirements of client's.	O	O	O	O	O	O	O
2.12	Management stimulates employees to deal with customer requirements.	O	O	O	O	O	O	O
2.13	Are there any other issues with regard to customer circumstance and your companies response that you might like to mention?							

Section: Capabilities

To support clients internationally, {provider} has specific capabilities in order to deliver IT services. Examples of capabilities are: business market knowledge, the knowledge and experience on managing IT infrastructure and applications, and on supporting adequate governance processes. The following questions regards to {provider's} capabilities to deal with changing client developments and needs. Please, could you assess the statements as you perceive it on a seven-point scale.

Number	Question	Strongly disagree	Disagree	Slightly disagree	Neither agree nor disagree	Slightly agree	Agree	Strongly agree
4.1	Present capabilities are regularly assessed in order to match client's business needs.	O	O	O	O	O	O	O
4.2	We at {provider} improve our capabilities continuously.	O	O	O	O	O	O	O
4.3	{Provider's} capabilities are regularly discussed with clients.	O	O	O	O	O	O	O
4.4.	We continuously adapt our capabilities to client shifting needs.	O	O	O	O	O	O	O
4.5	Within our company we know how to adapt our capabilities.	O	O	O	O	O	O	O
4.6	Changing client circumstances have an impact on the courses and training that are provided to {provider} employees.	O	O	O	O	O	O	O
4.7	Overall, {provider} accumulates relevant knowledge to effectively adapt to clients changing circumstances and needs.	O	O	O	O	O	O	O
4.8	Our management has expertise in coordinating capabilities required to offer services that fit the client.	O	O	O	O	O	O	O

Can you assess to what degree the capabilities within your department are affected by the following changing client circumstances?

Number	Question	Not at all	Slightly	To some degree	In a high degree	Very strong
5.1	The sourcing strategy (e.g. sole sourcing, multi vendor sourcing,	○	○	○	○	○
5.2	Client's need for innovation.	○	○	○	○	○
5.3	The required flexibility of your clients (e.g. start a project on a short notice, deploy additional resources).	○	○	○	○	○
6.1	Are there any other issues with regard to customer circumstances and your companies capabilities that you might like to mention?					

Section: Organizational structure

To support clients internationally, the organizational structure of {provider} facilitates the provisioning of IT services. Please, could you assess the statements as you perceive it on a seven-point scale.

Number	Question	Strongly disagree	Disagree	Slightly disagree	Neither agree nor disagree	Slightly agree	Agree	Strongly agree
7.1	Our management has expertise in reorganizing our company to adapt to customers circumstances and needs.	○	○	○	○	○	○	○
7.2	Our company facilitates employees with training to work in cross-functional teams.	○	○	○	○	○	○	○
7.3	Written rules and procedures improve the quality of IT services effectively.	○	○	○	○	○	○	○
7.4	Overall, decision-making is highly decentralized.	○	○	○	○	○	○	○
7.5	We can quickly adapt the numbers of hierarchical layers.	○	○	○	○	○	○	○
7.6	Overall, written rules and procedures are observed conclusively.	○	○	○	○	○	○	○
7.7	Our company stimulates employees to work in cross-functional teams.	○	○	○	○	○	○	○
7.8	Our managers are supportive of the decisions made by work teams.	○	○	○	○	○	○	○
7.9	{Provider} encourages handling job-related problems by ourselves.	○	○	○	○	○	○	○
7.10	Written rules and procedures guide creative problem solving.	○	○	○	○	○	○	○

Number	Question	Strongly disagree	Disagree	Slightly disagree	Neither agree nor disagree	Slightly agree	Agree	Strongly agree
8.1	{Provider} is a lean organization.	○	○	○	○	○	○	○
8.2	Communication between different levels in hierarchy within our company is easy.	○	○	○	○	○	○	○
8.3	Written rules and procedures enable employees to make suggestions for changes.	○	○	○	○	○	○	○
8.4	Overall, employees are authorised to correct problems when they occur.	○	○	○	○	○	○	○
8.5	Important tasks and activities are carried out by cross-functional teams.	○	○	○	○	○	○	○
8.6	Overall, strategic decisions are quickly passed on to relevant employees.	○	○	○	○	○	○	○
8.7	Overall, there are few hierarchical layers in our company.	○	○	○	○	○	○	○
8.8	Our employees can easily meet and communicate with top management.	○	○	○	○	○	○	○
8.9	Our management has expertise to lead various cross-functional teams.	○	○	○	○	○	○	○
8.10	Overall, among managers the communication is intensively.	○	○	○	○	○	○	○

Can you assess to what degree the organizational structure within your department is affected by the following changing client circumstances?

Number	Question	Not at all	Slightly	To some degree	In a high degree	Very strong
9.1	The sourcing strategy (e.g. sole sourcing, multi vendor sourcing, offshoring) of your clients.	○	○	○	○	○
9.2	Client's need for innovation.	○	○	○	○	○
9.3	The required flexibility of your clients (e.g. start a project on a short notice, deploy additional resources).	○	○	○	○	○
10.1	Are there any other issues with regard to customer circumstances and your organizational structure that you might like to mention?					

Section: Performance

The following questions refer to {provider} delivered performance of IT services towards clients.

Please, could you assess the statements as you perceive it on a seven-point scale?

Number	Question	Strongly disagree	Disagree	Slightly disagree	Neither agree nor disagree	Slightly agree	Agree	Strongly agree
11.1	The performance of {provider} IT services is regularly monitored.	○	○	○	○	○	○	○
11.2	The performance of {provider} IT services is regularly assessed.	○	○	○	○	○	○	○
11.3	The influence of capabilities on the performance is significantly.	○	○	○	○	○	○	○
11.4	The influence of organizational structure on the performance is significantly.	○	○	○	○	○	○	○
11.5	The fit between capabilities and their organizational structure has dramatically increased our performance.	○	○	○	○	○	○	○
11.6	The performance of the delivered IT services towards clients is durable	○	○	○	○	○	○	○

Can you assess to what degree the performance of the delivered services towards clients is affected by the following changing client circumstances?

Number	Question	Not at all	Slightly	To some degree	In a high degree	Very strong
12.1	The sourcing strategy (e.g. sole sourcing, multi vendor sourcing, offshoring) of your clients.	O	O	O	O	O
12.2	Client's need for innovation.	O	O	O	O	O
12.3	The required flexibility of your clients (e.g. start a project on a short notice, deploy additional resources).	O	O	O	O	O
13.1	You have answered all the questions and statements which are related to {provider's} performance. Does this give any additional suggestions or remarks?					

References

Alpert, S.R. and Gruenenberg, K. (2000). Concept mapping with multimedia on the web. *Journal of Educational Multimedia and Hypermedia*, 9, 313–30.

Anderson, J.C. and Gerbing, D.W. (1988). Structural equation modelling in practice: a review and recommended two-step approach. *Psychological Bulletin*, 103, 411–23.

Aubert, B.A., Rivard, S. and Patry, M. (2004). A transaction cost model of IT outsourcing. *Information and Management*, 41, 921–32.

Ausubel, D.P. (1963). The psychology of meaningful verbal learning. *Sloan Management Review*, 23(4), 35–43.

Bacharach, S.B. (1989). Organizational theories: some criteria for evaluation. *Academy of Management Review*, 14, 496–515.

Bagozzi, R.P. and Yi, Y. (1988). On the evaluation of structural equation models. *Journal of the Academy of Marketing Science*, 16(1), 74–94.

Barney, J.B. (1986). Organizational culture: can it be a source of sustained competitive advantage? *Academic Management Review*, 11, 656–65.

Barney, J.B. (1991). Firm resources and sustained competitive advantage. *Journal of Management*, 17, 99–120.

Barney, J.B. (1995). Looking inside the organization for competitive advantage. *Academic of Management Executive*, 9, 49–61.

Barney, J.B. and Arikan, A.M. (2001). *The Resource-based View: Origins and Implications.* Malden, MA: Blackwell Publishers.

Barthélemy, J. (2001). The hidden cost of IT outsourcing. *Sloan Management Review*, 42(3), 60–9.

Barthélemy, J. and Quelin, B.V. (2006). Complexity of outsourcing contracts and ex post transaction costs: an empirical investigation. *Journal of Management Studies*, 43, 1775–97.

Benbasat, I. and Zmud, R. W. (1999). Empirical research in information systems: the practice of relevance. *MIS Quarterly*, 23, 3–16.

Bensaou, M. and Venkatraman, N. (1996). Inter-organizational relationships and information technology: a conceptual synthesis and a research framework. *European Journal of Information Systems*, 5, 84–91.

Bergeron, F., Raymond, L. and Rivard, S. (2001) Fit in strategic information technology management research: an empirical comparison of perspectives. *Omega*, 29, 125–42.

Beulen, E. and Ribbers, P. (2003). A case study of managing IT outsourcing partnerships in Asia. *Communications of the Association of Information Systems*, 11, 357–76.

Beulen, E., Ribbers, P. and Roos, J. (2011). *Managing IT Outsourcing: Governance in Global Partnerships*, 2nd edn. London: Routledge.

Bourgeois, L.J., Mcallister, D.W. and Michell, T.R. (1978). The effects of different organizational environments upon decisions about organizational structure. *Academy of Management Journal*, 21, 508–14.

Bouwman, W.A.G.A., van den Hoof, B., van de Wijngaert, L. and van Dijk, J. (2006). *Information and Communication Technology in Organizations*. Thousand Oaks, CA and London: Sage Publications.

Burns, T. and Stalker, G.M. (1961). *The Management of Innovation*. London: Tavistock.

Busi, M. and McIvor, R. (2008). Setting the outsourcing research agenda: the top-10 most urgent outsourcing areas. *Strategic Outsourcing: An International Journal*, 1, 185–97.

Carmel, E. (1999). *Global Software Teams: Collaborating Across Borders and Time Zones*. Upper Saddle River, NJ: Prentice Hall PTR.

Carmeli, A. and Tishler, A. (2004). The relationships between intangible organizational elements and organizational performance. *Strategic Management Journal*, 25, 1257–78.

Carmel, E. and Tjia, P. (2005). *Offshore Outsourcing of Information Technology Work*. Cambridge: Cambridge University Press.

Carmel, E. and Espinosa, J.A. (2011). *I'm Working While They're Sleeping: Time Zone Separation Challenges and Solutions*. USA: Nedder Stream Press.

Charkravarthy, B.S. (1992). Adaptation: a promising metaphor for strategic management. *Academic Management Review*, 7, 35–44.

Clemons, E.K. and Row, M. (1991). Sustaining IT advantage: the role of structural differences. *MIS Quarterly*, 15, 275–92.

Cohen, L. and Young, A. (2006) *Multisourcing: Moving Beyond Outsourcing to Achieve Growth and Agility*. Boston, MA: Harvard Business School Press.

Cunningham, M.T. (1980). International marketing and purchasing of industrial goods-features of an European project. *European Journal of Marketing*, 14, 322–38.

Cunningham, M.T. and Tynan, C. (1993). Electronic trading, interorganizational systems and the nature of buyer-seller relationships: the need for a network perspective. *International Journal of Information Management*, 13, 3–28.

Currie, W.L. and Seltsikas, P. (2001). Exploring the supply-side of IT outsourcing: evaluating the emerging role of application service providers. *European Journal of Information Systems*, 10, 123–34.

Daft, R.L. (1995). *Organization Theory and Design*. St Paul, MN: West Publishing Company.

Dalton, D.R., Todor, W.D., Spendolini, M.J., Fielding, G.J. and Porter, L.W. (1980). Organizational structure and performance. *Academic of Management Review*, 5, 49–64.

Davenport, T. and Nohria, N. (1994). Case management and the integration of labor. *Sloan Management Review*, 35, 11–23.

De Looff, L.A. (1997). *Information Systems Outsourcing Decision Making: A Managerial Approach*. Hershey, PA: Idea Group.

Denzin, N.K. (1978). *The Research Act: A Theoretical Introduction to Sociological Methods*. New York, NY: McGraw-Hill.

Dibbern, J., Goles, T., Hirschheim, R. and Jayatilaka,B. (2004) Information systems outsourcing: a survey and analysis of the literature. *DATA BASE for Advances in Information Systems*, 34(4), 6–102.

Dierickx, I. and Cool, K. (1989). Asset stock accumulation and sustainability of competitive advantage. *Management Science*, 35, 1504–11.

DiRomualdo, A. and Gurbaxani, V. (1998). Strategic intent for IT outsourcing. *Sloan Management Review,* 39, 67–80.

Doll, W.J. and Vonderembse, M.A. (1991). The evolution of manufacturing systems: towards the post-industrial enterprise. *Omega,* 19, 401–11.

Drazin, R. and van de Ven, A.H. (1985). An examination of the alternative forms of contingency theory. *Academy of Management Review,* 30, 514–39.

Dent, E.B. and Galloway Goldberg, S. (1999) Challenging 'resistance to change'. *Journal of Applied Behavioural Science,* 35(1), 25–41.

Dubrin, A.J. and Ireland, R.D. (1993) *Management and Organisation,* 2nd edn. Cincinnati, OH: South-Western Publishing.

Dyer, J. (1997). Effective inter-firm collaboration: how firms minimize transaction costs and maximize transaction value. *Strategic Management Journal,* 18, 535–56.

Dyer, J. and Chu, W. (2003). The role of trustworthiness in reducing transaction costs and improving performance: empirical evidence from the United States, Japan, and Korea. *Organisational Science,* 14, 57–68.

Eisenhardt, K.M. and Martin, J.A. (2000). Dynamic capabilities: What are they? *Strategic Management Journal,* 21, 1105–21.

Ethiraj, S.K., Kale, P., Krishnan, M.S. and Singh, J. (2005). Where do capabilities come from and how do they matter? A study in the software services industry. *Strategic Management Journal,* 26, 25–45.

Feeny, D., Lacity, M. and Willcocks, L.P. (2005). Taking the measure of outsourcing providers. *Sloan Management Review,* 46(3), 41–8.

Feeny, D.F. and Ives, B. (1990). In search of sustainability: reaping long-term advantage from investments in information technology. *Journal of Management Information Systems,* 7, 27–32.

Field, A.P. (2005). *Discovering Statistics Using SPSS.* London: Sage Publications.

Fornell, C. and Larcker, D.F. (1981). Evaluating structural equation models with unobservable variables and measurement error. *Journal of Marketing Research,* 18, 39–50.

Galbraith, J.R. (1977). *Organization Design.* Reading, MA: Addison-Wesley.

Galliers, R.D. (1992). Choosing information systems research approaches. In R.D. Galliers (ed.), *Information Systems Research: Issues, Methods, and Practical Guidelines.* Oxford: Blackwell Scientific Publications, pp. 44–162.

Gartner (2009). Gartner on Outsourcing: 2008–2009. *ID Number: G00164206.*

Germain, R. (1996). The role of context and structure in radical and incremental logistics innovation adoption. *Journal of Business Research,* 35, 117–27.

Gietzman, M.B. (1996). Incomplete contracts and the make or buy decision: governance design and attainable flexibility. *Accounting, Organizations and Society,* 21, 611–26.

Glaser, B.G. and Strauss, A.L. (1967). *The Discovery of Grounded Theory: Strategies for Qualitative Research.* Chicago: Aldine.

Gonzalez, R., Gasco, J. and Llopis, J. (2006). IS outsourcing: a literature analysis. *Information and Management,* 43, 821–34.

Gosain, S., Malhotra, A. and Sawy, O.A.E. (2005). Coordinating for flexibility in e-business supply chains. *Journal of Management Information Systems,* 21, 7–45.

Grant, R.M. (1991). The resource-based theory of competitive advantage: implications for strategy formulation. *California Management Review,* 33, 114–35.

Griffin, R.W. (1993) *Management,* 4th edn. Boston: Houghton Mifflin.

Gupta, A.K. and Govindarajan, V. (194) Business units strategy, managerial characteristics, and business unit effectiveness at strategy implementation. *Academy of Management Journal*, 27, 25–41.

Gurbaxani, V. (1996). The new world of information technology outsourcing. *Communication of the ACM*, 39, 45–6.

Hakansson, H. (1982). *International Marketing and Purchasing of Industrial Goods: An Interaction Approach*. Chichester: John Wiley & Sons.

Helfat, C.E. and Peteraf, M.A. (2003) The dynamic resource-based view: capability lifecycles. *Strategic Management Journal*, 24(10), 997–1010.

Henderson, R. and Cockburn, I. (1994). Measuring competence? Exploring firm effects in pharmaceutical research. *Strategic Management Journal*, 15, 63–84.

Herriott, R.E. and Firestone, W. A. (1983). Multisite qualitative policy research: Optimizing description and generalizability. *Educational Researcher*, 12, 14–19.

Holway, R. (1998). *Software and Computing Services Industry in Europe: Markets and Strategies*. Munich: PAC Gmbh.

Huber, G.P. (1984) The nature and design of the post-industrial organization. *Management Science*, 30(8), 929–51.

Jones, W.O. (2009) Outsourcing in China: opportunities, challenges and lessons learned: Industry insight. *Strategic Outsourcing: An International Journal*, 2(2), 187–203.

Kaplan, R. and Norton, D. (1992) The balanced scorecard: measures that drive performance. *Harvard Business Review*, 70(1), 71–9.

Keen, P.G.W. (1981). Information systems and organisational change. *Communications of the ACM*, 24(1), 24–33.

Kern, T. (1997). The gestalt of an information technology outsourcing relationship: an exploratory analysis. *18th International Conference on Information Systems*. Atlanta, Georgia, 15–17 December.

Kern, T. and Willcocks, L.P. (2000). Exploring information technology outsourcing relationships: theory and practice. *Strategic Information Systems*, 9, 321–50.

Kern, T. and Willcocks, L.P. (2001) *The Relationship Advantage: Information Technologies, Sourcing and Management*. Oxford: Oxford University Press.

Kern, T. and Willcocks, L.P. (2002). Exploring relationships in information technology outsourcing: the interaction approach. *European Journal of Information Systems*, 11, 3–19.

Kettinger, W.J., Grover, V., Guha, S. and Segars, A.H. (1994) Strategic information systems revisited: sustainability and performance. *MIS Quarterly*, 18(1), 31–58.

King, A. and Zeithaml, C. (2001). Competencies and firm performance: examining the causal ambiguity paradox. *Strategic Management Journal*, 22, 75–99.

Klepper, R.W. and Jones, W.O. (1998). *Outsourcing Information Technology, Systems and Services*. Englewood Cliffs, NJ: Prentice Hall.

Kotlarsky, J. and Oshri, I. (2008). Knowledge sharing, social ties and successful collaboration in globally distributed system development projects. In J. Kotlarsky, I. Oshri and P.C.V. Fenema (eds), *Knowledge Processes in Globally Distributed Contexts*. London: Palgrave Macmillan.

Koufteros, X.A. and Vonderembse, M. A. (1998). The impact of organizational structure on the level of JIT attainment: towards theory development. *International Journal of Production*, 36, 2863–78.

Kreitner, R. (1992) *Management*, 5th edn. Boston: Houghton Mifflin.
Lacity, M.C. and Hirschheim, R. (1993). The information systems outsourcing bandwagon. *Sloan Management Review*, 35, 73–86.
Lacity, M. C., Willcocks, L.P. and Feeny, D. (1995). IT sourcing: maximize flexibility and control. *Harvard Business Review*, May/June, 84–93.
Lacity, M. and Willcocks, L.P. (1996) Interpreting information technology sourcing decisions from a transaction cost perspective: findings and critique. *Accounting Management and Information Technologies*, 5(3/4), 203–44.
Lacity, M. and Willcocks, L.P. (2001). *Global Information Technology Outsourcing: In Search of Business Advantage*. Chichester: John Wiley.
Lawrence, P.R. and Lorsch, J.W. (1967). *Organization and Environment*. Homewood, IL: Irwin.
Leek, S., Turnbull, P. and Naude, P. (2000). Is the interaction approach of any relevance in an IT/e-commerce driven world? *Proceedings of the 16th Annual International marketing and Purchasing Conference*. University of Bath, UK.
Leiblein, M.J. (2003). The choice of organizational governance form and performance: predictions from transaction cost, resourced-based, and real options theories. *Journal of Management*, 29, 937–61.
Levina, N. and Ross, J. (2003). From the vendor's perspective: exploring the value proposition in information technology outsourcing. *MIS Quarterly*, 27, 331–64.
Levina, N. and Su, N. (2008). Global multisourcing strategy: the emergence of a supplier portfolio in services offshoring. *Decision Sciences*, 39(3), 541–70.
Lieberman, M.B. and Montgomery, D.B. (1998). First-mover (dis)advantages: retrospective and link with the resource-based view. *Strategic Management Journal*, 19, 1111–25.
Lincoln, Y.S. and Guba, E.G. (1985). *Naturalistic Inquiry*. Beverly Hills, CA: Sage Publications.
Linder, J.C. (2004). Transformational outsourcing. *MIT Sloan Management Review*, 45, 52–8.
Loh, L. and Venkatraman, N. (1992). Diffusion of information technology outsourcing: influence sources and the Kodak effect. *Information Systems Research*, 3, 334–58.
Markus, M.L. (1983) Power, politics and MIS implementation. *Communications of the ACM*, 26(6), 430–44.
Martinsons, M., Davison, R. and Tse, D. (1999) The balanced scorecard: a foundation for the strategic management of information systems. *Decision Support Systems*, 25, 71–88.
McFarlan, F.W. and Nolan, R.L. (1995). How to manage an IT outsourcing alliance. *Sloan Management Review*, 36, 9–23.
McIvor, R. (2009). How the transaction cost and resource-based theories of the firm inform outsourcing evaluation. *Journal of Operations Management*, 27, 45–63.
Michell, V. and Fitzgerald, G. (1997). The IT outsourcing market-place: vendors and their selection. *Journal of Information Technology*, 12, 223–37.
Miles, M.B. and Huberman, A.M. (1994). *Qualitative Data Analysis: An Expanded Sourcebook*, 2nd edn. Thousand Oaks, CA and London: Sage Publications.
Miles, R.E. and Snow, C.C. (1978). *Organizational Strategy, Structure and Process*. New York, NY: McGraw-Hill.

Miller, D. and Friesen, P.H. (1980). Momentum and revolution in organisational adaptation. *Academy of Management Journal*, 23(4), 591–614.

Mintzberg, H. (1979). *The Structuring of Organizations*. Englewood Cliffs, NJ: Prentice Hall.

Mintzberg, H. (1983). *Structure in Fives: Designing Effective Organizations*. Englewood Cliffs, NJ: Prentice Hall.

Mohr, J.J. and Spekmann, R.E. (1996). Several characteristics contribute to successful alliances between channel members. *Marketing Management*, 4, 34–43.

Nahm, A.Y., Vonderembse, M.A. and Koufteros, X.A. (2003). The impact of organizational structure on time-based manufacturing and plant performance. *Journal of Operations Management*, 21, 281–306.

Neely, A.D., Adams, C.A. and Kennerley, M. (2002). *Performance Prism: The Scorecard for Measuring and Managing Business Success*. London: Financial Times/Prentice Hall.

Neman, W.L. (2000). *Social Research Methods: Quantitative and Quantitative Approach*. Boston: Allyn and Bacon.

Novak, J.D. and Gowin, D.B. (1984). Learning how to learn. In J. Kotlarsky, I. Oshri and P.C.V. Fenema (eds), *Knowledge Processes in Globally Distributed Contexts*. London: Palgrave Macmillan.

Novak, J.D. (1990). Concept maps and Vee diagrams: two metacognitive tools to facilitate meaningful learning. *Instructional Science*, 19, 19–52.

Oktemgil, M. and Greenley, G. (1997). Consequences of high and low adaptive capability in UK companies. *European Journal of Marketing*, 31, 445–66.

Oshri, I., Kotlarski, J. and Willcocks, L. (2009). *The Handbook of Global Outsourcing and Offshoring*. London: Palgrave Macmillan.

Oshri, I., Kotlarski, J. and Willcocks, L. P. (2007). Managing dispersed expertise in IT offshore outsourcing: Lessons from Tata Consulting Services. *MIS Quarterly Executive*, 6, 53–65.

Paswan, A.K. and Dant, R.P. Lumpkin, J.R. (1998). An empirical investigation of the linkages among relationalism, environmental uncertainty, and bureaucratization. *Journal of Business Research*, 43, 125–40.

Penrose, E.G. (1959). *The Theory of the Growth of the Firm*. New York, NY: John Wiley.

Plugge, A.G., Wijers, G. and Wagenaar, R.W. (2008). Exploring IT outsourcing: how client developments affect supplier capabilities. In I. Oshri, J. Kotlarsky and L.P. Willcocks (eds), *Outsourcing Global Services: Knowledge, Innovation and Social Capital*. London: Palgrave Macmillan, pp. 71–95.

Plugge, A.G. and Bouwman, W.A.G.A. (2009). Developing an IT outsourcing service provider fit between sourcing capabilities and organizational structure: a comparative study. Paper presented at the Third Global Sourcing Workshop (22–5 March). Keystone, CO, USA.

Plugge, A.G. and Janssen, M.F.W.H.A. (2009). Managing change in IT outsourcing arrangements: an offshore service provider perspective on adaptability. *Strategic Outsourcing: An International Journal*, 2, 257–74.

Podsakoff, P.M., Mackenzie, S.B., Lee, J. and Podsakoff, N.P. (2003). Common method biases in behavioral research: A critical review of the literature and recommended remedies. *Journal of Applied Psychology*, 20, 879–903.

Polanyi, M. (1966). *The Tacit Dimension*. London: Routledge & Kegan Paul Ltd.

Poppo, L. and Zenger, T. (1998). Testing alternative theories of the firm: transaction cost, knowledge-based, and measurement explanations for make-or-buy decisions in information services. *Strategic Management Journal*, 19, 853–77.

Porter, M.E. (1980). *Generic Competitive Strategies*. New York: Free Press.

Porter, M.E. (1991). Towards a dynamic theory of strategy. *Strategic Management Journal*, 12, 95–117.

Prahalad, C.K. and Hamel, G. (1990). The core competence of the corporation. *Harvard Business Review*, 68, 79–93.

Prescott, J.E., Kohili, A.K. and Venkatraman, N. (1986). The market share–profitability relationship: an empirical assessment of assertions and contradictions. *Strategic Management Journal*, 7, 377–94.

Quinn, J.B. (1999). Strategic outsourcing: leveraging knowledge capabilities. *Sloan Management Review*, 40, 9–21.

Robins, J. and Wiersema, M.F. (1995). A resource-based approach to the multibusiness firm: empirical analysis of portfolio interrelationships and corporate financial performance. *Strategic Management Journal*, 16, 277–99.

Robinson, M., Kalkola, R. (2004). *Offshore Outsourcing, Business Models, ROI and Best Practices*. Apharetta, GA: Mivar Press.

Rossman, G.B. and Wilson, B.L. (1984). Number and words: combining quantitative and qualitative methods in a single large-scale evaluation study. *Evaluation Review*, 9, 627–43.

Rossman, G.B. and Wilson, B.L. (1991). Numbers and words revisited: being 'shamelessly eclectic'. *Evaluation Review*, 28, 315–27.

Rottman, J.W. (2008). Successful knowledge transfer within offshore supplier networks: a case study exploring social capital in strategic alliances. *Journal of Information Technology*, 23, 31–43.

Rottman, J.W. and Lacity, M.C. (2009). Outcomes from offshore outsourcing: evidence from a client's perspective. In Leslie P. Willocks and M. Lacity (eds), *The Practice of Outsourcing: From Information Systems to BPO and Offshoring*. London: Palgrave Macmillan, pp. 389–445.

Roy, V. and Aubert, B.A. (2002). A resource-based analysis of IT sourcing. *The DATA BASE for Advances in Information Systems*, 33(2), 29–40.

Ruekert, R.W., Walker, O.C. and Roering, K.J. (1985). The organization of marketing activities: a contingency theory of structure and performance. *Journal of Marketing*, 49, 13–25.

Safayeni, F.N., Derbentseva, A.J. and Canas, A. (2005). A theoretical note on concepts and the need for cyclic concept maps. *Journal of Research in Science Teaching*, 42(7), 741–66.

Sanchez, R. (1996). Strategic product creation: managing new interactions of technology, markets and organizations. *European Management Journal*, 14(2), 121–38.

Schendel, D.E. and Hofer, C.W. (1979). *Strategic Management: A New View of Business Policy and Planning*. Boston: Little, Brown.

Slotte, V. and Lonka, K. (1999). Spontaneous concept maps aiding the understanding of scientific concepts. *International Journal Scientific Education*, 21, 515–31.

Speklé, R.F. (2001). Explaining management control structure variety: a transaction cost economics perspective. *Accounting, Organizations and Society*, 26(4–5), 419–41.

Tan, C. and Sia, S.K. (2006). Managing flexibility in outsourcing. *Journal of the Association for Information Systems*, 7, 179–206.

Teece, D., Pisano, G. and Shuen, A. (1997). Dynamic capabilities and strategic management. *Strategic Management Journal*, 18(7), 509–33.

Tergan, S.O. (2005). *Digital Concept Maps for Managing Knowledge and Information*. Berlin and Heidelberg: Springer-Verlag.

Van de Ven, A.H. and Poole, M.S. (1995). Explaining development and change in organizations. *Academy of Management Review*, 20(3), 510–40.

Van Dijk, T.A. and Kintsch, W. (1983). *Strategies for Discourse Comprehension*. New York: Academic Press.

Venkatraman, N. (1989). The concept of fit in strategy research: toward verbal and statistical correspondence. *Academy of Management Review*, 14(3), 423–44.

Volberda, H.W. (2003). *Strategic Flexibility: Creating Dynamic Competitive Advantages*. Oxford: Oxford University Press.

Wade, M. and Hulland, J. (2004). The resource-based view and information systems research: review, extension, and suggestions for further research. *MIS Quarterly*, 28(1), 107–42.

Walton, R.E. (1985). From control to commitment: transforming work force management in the United States. In K. Clark, R. Hayes and C. Lorenz (eds), *The Uneasy Alliance: Managing the Productivity–Technology Dilemma*. Boston, MA: Harvard Business School Press.

Watjatrakul, B. (2005). Determinants of IS sourcing decisions: a comparative study of transaction cost theory versus the resource-based view. *Journal of Strategic Information Systems*, 14(4), 389–415.

Wernerfelt, B. (1984). A resource-based view of the firm. *Strategic Management Journal*, 5(2), 171–80.

Wigand, R., Picot, A. and Reichwald, R. (1997). *Information, Organization and Management*. New York: John Wiley and Sons.

Willcocks, L.P. and Lacity, M.C. (2009). *The Practice of Outsourcing: From Information Systems to BPO and Offshoring*. London: Palgrave Macmillan.

Williamson, O.E. (1975). *Markets and Hierarchies*. New York, NY: Free Press.

Williamson, O.E. (1979). Transaction cost economics: the governance of contract relations. *Journal of Law and Economics*, 22, 233–61.

Williamson, O.E. (1981). The economics of organization: The transaction cost approach. *American Journal of Sociology*, 87(3), 548–77.

Winter, S.G. (2005) Understanding dynamic capabilities. *Strategic Management Journal*, 24(10), 991–5.

Yin, R.K. (1994). *Case Study Research: Design and Methods*. Thousand Oaks, CA: Sage Publications.

Zajac, E.J., Kraatz, M.S. and Breser, R.K.F. (2000). Modelling the dynamics of strategic fit: a normative approach to strategic change. *Strategic Management Journal*, 21(4), 429–54.

Zammuto, R.F. and O'Conner, E.J. (1992). Gaining advanced manufacturing technologies benefits: the roles of organizational design and culture. *Academy of Management Review*, 17(4), 701–28.

Zollo, M. and Winter, S.G. (2002). Deliberate learning and the evolution of dynamic capabilities. *Organization Science*, 13(3), 339–51.

Index